GODS AND DEMONS, PRIESTS AND SCHOLARS

GODS AND DEMONS,

PRIESTS AND SCHOLARS

Critical Explorations in the History of Religions

BRUCE LINCOLN

‡

THE UNIVERSITY OF CHICAGO PRESS ‡ CHICAGO AND LONDON

BRUCE LINCOLN

is the Caroline E. Haskell Professor of the History of Religions, Middle Eastern Studies, and Medieval Studies at the University of Chicago, where he is also an associate in the Departments of Anthropology and Classics. He is the author of nine books, most recently *Religion, Empire, and Torture: The Case of Achaemenian Persia*, also published by the University of Chicago Press.

*

The University of Chicago Press, Chicago 60637
The University of Chicago Press, Ltd., London
© 2012 by The University of Chicago
All rights reserved. Published 2012.
Printed in the United States of America

21 20 19 18 17 16 15 14 13 12   2 3 4 5

ISBN-13: 978-0-226-48186-9 (cloth)
ISBN-13: 978-0-226-48187-6 (paper)
ISBN-10: 0-226-48186-7 (cloth)
ISBN-10: 0-226-48187-5 (paper)

†

THE UNIVERSITY OF CHICAGO PRESS
gratefully acknowledges the generous support of
THE DIVINITY SCHOOL AT THE UNIVERSITY OF CHICAGO
toward the publication of this book.

‡

LIBRARY OF CONGRESS CATALOGING-IN-PUBLICATION DATA
Lincoln, Bruce.
    Gods and demons, priests and scholars : critical explorations in the
history of religions / Bruce Lincoln.
        p.   cm.
    Includes bibliographical references and index.
    ISBN-13: 978-0-226-48186-9 (hardcover : alk. paper)
    ISBN-10: 0-226-48186-7 (hardcover : alk. paper)
    ISBN-13: 978-0-226-48187-6 (pbk. : alk. paper)
    ISBN-10: 0-226-48187-5 (pbk. : alk. paper)   1. Religion—History—
Study and teaching.   2. Religion—History—Study and teaching —
Methodology.   I. Title.
BL41.L56 2012
200.71—dc23   2011026886

for

CHRIS AND SUSAN FARAONE

CONTENTS

ILLUSTRATIONS

TABLES

PREFACE

THIS IS NOT A RELIGIOUS BOOK. Rather, it is a book about religion. Insofar as it aspires to *truth*, said truth is strictly provisional and mundane. At best, I would hope to provide nothing save accuracy in reporting and, *Deo volente*, a bit of perspicacity in interpreting what certain humans have thought, said, and done at one time or another.

Conceivably, Thales was right and gods fill the cosmos. The same can be said of demons. The religious have spent much time on this and tend to have strong opinions, but I have encountered little direct evidence and regard the question as beyond certainty of answer. On principle, I am disinclined to rely on the testimonies of others, which—their sincere claims notwithstanding—often recirculate the testimonies and claims of others still, particularly those backed by strong institutions, charismatic leaders, and texts constituted as "sacred."

Fortunately, the question of whether spiritual entities exist falls outside my professional purview. As I understand it, historians of religions ought to concern themselves with such things *only at second hand*, for "religion" is not the sphere permeated by gods, demons, or spirits of whatever kinds. Rather, it is the sphere of people who discuss and ponder such matters and try to live their lives consistent with the kind of world they describe and imagine. Whether or not gods fill the cosmos, they populate a good many conversations.

In their conversations on such topics, priests, theologians, and those for whom religion is a matter of commitment rather than an object of disinterested and/or critical study focus on that which they take to be eternal, transcendent, ineffable, sacred, absolute, and sublime: lofty considerations all. Historians share a different perspective, determined by—and consistent with—a different regime of truth. Like all proponents of the social and not the divine sciences, they study human subjects: finite, fallible mortals who occupy specific coordinates in time and space as adherents (and advocates) of particular communities, who operate with partial knowledge and contingent interests (material and nonmaterial) to advance various goals. In this, the students are very like those whom they study.

The chapters that follow were written in this spirit, and were produced for various occasions, beginning with the "Theses on Method" (chapter 1), which I first nailed (well, thumbtacked) to my office door in the early 1990s.[1] Most are more recent, however, dating from the last several years, and roughly half are published here for the first time, including chapter 13, "The (Un)discipline of Religious Studies," where I consider the failings of other, distinctly uncritical and nonhistorical approaches to the study of religion.

Those who provided me with opportunities to present these researches and who offered useful feedback on them include Clifford Ando, Nicole Belayche, Maurizio Bettini, Ra'anan S. Boustan, Claude Calame, Francis X. Clooney, Marcel Detienne, Nicholas Dirks, Chris Faraone, Fritz Graf, Frantz Grenet, François Hartog, Clarisse Herrenschmidt, Greg Johnson, Sarah Iles Johnston, Jean Kellens, Jacob Olupona, Wayne Proudfoot, James Redfield, Cal Roetzel, Rick Rosengarten, Erik Sand, Barry Saunders, John Scheid, Stefanie von Schnurbein, Brian K. Smith, Jørgen Podemann Sørensen, Mark Taylor, Hugh Urban, Priscilla Wald, Margit Warberg, and Morten Warmind. I am grateful to them all, as also to Jay Munsch, who served as my research assistance, and Margaret Mitchell, Dean of the University of Chicago Divinity School, who provided financial support for this book, along with collegiality and friendship. My deepest and fullest thanks go to Louise Lincoln, whose support, understanding, and encouragement have sustained me through these years and many more.

Last words of appreciation go to Carsten Colpe, who was one of my most important teachers, and to Cristiano Grottanelli, who was my most valued colleague for decades. Both were scholars whose knowledge was much wider and wisdom much deeper than my own. Colpe was the very model of responsibility and rigor; Grottanelli a marvel of originality, acumen, and intellectual daring. I learned much from both, treasured their friendship, and took inspiration from their examples. Their recent deaths are terrible losses to me and to scholarship in general.

*

Chicago, February 2, 2011

CHAPTER ONE

THESES ON METHOD

History can encompass history

(1) The conjunction *of* that joins the two nouns in the disciplinary ethnonym "History of Religions" is not neutral filler. Rather, it announces a proprietary claim and a relation of encompassment: *History* is the method and *Religion* the object of study.

(2) The relation between the two nouns is also tense, as becomes clear if one takes the trouble to specify their meaning. Religion, I submit, is that discourse whose defining characteristic is its desire to speak of things eternal and transcendent with an authority equally transcendent and eternal. History, in the sharpest possible contrast, is that discourse which speaks of things temporal and terrestrial in a human and fallible voice while staking its claim to authority on rigorous critical practice.

must change to think religion is

(3) History of religions is thus a discourse that resists and reverses the orientation of that discourse with which it concerns itself. To practice history of religions in a fashion consistent with the discipline's claim of title is to insist on discussing the temporal, contextual, situated, interested, human, and material dimensions of those discourses, practices, communities, and institutions that characteristically represent themselves as eternal, transcendent, spiritual, and divine.

(4) The same destabilizing and irreverent questions one might ask of any speech act ought to be posed of religious discourse. The first of these is Who speaks here?—that is, what person, group, or institution is responsible for a text, whatever its putative or apparent author. Beyond that, To what audience? In what immediate and broader context? Through what system of mediations? With what interests? And further, Of what would the speaker(s) persuade the audience? What are the consequences if this project of persuasion should happen to succeed? Who wins what, and how much? Who, conversely, loses?

ethical truth > politeness

(5) Reverence is a religious and not a scholarly virtue. When good manners and good conscience cannot be reconciled, the demands of the latter ought to prevail.

(6) Many who would not think of insulating their own or their parents' religion against critical inquiry still afford such protection to other people's faiths, via a stance of cultural relativism. One can appreciate their good intentions while recognizing a certain displaced defensiveness, as well as the guilty conscience of Western imperialism.

(7) Beyond the question of motives and intentions, cultural relativism is predicated on the dubious—not to say fetishistic—construction of "cultures" as if they were stable and discrete groups of people defined by the stable and discrete values, symbols, and practices they share. Insofar as this model stresses the continuity and integration of timeless groups, whose internal tensions and conflicts, turbulence and incoherence, permeability and malleability are largely erased, it risks becoming a religious and not a historic narrative: the story of a transcendent ideal threatened by debasing forces of change.

culture is not a static thing to revere, they change constantly + are constructed by people

(8) Those who sustain this idealized image of culture do so, inter alia, by mistaking the dominant fraction (sex, age group, class, and/or caste) of a given group for the group or "culture" itself. At the same time, they mistake the ideological positions favored and propagated by the dominant fraction for those of the group as a whole (e.g. when texts authored by Brahmins define "Hinduism," or when the statements of male elders constitute "Nuer religion"). Scholarly misrecognitions of this sort replicate the misrecognitions and misrepresentations of those the scholars privilege as their informants.

be weary of people trying to speak on behalf of

authority + knowledge of truth

be careful abt discourses of identity

(9) Critical inquiry need assume neither cynicism nor dissimulation to justify probing beneath the surface, and ought to probe scholarly discourse and practice as much as any other.

(10) Understanding the system of ideology that operates in one's own society is made difficult by two factors: (a) one's consciousness is itself a product of that system, and (b) the system's very success renders its operations invisible, since one is so consistently immersed in and bombarded by its products that one comes to mistake them (and the apparatus through which they are produced and disseminated) for nothing other than "nature."

(11) The ideological products and operations of other societies afford invaluable opportunities to the would-be student of ideology. Being initially unfamiliar, they do not need to be denaturalized before they can be examined. Rather, they invite and reward critical study, yielding lessons one can put to good use at home.

(12) Although critical inquiry has become commonplace in other disciplines, it still offends many students of religion, who denounce it as "reductionism." This charge is meant to silence critique. The failure to treat religion "as religion"—that is, the refusal to ratify its claim of transcendent nature and sacrosanct status—may be regarded as heresy and sacrilege by those who construct themselves as religious, but it is the starting point for those who construct themselves as historians.

(13) When one permits those whom one studies to define the terms in which they will be understood, suspends one's interest in the temporal and contingent, or fails to distinguish between "truths," "truth claims," and "regimes of truth," one has ceased to function as historian or scholar. In that moment, a variety of roles are available: some perfectly respectable (amanuensis, collector, friend and advocate), and some less appealing (cheerleader, voyeur, retailer of imported goods). None, however, should be confused with scholarship.

CHAPTER TWO

HOW TO READ A RELIGIOUS TEXT

I

As a first principle, noncontroversial in itself (I hope) but far reaching in its implications, let me advance the observation that, like all other texts, those which constitute themselves as religious are human products. Yet pursuing this quickly leads us to identify the chief way religious texts are unlike all others: the claims they advance for their more-than-human origin, status, and authority. For characteristically, they connect themselves—either explicitly or in some indirect fashion—to a sphere and a knowledge of transcendent or metaphysical nature, which they purportedly mediate to mortal beings through processes such as revelation, inspiration, and unbroken primordial tradition. Such claims condition the way devotees regard these texts and receive their contents: indeed, that is their very raison d'être. Scholars, however, ought not to replicate the stance of the faithful or adopt a fetishism at second hand. Intellectual independence, integrity, and critical spirit require that we treat the "truths" of these texts more cautiously (and more properly) as "truth claims." Such a stance obliges us, moreover, to inquire about the human agencies responsible for the texts' production, reproduction, dissemination, consumption, and interpretation. As with secular exercises in persuasion, we need to ask, Who is trying to persuade whom of what in this text? In what context is the attempt situated, and what are the consequences should it succeed?

As a case in point, I would like to consider a brief passage from the *Chandogya Upaniṣad*, one of the longest, oldest, and most prestigious texts of this category: a crowning accomplishment of Vedic religion. Like the other principal Upaniṣads, the *Chandogya* is hard to date with certainty, but probably took shape in Northern India sometime in the middle of the first millennium BCE. Assembled from preexisting materials and participating in the tradition of the *Sāma Veda*, it is a work of vast scope and intellectual daring, marked by both rigor and imagination. Along with the *Bṛhadāraṇyaka Upaniṣad* (itself in the tradition of the *White Yajur Veda*), the *Chandogya* establishes the great themes of Upaniṣadic thought, attempting to identify esoteric patterns in the arcane details of sacrificial practice and to forge from these a unified understanding of the cosmos, the self, and the nature of being.[1]

Some years ago, I contributed a brief study of the sixth chapter (*adhyāya*) of the *Chandogya*, a text that works out one such pattern.[2] There, all existence is said to be composed of three basic qualities or elements. Most often, these include—in ranked order—(1) Brilliance (*tejas*), (2) Water (*āpas*), and (3) Food (*annam*). At times, however, variant forms of the set appear, including (1) Speech (*vāc*), (2) Breath (*prāṇa*), and (3) Mind (*manas*), which are understood as the essences of the basic categories. Thus, Speech is the essence of Brilliance (i.e. the loftiest, most rarefied, most brilliant of all things); Breath, the essence of Water (being the loftiest and most rarefied of life-sustaining fluids); and Mind, the essence of Food (being the loftiest and most rarefied of life-sustaining solid matter). A system of three colors—(1) Red, (2) White, (3) Black—provides another means to describe this system; and to demonstrate the system's universal applicability, the text treats several concrete examples. Thus, for instance, it describes how Fire is properly understood as consisting of Brilliance (= the red portion, flame), Water (= the white portion, smoke, conflated with clouds and steam), and Food (= the dark wood that fire "eats" and the ashes it produces [= the fire's excrement]).

This analysis further connects fire—and the givens of the system—to the three levels of the cosmos, homologizing Heaven, home of the red sun, to Brilliance; Atmosphere, home of the white clouds, to Water; and Earth, home of the dark soil and the plants that grow from it, to Food. Similarly, it can account for the social order as a set of hierarchized strata: (1) Priests (Brāhmaṇas), associated with the heavens, the flame of the sacrificial fire, and Brilliance; (2) Warriors (Kṣatriyas), with the atmosphere, lightning bolt, storm clouds, and Water; and (3) Commoners (Vaiśyas), with the dark earth, agricultural labor, dirt, excrement, and Food.

Such an analysis helped sustain the social order by naturalizing its categories and the rankings among them. Rather than understanding the tripartite *varṇa* ("caste," but more literally "color") system of Priests, Warriors, Commoners as the product of human institutions, conventions, and practices—or, alternatively, as the residue of past history and struggles— the *Chandogya* represents it as one more instance of the same pattern that determines the cosmos and everything in it. When arguments of this sort are advanced, accepted, and invested with sacred status, the stabilizing effects are enormous.

There are, however, other possibilities. If religious texts can help reinforce and reproduce the social order, they can also be used to modify it, either by agitating openly against its sustaining logic or, more modestly and more subtly, by using that same logic to recalibrate the positions assigned to given groups, shifting advantage from some to others. The passage I will cite, *Chandogya Upaniṣad* 1.3.6–7, provides a convenient example. Briefly, it adopts a variant on the system of three ranked categories—its version is (1) Breath, (2) Speech, (3) Food—and it aims its intervention not at the *varṇa* system but at a lower level of social classification: that which ranks different categories of priests in roughly parallel fashion.

To appreciate the skill of this maneuver, one must set it against the normative order, in which the Hotṛ ("Invoker") priests responsible for the hymns of the *Ṛg Veda* are accorded the paramount position. Udgātṛ ("Chanter") priests, responsible for the *Sāma Veda*, rank second, since their texts quote verses from—that is, are dependent on—the fuller compositions of the *Ṛg Veda*. Finally, there are the Adhvaryu priests, responsible for the *Yajur Veda*. In contrast to the other two collections, this text is in prose, from which the Adhvaryus—who are responsible for the physical actions involved in sacrifice (building the altar, pouring libations, killing and dismembering animal victims, etc.)—quote the formulae deemed appropriate to accompany each discrete step of the process (table 2.1).

Making matters more complicated still, the Sāman chants have multiple parts, which can be performed in more- and less-elaborate fashion, with different sections assigned to various assistants of the Udgātṛ. At the center of each performance, however, is the "Loud Chant" or "High Chant" known as the Udgītha, which is introduced by the most sacred of all syllables (*oṃ*) and is sung by the Udgātṛ himself.[3] The *Chandogya Upaniṣad*—which, as I noted earlier, is a text connected to the *Sāma Veda* and, as such, a possession of the Udgātṛ priests—is particularly concerned to assess the profound significance and esoteric power of the Udgītha chant. Whence the following passage.

TABLE 2.1 Normative ranked order among Vedic priests. *Note:* The "qualities" listed here are those that appear in *Chandogya Upaniṣad* 6, for which other like sets could be substituted, for example Purity (*sattva*)/Energy (*rajas*)/Darkness (*tamas*) or Speech (*vāc*)/Breath (*prāṇa*)/Mind (*manas*).

Rank	Quality	Priest	Veda	Genre	Action
1	Brilliance	Hotṛ	*Ṛg*	Hymns	Invoking
2	Water	Udgātṛ	*Sāma*	Chants	Chanting
3	Food	Adhvaryu	*Yajur*	Prose formulae	Physical action

One should homologize the syllables of [the name] "Udgītha" in this fashion: ud- is really Breath. Truly, one stands up [ud-tiṣṭhati] by the breath. gī- is Speech. Truly, speeches are regarded as words [giras]. tha is Food. Truly, all this [= the body] is established [sthitam] on food. Heaven is really ud, the atmosphere gī, the earth tha. The sun is really ud, the wind gī, the fire tha. The Sāma Veda is really ud, the Yajur Veda gī, the Ṛg Veda tha.[4]

In a tour de force of Upaniṣadic argumentation, this brief passage treats the word Udgītha as if each of its syllables had its own profound inner essence, and it uses a pseudophilological analysis to show that these are the three basic qualities of existence. The word as a whole—and thus, a fortiori, the "Udgītha" chant—is consequently seen to contain everything necessary to sustain the cosmos. And before it is finished, the text homologizes the syllables ud, gī, tha to the elemental qualities, the levels of the cosmos, the core entity of each cosmic level, and the three Vedas (table 2.2).

Two innovations are striking here. First, although most other texts tend to rank Speech above Breath, treating the latter as a coarser, more material substance that provides a foundation for the more rarefied, sublime existence of the former, this passage reverses those relations.[5] In doing so, it introduces a certain confusion, for Breath would seem to be more easily homologized to Atmosphere and Wind (as it regularly is elsewhere) than to Heaven and Sun (as is the case here).[6] In support of this move, the text offers a bit of wordplay. Grammatically, the syllable ud- is a preverb that adds the sense of "up" to the verbs it modifies. The text uses this suggestion of height to make the connection between ud and Heaven, highest of the cosmic strata, then argues for the association to Breath by observing that it is Breath that provides all vital force, permitting one to "stand up" (ud- √sthā-). The argument is forced, but mildly ingenious, at least within the rules of the game. Were one not paying close attention, it could pass unnoticed. And even should it be caught, one might be inclined to let it go, since nothing vital seems at stake in the matter.

TABLE 2.2 Homologies connecting the three syllables in the name of the Udgītha chant to other dimensions of existence. Note: According to the analysis of Chandogya Upaniṣad 1.3.6–7.

Rank	Syllable	Quality	Cosmic level	Defining object	Veda
1	ud	Breath	Heaven	Sun	Sāma
2	gī	Speech	Atmosphere	Wind	Yajur
3	tha	Food	Earth	Fire	Ṛg

Not so the case with the second, more provocative innovation, which turns the normal ranking of priests topsy-turvy. Two classes of priest—the Udgātṛ and Adhvaryu—both move up a notch, while the ordinarily paramount Hotṛ priest tumbles to last position. Tumbles? The metaphor is misleading, for the man was positively pushed. Pushed into the Food, what is more, which is to say—following the logic of the text—into the material realm of earth, dirt, and shit. Moreover, it was the *Chandogya Upaniṣad*—an extension of the *Sāma Veda*, product and instrument of the Udgātṛ priests—that performed this exquisitely cerebral act of pushing.

II

In an earlier work, I offered a protocol for dealing with texts like the one we have just considered. For the sake of explicitness, let me restate the steps involved in this method of analysis.[7]

1. Establish the categories at issue in the text on which the inquiry is focused. Note the relations among these categories (including the ways different categorical sets and subsets are brought into alignment), as well as their ranking relative to one another, also the logic used to justify that ranking.
2. Note whether there are any changes in the ranking of categories between the beginning of the text and its dénouement. Ascertain the logic used to justify any such shifts.
3. Assemble a set of culturally relevant comparative materials in which the same categories are at issue. Establish any differences that exist between the categories and rankings that appear in the focal text and those in these other materials.
4. Establish any connections that exist between the categories that figure in these texts and those which condition the relations of the social groups among whom the texts circulate.
5. Establish the authorship of all texts considered and the circumstances of their authorship, circulation, and reception.
6. Try to draw reasonable inferences about the interests that are advanced, defended, or negotiated through each text. Pay particular attention to the way the categories constituting the social order are redefined and recalibrated, such that certain groups move up and others move down within the extant hierarchy.

Some may charge that an approach of this sort shows disturbing cynicism, insofar as I focus on social, also material issues and on the will to power, while ignoring all that they consider truly and properly religious. Although rigorous definitions of the latter category rarely accompany such defensive reactions, I imagine my critics would emphasize such things as the cosmic sensibility, moral purpose, and spiritual yearning they take to be constitutive of the religious or the sense of reverence and wonder they find in religious texts.

Surely, I would not deny that such characteristics often figure prominently in religious discourse. It is hardly my intention to renew vulgar anticlerical polemic by asserting that religion is always venal, petty, pretentious, or deceitful. Rather, my point is the more basic and, I trust, more nuanced observation with which I began: religious texts are human products. Like all that is human, they are capable of high moral purpose *and* crass self-promotion, spiritual longing *and* material interest. When both these possibilities assert themselves, however, religious texts take considerable pains to contain, elide, or deny the resultant contradiction, which impeaches—or at least complicates—the idealized self-understanding religion normally cultivates.

The examples that fascinate me—*Chandogya Upaniṣad* 1.3.6–7, for instance—tend to be those in which this kind of contradiction proves uncontainable and bursts into view, if only one has knowledge enough to see it. Admittedly, these are extreme, and not typical cases. For that precise reason, however, they are analytically revealing, since they mark the limit point where texts that characteristically misrecognize their nature as human products are forced to acknowledge their human instrumentality and interests. My goal in treating such examples is not to replace our discipline's traditional concern for the metaphysical content of religious texts with an equally one-sided focus on their physical preconditions and consequences. Rather, I want to acknowledge both sides and understand how they are interrelated: the discursive and the material, the sacred and the social, or—to put it in Upaniṣadic terms, the realm of "Speech," "Breath," or "Brilliance" in its relation to the realm of "Food." And here, another passage from the *Chandogya* holds considerable interest.

III

This is *Chandogya Upaniṣad* 1.10–11, which tells the story of Uṣasti Cākrāyaṇa, "a needy man who dwelt in a wealthy village."[8] Wealthy though the village may normally have been, the narrative describes it when it had been devastated by hail[9] and its food supply was badly strained. We thus meet our hero in the act of begging from a "rich man," though circumstances have not been kind to the latter, who is reduced to eating a bowl of bad grain.[10] From this, however, he gives Uṣasti Cākrāyaṇa enough to eat and still take home a bit for his wife. But as it turned out, she had had success in her own begging, so she stores this bit of food, now thrice left over: once by the rich man, once by her husband, and once by the woman herself.[11]

Waking early the next morning, Uṣasti Cākrāyaṇa remarks to his wife, "Ah! If we had some food, we could get some money. The king is going to sponsor a sacrifice. He might select me for all the priestly duties."[12] So the good woman gives her husband the leftover grain, and after eating, he makes his way to the sacrifice, which is already in progress.[13] Sitting down beside the Udgātṛ and his two assistants, he warns them not to sing the chants with which they were charged, since they do not know the real deity associated with these verses.[14] The resultant commotion attracts the notice of the king, who is patron (*yajamāna*) of the sacrifice, which is probably just what Uṣasti Cākrāyaṇa wanted. Be that as it may, discussions follow, at the end of which he is hired to instruct the three *Sāma Veda* priests, and the king agrees to pay him the same salary as each of these worthies.[15]

So it is that Uṣasti Cākrāyaṇa comes to tell the Prastotṛ priest that Breath is the true deity of his Prastāva chant (i.e. the introductory praise hymn). By way of explanation, he notes that the word for "Breath"—Sanskrit *prāṇa*—has the same first element as do the priest's title (*pra-stotṛ*) and that of his chant (*pra-stāva*).[16] In similar fashion, he teaches the Udgātṛ that the true deity of the Udgītha is Sun (*āditya*), as indicated by the resemblance of the two words. And finally, he tells the Pratihartṛ that Food (*annam*) is the deity of his Pratihāra chant (i.e. the response that is the last phase of Sāman recitation), although here he has to work a bit harder to produce a philological justification. "Truly, all these beings live by obtaining food [*annam ... pratiharamāṇāni*]. That is the deity connected to the Pratihāra."[17] With this piece of esoteric wisdom the story comes to a close.

While the priests seem to have accepted the teachings of Uṣasti Cākrāyaṇa with gratitude, we might hesitate briefly before following their lead. Thus, although Breath and Food are often associated, nowhere else in Vedic literature does his triad of Breath/Sun/Food appear. Further, the insertion of Sun seems forced and a bit confused, since it is set in the second position rather than the first, which it normally occupies by virtue of its association with Heaven.[18] To cite the most relevant comparative example, the much fuller, more rigorous, and more orthodox discussion of *Chandogya Upaniṣad* 2.2–19 homologizes Sun to the Prastāva, not the Udgītha, as Uṣasti Cākrāyaṇa has it (table 2.3). The reputation of the latter sage—if sage he be—only compounds the difficulty, for he makes only one other appearance in all Vedic literature, in a passage where he plays a weak foil to the infinitely more learned Yajñavalkya.[19]

If close inspection shakes one's faith in the doctrine a bit, the frame story raises the suspicion that this is no esoteric wisdom at all, merely the simulacrum of same, invented by a poor, hungry, and clever man.[20] That

TABLE 2.3 Homologies posited by Uṣasti Cākrāyaṇa. *Note*: According to the narrative of *Chandogya Upaniṣad* 1.11.4–9, compared to those developed in greater detail in the same text, 2.2.2–19.2. Note the different placement of Sun in the two systems.

	1	*2*	*3*
Chandogya Upaniṣad 1.11.4-9	Prastāva	Udgītha	Pratihāra
	Breath	Sun	Food
Chandogya Upaniṣad 2.2.2-19.2	Prastāva	Udgītha	Pratihāra
	Sun	Atmosphere	Fire
	Cloud	Rain	Lightning
	Summer	Rainy season	Autumn
	Sunrise	Noon	Afternoon
	Speech	Sight	Hearing
	Skin	Flesh	Bone

Uṣasti Cākrāyaṇa was not above exploiting the opportunities presented by a royal sacrifice is surely suggested by his words to his wife: "If we had some food, we could get some money" (yad batānnasya labhemahi, labhemahi dhanamātrām).[21]

Food is convertible to money, the story shows us, via several mediations. Thus, as other portions of the *Chandogya* suggest, food is the material basis that makes breath and speech possible.[22] Under the right circumstances, speech is then convertible to wealth, for as the vehicle of wisdom and the necessary accompaniment to sacrificial practice, priestly speech wins compensation from wealthy patrons. But, as our story ever so slyly hints, pretentious chatter can also win money, provided it conveys the *semblance* of wisdom to gullible priests and patrons.

IV

Again, it is possible that I may be charged with cynicism or with abusively misinterpreting this text. Perhaps it is so. The chapter which immediately follows the story of Uṣasti Cākrāyaṇa, however, provides an indigenous commentary similar to my own, while surpassing the latter in its cynicism. *Chandogya Upaniṣad* 1.12—perhaps the most scandalously irreverent passage in all Vedic literature, sufficiently rich in truth and irony to have won the admiration of Kafka—reads as follows:[23]

> Now, there is the Udgītha of dogs. One day Baka Dālbhyo (or Glāva Maitreya) left home for his Vedic recitation. A white dog appeared to him. Other dogs gathered around him and said: "Good sir, obtain food for us by chanting. We are very hungry." He said to them: "Approach me together, early in the morning." So

Baka Dālbhya (or Glāva Maitreya) kept watch. Just as [priests] who chant the Bahiṣpavamāna praise hymn file in, each one holding the shoulders of the man in front of him, in this fashion the dogs filed in. Having sat down, they [began the sāman chant by] pronouncing the syllable *Hum.* Then they chanted: "Om. Let us eat! Om. Let us drink! Om. May the gods Varuṇa, Prajāpati, and Savitṛ bring food here! O Lord of food, bring food here! Om!"[24]

If Uṣasti Cākrāyaṇa is a dubious source, Baka Dālbhyo holds a rather different status. When presenting the mythic genealogy of the Udgītha chant, the *Chandogya* names three quasi-divine figures as its original masters (Aṅgiras, Bṛhaspati, Ayāsya), after which our man is listed as the first Udgātṛ priest of the Naimiṣa people. In this capacity, he won fulfillment of all his people's desires for them by the force of his chanting and the depth of his sacred knowledge, thereby establishing himself as the paradigmatic model for all subsequent Udgātṛs.[25]

By citing Baka Dālbhyo as the witness to "the Udgītha of dogs" (*śauva udgīthah*), the text plays with our sensibilities by attributing a seemingly parodic story to an unimpeachable source.[26] Whatever its origins, genre, or intent, the narrative is striking for the way it inverts the normal relations between the categories of Food and Speech, for in so doing it entertains a novel system of value, much as Uṣasti Cākrāyaṇa had done. Comparing the three systems is instructive (table 2.4).

In effect, these passages represent not just different systems of value but rival economic orders. Thus, the standard view makes the capacity to produce speech, more specifically learned and ritual speech, the highest value and primary form of capital while assigning a subordinate position to the production and consumption of material sustenance, here treated as simply the means to an end. Uṣasti Cākrāyaṇa keeps this order intact, but introduces a new category in the paramount position, thereby transforming an economy of priestly distinction into a monetized economy, open to entrepreneurship (such as his own) with unexpected profits, losses, and op-

TABLE 2.4 Recalibration of standard Upaniṣadic values in *Chandogya Upaniṣad* 1.10–11 (Uṣasti Cākrāyaṇa) and 1.12 (the Udgītha of Dogs)

Standard view	Uṣasti Cākrāyaṇa	Udgītha of Dogs
1. Speech	1. Money	1. Food
2. Breath	2. Speech	2. Speech
3. Food	3. Breath	3. Breath
	4. Food	

portunities for accumulation. Finally, the narrative of the dogs entertains an economy more imaginary than real, which inverts the standard order. This is an economy of consumption and pleasure, where priestly speech—and not food—is simply the means to an end. In this alternate universe, the ultimate beneficiaries and ruling stratum are those whom other systems judge to be "animals": those for whom material existence and bodily pleasure are not degraded and degrading, but the goal and supreme joy of existence. Dancing, singing, and feasting together, they inhabit a world whose supreme deity is "Lord of food" (*annapati*), and their most sacred chant has as its refrain "Om. Let us eat! Om. Let us drink!"[27]

<h1 style="text-align:center">V</h1>

By way of conclusion, let me return to the question of how the metaphysical and the physical—or, more precisely, the speculative and the sociopolitical—interpenetrate in texts of the sort we have been discussing. The conscious goal of the Upaniṣads, as I understand them, is *not* to provide ideological support for a discriminatory social hierarchy. Rather, the authors of these texts struggled to explicate the fundamental unity and essential nature of all being. And given the total nature of their inquiry, most of the domains for which they offered analysis—the levels of the cosmos or the constituent elements of the sacrificial fire, for instance—are not themselves affected by such theorizing. People influenced by it, however, ought to change the way they regard these (and all other) entities. This is to say that the prime effects of such discourse are on consciousness. Only through the mediation of human subjects does it reach and potentially reshape other parts of the cosmos. Its capacity to do this, moreover, varies with the nature of the entity in question. No matter how many people a given text reaches and influences, it will not change the position of the sun in the heavens. Nor will it change the fire's need for oxygen and fuel, although it can change the way people build fires: the kinds of fuel they use, the shape in which they build hearths and altars, and so on.

If texts acquire their agency only through the mediation of those subjects whose consciousness they reshape, it follows that they have their greatest effects on entities which are themselves most fully the product of human activity. The shape of houses and cities, for instance, is more open to human intervention than is the shape of a fire. The extreme case here is the way humans organize themselves and their relations with others. Rather than treating this as an extreme case, however, the Upaniṣads treat the social order as *a case like any other*, one more instance of the same overarching pattern that undergirds the entire cosmos. In this moment, they simultaneously collapse the physical in the metaphysical and naturalize the social. Those whose consciousness has been shaped by such a vision are conditioned to see, accept, ponder, and admire the same "cosmic" order in all its (putative) instantiations. They are also conditioned to reproduce that order through their conscious interpretations and, where relevant, also their active labor. Insofar as they do this in their relations with other (similarly conditioned) subjects, they create a social order. Moreover, they experience that order as one more confirmation of the pattern they have learned to identify with the nature of the cosmos, for all that it is the product of their own discourse and practice.

The point of critical analysis, then, is not to question the sincerity or integrity of those who speculate about the nature of the cosmos, nor is it to charge them, ad hominem, with bad faith. Rather, it is to suggest that the nature of their speculation is informed and inflected by their situation of interest, which has always already been normalized and naturalized by the prior speculations of others like them. Beyond this, one must realize that the nature of the cosmos is not significantly affected by the content of human speculation. The nature of society, in contrast, exists only insofar as it is continually produced and reproduced by human subjects, whose consciousness informs their constitutive actions, perceptions, and senti-ments. When any given discourse—metaphysical or cosmological, as well as explicitly sociological—succeeds in modifying general consciousness, this can have profound consequences for social reality, even if cosmic reality remains serenely unaffected.

CHAPTER THREE

NATURE AND GENESIS OF PANTHEONS

I

It is generally taken for granted that Greeks, Romans, Hindus, and countless others have found polytheism "good to think." The same goes for scholars of religion, although presumably with a bit more critical distance. Beyond the obvious question—Just what do we mean by *pantheon*?—one might also ask whether all polytheistic religions possess a pantheon, and if so, are all of the same type? Further, if—as we commonly assume—a pantheon has (is?) a structure and a system, precisely who constitutes it as such and endows the structure with its coherence? How systemic are these structures and how stable are these systems?

To begin engaging these issues, it is heuristically useful to differentiate three types of pantheons (and their three associated modes of pantheon production). The first step is to distinguish pantheons that are given relatively full and explicit articulation by a Hesiod, for example, from others that have no such formal, authoritative encoding. The latter might be considered "implicit pantheons," but one might also term them "prepantheons," "protopantheons," or something of the sort, since they provide the basis from which their more fully, consciously, and explicitly theorized counterparts are generated.

Pantheons of the implicit sort are a byproduct of the ongoing religious activity of a polytheistic population, representing the sedimented results of informal discourse and practical experimentation. Thus, as ordinary people gravitate toward specific deities for specific purposes, based on a god's existing reputation and recent record of success, the divinities assume ever-more-distinct identities. Some grow in popularity, and their areas of (putative) expertise expand as reports of their powers circulate. Conversely, other gods' spheres of activity contract, and these deities may even face obsolescence as fewer supplicants seek their assistance for a diminished number of concerns. Over time, as people ceaselessly report their experiences to one another, exchanging and reshaping their opinions in the process, a collective imaginary gradually takes shape, within which the division of divine labor assumes ever-more-standardized form as people reach relative agreement about the nature of the various deities (especially the interests, capabilities, and range of activity imputed to each) and the potential relations among them (as, for instance, when the logical affinity between certain abstract principles is encoded as family relation, friendship, cooperation, or erotic attraction between the deities manifesting those qualities).

Inevitably, analogies drawn from human social and political institutions will inform discussions where the divine is imagined, at which point a previously loose, even amorphous collection of gods can acquire aspects of a celestial family, royal court, incipient bureaucracy, or some other culturally appropriate patterned structure. In this moment, a pantheon has taken relatively coherent shape, even if no indigenous actor or text has ever theorized it as such or articulated it in its entirety. It is, however, less a fixed system and enduring structure than a repertoire or anthology that remains always-evolving.

I am inclined to think any population that entertains more than one god will develop such an implicit pantheon. Less common, however, are pantheons that have acquired fuller and more explicit form, such that their constituent pieces are integrated within some overarching schema that is relatively complex and that has become an object of interest in itself, quite apart from its practical implications. Although there are probably exceptions to this rule, a well-structured, comprehensive pantheon is likely to be the result of conscious, sustained theoretical labor carried out by specialists (such as priests, poets, theologians, and shamans) who make it their task to refine, systematize, complete, and perfect the more diffuse intuitions of the implicit pantheon.

Those who produce explicit pantheons are not just specialists in speculation, however. In addition, they must have access to prestigious and enduring means of communication. The production of written texts is the most obvious case, but inspired poetry, oracular proclamation, temple architecture, and iconography, for instance, can play similar roles. Ultimately, both theorists and their favored media must wield sufficient authority to secure wide acceptance and high respect for the pantheons they produce and disseminate.

Not every polytheistic religion develops an explicit pantheon, and many—perhaps most—make do with the partial understandings that percolate through a steady stream of informal conversations. When an explicit pantheon does emerge, it does not fully supplant its implicit predecessor, since unsystematic assumptions persist and informal conversations continue. The explicit pantheon does inflect and constrain such conversations, however, establishing what assumptions are commonly made while rendering others less acceptable or likely. In this fashion, it stabilizes the population's understanding of its gods, establishing a norm that serves as the basis for further discussions. This does not necessarily constitute an orthodoxy or canon, but it approaches that status, as it becomes an ordered system, encoded in prestigious genres, backed by authoritative specialists, widely diffused and commonly accepted.

Beyond the distinction between "implicit" and "explicit" pantheons, one must also differentiate between pantheons produced by indigenous theorists, who are concerned to organize their own beliefs and those of their coreligionists, and those worked out by scholars of a later era (or different culture), whose business it is to "study" the gods of others (fig. 3.1).

No less than colleges of ancient priests, modern researchers also collect evidence from implicit pantheons and subject this to such theoretical operations as synthesis, extrapolation, abstraction, analogy, clarification, and schematization. If all goes well, at the end of such labors they provide a coherent, well-structured system: an explicit—but exogenous—pantheon, whose goals are descriptive (not prescriptive), whose claims to truth are historical (not religious), and whose authority derives from scholarly rigor (not poetic inspiration, priestly devotion, visionary experience, or the like).

Clearly, indigenous and exogenous theorists can produce pantheons that are near identical in their form and content, for they work from the same raw material with similar goals and methods, attempting to provide a thorough, elegant, schematic overview of the way the deities are more haphazardly imagined by the population at large. Where the two differ most strongly, however, is the way their results do—or do not—filter back to that general

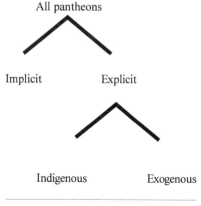

FIGURE 3.1 Subcategories of pantheons.

population. Thus, an indigenous pantheon does not just draw information from its implicit predecessor while leaving the latter unmodified. Rather, as the explicit version permeates general consciousness, it stabilizes popular thinking about the gods, which, as a result, becomes less amorphous and labile. In the sharpest possible contrast, exogenous pantheons ordinarily have little effect on the populations whose beliefs they describe. (For obvious reasons, this is particularly true for those produced by students of ancient religions.)

The preceding discussion prompts three generalizations:

1. Implicit pantheons, which are relatively ubiquitous, remain fairly flexible and open to change until indigenous specialists produce an explicit pantheon (something that does not happen among all peoples).
2. An explicit pantheon gives more rigorous, systematic, comprehensive, and schematic expression to the way the gods are popularly imagined, stabilizing the divine order by narrowing the range and slowing the rate of religious change (but never eliminating change altogether).
3. If a society produces no explicit pantheon of its own, exogenous theorists may take up that task, even many centuries later. What they produce, however, will influence no community of believers and will have no stabilizing effects (except in the scholarly literature).

At best, an exogenous pantheon can generate the formal results that indigenous theory might have produced at one particular moment in time. But in the absence of indigenous theory, implicit pantheons will continue to develop in unpredictable ways that are hard to capture—and impossible to arrest—by any exogenous theoretician. Exogenous theorists thus deceive themselves when they believe too strongly in their own pantheons and mistake these artificial scholarly constructions for faithful *re*-constructions of anything that had more than potential or evanescent existence.

II

As a case in point, let us consider Old Norse or *altgermanische* religion, which developed an indigenous pantheon only very late in its history. Earlier, there is evidence of an implicit pantheon alongside the efforts of two exogenous theorists: Caesar and Tacitus. Surviving evidence of the implicit pantheon is abundant enough, consisting of inscriptions (in Latin and Runic); theophoric personal and place-names; pictorial representations on bracteates, rune stones, and the like; and a great body of prose and poetry in which various gods make their appearance and have their adventures. In none of these data, however, are the several-score individually named gods ever theorized as a set.[1]

This variety, abundance, and confusion notwithstanding, Caesar simplifies ruthlessly: "They admit to the company of the gods only those whom they perceive with their senses and from whose works they clearly derive benefit: Sun, Vulcan, and Moon. They have not heard of the rest, even by rumor."[2] All three of those Caesar names do show up as minor deities in Germanic sources (e.g. Old Norse Sól, Máni, and Völundr), but the utilitarian principle he articulates finds no indigenous support, and his denial of other deities is flatly contradicted not only by the inscriptional evidence but by the better-informed testimony of Tacitus, written a century and a half later (98 or 99 CE).

> Among the gods, they attend to Mercury most highly and on certain days they have the obligation to offer sacrifice to him with human victims. They placate Hercules and Mars with animal offerings. Some of the Suebi sacrifice to Isis.[3]

There is reasonable scholarly agreement that the Germanic gods of Tacitus's *interpretatio romana* were Mercury = *Wóðanaz (Old High German Wuotan, Anglo-Saxon Woden, Old Saxon Uuoden, Old Norse Óðinn), Hercules = *Thunraz (Old High German Donar, Anglo-Saxon Thunor, Old Norse Thórr), and Mars = *Teiwaz (Old High German Ziu, Anglo-Saxon Tíw ~ Tíg, Gothic Tius, Old Norse Týr), although Isis remains more elusive. Like Caesar, Tacitus made a selection among the attested Germanic deities, singling out several to be organized in a structure reminiscent of the Roman Capitoline triad. In contrast to Caesar's (mini)pantheon, however, that assembled by Tacitus does actually resemble certain divine groups attested among the Germans.

Three comparanda are regularly cited, although none matches the Tacitean system exactly and all differ somewhat from each other.[4] Temporally closest is an inscription found at Remagen, where members of the XXXth Roman Legion—which was stationed in Germania inferior and included German soldiers among its number—that dedicates their cause to I(ovi) O(ptimo) M(aximo) et Genio loc(i) Marti Hercul(i) Mercurio Ambiomarcis.[5] This supplies the closest match, since the three gods named by Tacitus are all present. They appear, however, in inverse order and Mercury is no longer paramount, that role now being assigned to Jupiter (whose omission from the Tacitean version served to identify the Germans as religiously defective). The local deity (*genius loci*) is accorded second place, followed by Mars, Hercules, Mercury, and the otherwise obscure Ambiomarcis, whose name suggests he was a Gallic and not a German deity.[6]

Second, there is the Old Saxon baptismal vow, dating to the latter part of the ninth century, in which the new convert was obliged to abjure the old gods, stating, "I forsake all the devil's words and works: Thunaer and Uuoden and Saxnōt and all the unholy beings who are their companions."[7] Here, Thunaer—not Uuoden—is given first place, reflecting the latter god's relative unimportance among the continental Germans.[8] What is more, the third member of the triad has no relation to either "Mars" or *Teiwaz, for Saxnōt is the national god (i.e. the eponymous divine representation) of the Saxon people.[9] As such, he resembles the genius loci of the Remagen inscription more than any of the figures mentioned by Tacitus.

Finally, there is the group of cult statues at the Uppsala Temple, as described by Adam of Bremen around 1070, where Thor was placed in the middle, with Odin and Fricco on either side.[10] Again, the first two figures provide a reasonable match for the Tacitean set, albeit with a shift in hierarchy, since Adam identified Thor as most powerful (potentissimus eorum). Complicating matters further, Adam identified Thor with Jupiter (not Hercules) and Odin with Mars (not Mercury).[11] For his part, Fricco was given no interpretatio romana and apparently resembled no Roman god. Endowed with an enormous phallus, presiding over marriages, ensuring peace and pleasure, he represents a local version of the Old Norse Freyr, the fertility/prosperity god from whom Swedish kings claimed descent.[12]

It would seem that Tacitus had reasonable but imperfect and incomplete information about a tendency of the ancient Germans to organize their gods in triads, at least for some purposes and on some occasions. That this was not the only pattern they utilized and that these three gods were not the only ones worshipped must have been clear to him, for he names nine other deities elsewhere in the Germania.[13]

It thus appears that the triad of Germania 9 is best regarded as one variant on one common pattern that was part—but not all—of the implicit pantheon. As an exogenous product, the Tacitean version simplified a body of discourse that was more complex, schematized an understanding of deities that was more diffuse, and suggested more stability in Germanic constructions of the divine order than was ever actually present. Nor did the publication of this variant have any stabilizing effect on the implicit pantheon. Informal conversations continued, and Germans continued to reimagine the way their gods might be fitted into triads and other structures, as attested by the three variants we have considered, all of which postdate Tacitus and differ from his in the ways I have suggested (table 3.1).

III

To judge from surviving records, only one indigenous pantheon was ever proposed for the Old Norse gods: that of Snorri Sturluson's Prose Edda,

TABLE 3.1 Texts that constitute the Germanic pantheon in (semi-)triadic fashion. *Note*: Gods explicitly identified as having primacy are represented in capital letters.

Tacitus, *Germania* 9 (98 CE)		1. Mercury (=*Wóðanaz)	2. Hercules (=*Thunraz)	3. Mars (=*Teiwaz)	4. Isis	
Remagen inscription (*ca.* 300 CE)	1. Jupiter Optimus Maximus	5. Mercury	4. Hercules	3. Mars	2. *genius loci*	6. Ambiomarcis
Saxon baptismal formula (*ca.* 900 CE)		2. Uuoden	1. Thunaer		3. Saxnōt	
Uppsala temple statues (*ca.* 1070 CE)		2. Odin (= Mars)	1. THOR (= Jupiter)		3. Fricco	

written around 1220. This is perhaps the last moment such an attempt could have been made, since it dates more than two centuries after Iceland converted to Christianity. Snorri himself was not an active "pagan" believer but a serious antiquarian, determined not to let the old religion fade into oblivion.[14] Toward that end, and possibly inspired by Greco-Roman models,[15] he wove information he garnered from older poetry and surviving oral traditions into a textbook of sorts that identified twelve primary gods (Æsir) and fourteen goddesses (Ásynjurnar), detailing the complex relations that bound them together, including ties of birth, marriage, courtship, erotic dalliance, oath, treaty, rivalry and conflict, propinquity in residence, shared travels and adventures, and familial obligations of vengeance.[16]

Like Hesiod, whom he resembles in many ways, Snorri drew together all manner of fragmentary and inconsistent testimonies of the earlier implicit pantheon, conferred on them a definitive shape and structure, then embedded the results in a text destined to exercise enormous influence for many centuries thereafter. Often, his treatment of source material was meticulous and reverent, but he also remodeled the older traditions, and he could be extremely inventive. It is impossible to give a full picture of his efforts here, but the way he handled the moderately obscure deity Ullr provides an instructive example.

Several dozen toponyms show that Ullr was widely worshipped across Norway and Sweden, but with much less representation in Iceland and Denmark (fig. 3.2). None of the specific names reveal much, however, about the way this deity was imagined.[17] Similarly, an inscription recovered from the Thorsberg moor in Schleswig-Holstein confirms that he was already worshipped as early as 200 CE, but says nothing of the god himself.[18] His name

FIGURE 3.2 Distribution of toponyms containing the name of Ullr; from Jan de Vries, *Altgermanische Religionsgeschichte*, 3rd ed. (Berlin: Walter de Gruyter, 1970), 2: 155. Courtesy of Walter de Gruyter GmbH & Co.

offers some help, perhaps, for its Germanic cognates denote "glory."[19] Still, none of the philological, epigraphic, onomastic, or archeological evidence provides insight into the qualities, character, or range of activities attributed to this elusive god. For that, we must turn to the relatively small number of texts in which Ullr appears. The information they offer is so disparate, however, that one gets no sense of coherence, *and that is precisely the point.*[20]

Skaldic references dwell on a finite number of themes, speaking of Ull's general prowess in battle (*Ullar él, Ullr böð-gefnar, Ullr egg-hrídar hjaldr-Ullr, hríð-Ullr*, etc.) and mentioning a finite number of attributes, above all his shield, which he seems to have used as a mode of transport (over sea, or perhaps over ice) in some lost myth, since any ship can be called Ull's shield (*Ullar kjóll*). His weapons also get mentioned on occasion, most often a sword (*Ullr brands, Ullr branda, Ullr benloga*) and on one occasion a bowstring (*Ullr álmsíma*).[21] In contrast, eddic poetry makes no mention of Ull's weapons or mode of travel. Rather, the three verses in which he appears treat an oath sworn by his ring;[22] a hall he built named "Yew-dales" (*Ýdalir*);[23] and the favor he grants those who handle fire in some ritual fashion.[24] Finally, there is a narrative recounted by Saxo Grammaticus, in which a euhemerized Ollerus (= Ullr) is elected to take the place of King Othinus (= Óðinn) when the latter is forced into exile. He hold royal office and honors for ten years, until Othinus was restored, perhaps as the result of bribery. Thereafter, Ollerus retired to Sweden, where he was killed while trying to reassert his good reputation.[25] To this, Saxo appends a bit of information, which he characterizes as a rumor (*fama*): "The rumor is that he was so skilled in the use of magic tricks [*præstigiarum usu*] that for crossing the seas, instead of a ship, he employed a bone that he had sealed with dread incantations [*diris carminibus obsignavisset*]."[26]

Warfare, oaths, rituals, kingship, magic, runes, swords, shields, ships, and sea voyages: the list is disparate indeed. One gets the impression that Ullr was perceived as an ill-defined jack-of-all-(male)-trades or, to put it differently, his position was constantly shifting within the implicit pantheon as people turned to him for one need or another. Working with the materials we have assembled and perhaps others now lost to us, Snorri produced the following portrait:

> One [of the gods] called Ullr is Sif's son and Thor's stepson. He is so good an archer and skier that no one can compete with him. He is fair in appearance and has the skills of a warrior. He is also a good god to invoke in a duel.[27]

At certain points one can see precisely how Snorri transformed the information he took from his sources. Particularly instructive, for instance, is the way he revised Ull's place in the divine kinship system. Thus, several skaldic verses cited by Snorri refer to Ullr as Thor's *mágr*, a term that denotes males whose relation to each other is mediated through marriage and one that is used for fathers- and sons-in-law alike, also for sisters' husbands and wife's brothers.[28] It is thus ambiguous as regards the relative age and hierarchic order of the two men so designated, an ambiguity Snorri found intolerable. Determined to assert Thor's superior status, in his own text he describes Ullr not as Thor's indeterminate in-law (*mágr*) but as his stepson (*stjúpsonr, stjúpr*), something unattested in all surviving sources.[29] He then portrays Ullr as the son of Sif, Thór's wife, implying that (1) she had an earlier marriage, of which Ullr was the product; (2) that marriage dissolved, after which Sif married Thor; and (3) Thor adopted her child to consolidate the new family.[30] For none of this is there any prior evidence, but it was part of the theoretical labor Snorri found necessary to produce a fuller, richer, more schematic and properly ordered—that is, more explicit—pantheon than had previously existed.

Something similar is evident when Snorri amplifies the lone skaldic reference (or at least the only one that has survived) to Ull's "bowstring" (*álmsíma*) and makes the bow his iconic weapon (describing him as *bogmaðr*, "bow-man" or "archer").[31] Like most Norse gods, Ullr was frequently associated with blades and shields in skaldic verse, but this reference to a bow is more unusual. However isolated it may be, it helped distinguish him from the other martial figures and let Snorri endow him with a more distinctive identity.

Snorri's reasons for describing Ullr as one who "travels on skis" (*skíðfœrr*)[32] were probably similar, although his basis for this is quite unclear, since none of the surviving sources say anything of the sort. Accordingly, some ingenious scholars have suggested that the magic bone Saxo's rumor credited to Ollerus was actually the blade of a preindustrial ice skate (made of bone), and that his rapid ocean voyages were winter trips across frozen seas.[33] The argument seems strained, but the problem is real, since one presumes Snorri must have had some basis for his view of Ullr as master skier. Others have cited a Viking-age rune stone from Böksta (ca. 1050 CE) in this regard, since it shows an archer on skis, although nothing in the image (a hunting scene) or the accompanying text identifies this figure as Ullr (plate 1). Even if it were so, and even if Snorri knew of this image (or the tradition that informed it), one still must understand that Snorri chose to ignore most other aspects of Ullr that were known to him from various sources (oaths, rings, magic, kingship, runes, etc.) and created a distinctive identity for Ullr by making {skis + archery} his prime attributes.[34]

Regardless of how one imagines Snorri's motives and modus operandi, one can recognize how the relative fluidity of Ullr's image in earlier centuries gave way to one that was quite fixed after Snorri's model of the pantheon became standard. This only happened belatedly, however, for Snorri's attempt to rekindle his contemporaries' interest in old poetry and old gods fell on relatively deaf ears, and his work was largely ignored in the centuries following his assassination in 1241.

Only centuries later—in 1643, to be exact—were manuscripts of Snorri's *Edda* rediscovered. Almost immediately, however, this text sparked considerable interest, as evidenced by the *Edda oblongata*, where an artist of about 1680 produced twenty-three drawings of the old gods, based on Snorri's descriptions. There, Ullr holds a ski pole in his left hand and stands on skis that have been bent in an arc and tied with a cord, thereby forming an ambiguous image—or visual pun—uniting his attributes of bow and skis (plate 2).

Eighteenth-century publications of the *Prose Edda* also bore images of the deities, consistent with Snorri's descriptions. In these, Ullr always appears on skis, with bow in hand (plates 3 and 4).

Subsequent publications followed much the same pattern, although occasionally they combined attributes drawn from Snorri with others, as in an 1882 etching by Friedrich Wilhelm Heine, which gives Ullr his now-standard bow, but puts him on skates rather than the more usual skis (plate 5); or an illustration in Fredrik Sander's 1893 translation of the *Poetic Edda*, which gives him not only bow and skis but a torch and a bird on his helmet (plate 6). Neopagan groups, which have flourished in Europe and North America during the twentieth and twenty-first centuries, have largely followed the kind of iconography, style, and somber mood evident in Heine's engraving, while refashioning Ullr—like the other Scandinavian gods—as an instantiation of their idealized Nordic masculinity: powerful of body, serious of visage, ready (and able) to kill when necessary for the benefit of his kindred and race. Within neopagan ideology, the gods share and model this responsibility, and they are differentiated from one another largely by the iconic weapons they employ. Ullr's bow thus comes to overshadow his skis, which are often relegated to the background in neopagan images of him (plates 7 and 8). At times, the skis disappear altogether, so that his identity as Ullr the resolute hunter can emerge undiluted (plate 9), as in this "Ode to the Hunting God" composed by one "Cullyn Ullrson," Chieftain of the Eagle Hearth of Brisbane, Australia, and—to judge from the name he constructed for himself, a self-styled son of the deity :

Ullr guide skilled hand and sharp eye,
With bow, arrow, knife and spear
To be ready for all tasks at hand
As the time of the hunt grows near.

Ullr guide me to feed hearth, clan, kin
Life must feed on life.
Teach patience and knowledge
Of my place in the weaving of life's design
For through this action I alter my wyrd
A thread to be plucked at any time.

Ullr guide me to be devoid of ego
And to take only what I need
To survive the hard times.[35]

It is not just neopagans who show a certain renewed devotion to Ullr, however. In recent decades he has also been embraced—albeit with less seriousness and self-consciously grim determination—by ski enthusiasts, who have made him their patron deity of snow and winter sports.[36] Playful images of an unthreatening, whimsical, occasionally debauched, Dionysiac Ullr are now ubiquitous in logos, medallions, T-shirts, jewelry, theme beverages, and winter festival celebrations. For this puckish deity, skis and not bow are indispensable. The bow remains a frequent attribute, although rarely used in earnest (plates 10 and 11), and sometimes it disappears entirely, having been supplanted in some ways by the rather clownish Viking helmet with which this Ullr is now often equipped (plates 12–14).

If one can distinguish between the contemporary cult of Ullr the Dread Hunter (bow accentuated, skis relegated to the background) favored by neopagans and that of Ullr the Playful Patron of Winter Sports (skis accentuated, bow deemphasized or displaced by helmet) favored by alpine revelers, the two are equally rooted in the indigenous pantheon established by Snorri in the thirteenth century. Devotees can shift their emphasis from one of the now-mandatory attributes to the other, but their range of invention has been constrained by the authority of Snorri's version. Artists working in the fantasy genre, however, are not so tightly bound to established conventions, and are capable of reimagining the god in rather novel fashion, as in a strikingly aggressive rendering that gives him a brutal war axe in place of his bow, along with ravens and wolves for companions (plate 15). Equally original, if radically different in its conceptualization and style, is an image of Ullr as a slender, almost androgynous albino who grips his bow with steadfast determination (plate 16).

One could multiply these examples many times over, but the set I have assembled is sufficient for our present purposes. What I should like to have demonstrated is the relative consistency of the way Ullr has been imagined since the recovery of Snorri's *Edda* in the mid-seventeenth century. Once that text became available, it served as the prime point of reference for anyone concerned with the Old Norse gods, providing an indigenous pantheon after the fact. On rare occasion, an intrepid neopagan stumbles across one of the earlier sources and reconsiders Ullr's association with rings, ships, shields, or magic bones.[37] Even rarer is a believer—or simply an experimenter—who entertains the possibility that Ullr might have efficacy, applicability, or interest in some novel realm of endeavor. Such things do happen, to be sure, for novelty and human invention can never be closed down altogether.[38] That having been said, the point remains: an indigenous pantheon is not just a system or a structure but an instrument for the relatively stable reproduction of the divine order, which exercises its potent effects by establishing the parameters within which imagination, devotion, experimentation, and debate will be conducted thereafter.

CHAPTER FOUR

THE COSMO-LOGIC OF PERSIAN DEMONOLOGY

I

Although demonology was—and remains—a major part of many religions and cultures, the topic has received less scholarly attention than one might expect. The bases of demonological discourse having been discredited during the Enlightenment, it would seem the topic has been drained of all save antiquarian interest. With few exceptions, most studies are condescending in tone and superficial in their engagement, as if reflecting residual anxiety that such foolishness might be contagious or—a less magical construction of the same dynamic—that evincing too much interest can damage one's reputation.[1]

As the result of such skittishness, our understanding of many cultures and historic eras remains impoverished, for some of the best minds of numerous peoples were devoted to demonology. However much we may reject the foundational assumptions of this discourse, this hardly forces the conclusion that speculation on the demonic is necessarily naïve, "superstitious," or infantile. As a working hypothesis, I assume that the demonological components of any religion are no less intelligent than those of its other constituent parts and (therefore) deserve equally serious study.

Let me suggest that where it thrives, demonology constitutes something like a unified field theory of what we treat separately under the rubrics of bacteriology, epidemiology, toxicology, teratology, criminology, Marxism, psychoanalysis, and others, for it is an unflinching attempt to name, comprehend, and defend against all that threatens, frightens, and harms us. While such a project has clear import for questions of ethics, it goes well beyond that relatively narrow domain, stretching into physics, metaphysics, cosmology, and ontology, as I hope to show by examining a reasonably well-attested and historically important example, that of pre-Islamic (or: Mazdaean) Iran.[2]

II

Mazdaean literature (i.e. Zoroastrian texts plus Achaemenian royal inscriptions, which may or may not be Zoroastrian) on the demonic is large but diffuse, and the topic permeates virtually all other concerns, as we will ultimately see. To treat this in anything approaching comprehensive fashion goes far beyond my ambitions in this essay, where, by way of example, I will focus on just a few texts and demons. The first passage of interest is *Yašt* 18.1–2, a hymn of the Avesta (i.e. the older Zoroastrian scriptures) where demonology informs the sociopolitical imaginary.

> The Wise Lord said to Zarathuštra: "I created the Aryan royal glory, rich in cattle, with many pastures, with many riches, which conveys much wisdom/ spiritual power, which conveys much wealth, suppressor of Appetite, suppressor of bad spirits. It overcomes the extremely deadly Evil Spirit. It overcomes Rage of the bloody club. It overcomes yellow Torpor. It overcomes Ice that makes things rigid. It overcomes the demon Drought. It overcomes the non-Aryan countries."[3]

Most immediately, this passage treats the question of royal legitimacy, which it theorizes as a radiant charisma or "glory" (Avestan *x*ᵛ*arənah*) bestowed on rightful kings by God himself. Here and in related texts, this supreme form of legitimate power is construed as a monopoly of the Aryan (= Iranian) people and is said to convey benefits that include wisdom, wealth, and the ability to prevail over a host of menacing evils.[4] Six such menaces are specified by name, and non-Aryans are associated with these qualities and dangers. One of these—Rage—suggests that foreigners lack emotional control and are prone to violence, while two of the others—Ice and Drought—associate them with the elemental qualities of cold and dryness, which countless other texts define as antithetical to the flourishing of life, in pointed opposition to the divine, life-sustaining qualities of warmth and moisture.[5] Two others we will consider more thoroughly, but let us begin with the "Evil Spirit," elsewhere called "the demon of demons,"[6] who is the source of all others.

III

Invariably, the Evil Spirit (Avestan Aŋra Mainyu = Pahlavi Ahreman, also referred to as "the Foul Spirit" [Pahlavi *Gannāg Mēnōg*], "the Adversary" [Pahlavi *Petyārag*], or "the Lie" [Pahlavi *Druz* = Old Persian *Drauga*, Avestan *Drug*]) is set in binary opposition to the Wise Lord (Avestan and Old Persian Ahura Mazdā = Pahlavi Ohrmazd). These two—and they alone—exist from eternity, occupying opposite quadrants of the cosmos. As the opening passage of the *Bundahišn* specifies, they are diametrically opposed in their nature although they share one important characteristic: neither is omnipotent, each being limited by the existence and power of the other (a point that exculpates the deity from any responsibility for evil).

> It is revealed thus in the good religion: Ohrmazd exists in the highest height, in omniscience and goodness, forever in the light . . . Ahreman exists in darkness, in ignorance and love of destruction, in the station of the depths.[7]

The contrast between the two is overdetermined, and other passages work further binaries into this structure of opposition: light versus darkness, high versus low, all-knowing versus utterly ignorant, good versus evil, the benevolent powers of creation versus malevolent delight in destruction, fragrance versus stench, hot versus cold, and moist versus dry.[8] Mazdaean creation mythology thematizes these contrasts in what one might call the mother of all "outbreak narratives," to use Priscilla Wald's evocative terminology.[9] Although the story has many episodes and variants, let us note that the Wise Lord created an ideal world in which plants, animals, and humans initially enjoyed a perfect existence: without sickness, death, or suffering of any sort, also without the need to eat or reproduce.[10] Jealous, the Evil Spirit launched an attack from his dark depths, and to assist in the coming battle he fabricated the first demons. Most texts say he used darkness as the raw material for this act of "miscreation,"[11] and some hint that this was done via masturbation[12] or self-sodomy.[13] One way or another, the demons resembled their maker and material of origin, being not just dark, but "destructive creatures . . . terrible, foul, and vile in their evil."[14] With these for his troops, weapons, and allies, the Evil Spirit then assaulted the Wise Lord's creatures.

> He set loose Appetite, Deprivation, Distress, Pain, Sickness, Lust, and Torpor on the First Animal and the First Man.[15]

This is the start of all physical and moral evils that afflict embodied creatures: a list of seven demonic—what? Beings? Forces? Personified states? Abstract qualities? Like most Mazdaean discussions, this text defies such questions, for its categories do not correspond neatly to ours. In a moment, we will have to consider the construction of demons as *spritual* beings and the sweeping implications such an understanding entails. Yet before we do so, let us note that the first and last demons the Evil Spirit unleashed—Appetite and Torpor—recur in the list of demons associated with non-Aryan peoples. These are the two we will consider more fully.

First, however, we need to understand that Mazdaean cosmology was dualistic—fittingly enough—in two different senses. Thus, it posited a stark ethical opposition of good versus evil alongside an equally strong metaphysical distinction between spiritual (Pahlavi *mēnōg* = Avestan *main-iiauua*) and material (Pahlavi *gētīg* = Avestan *gaēθa*) planes of existence. The spiritual is theorized as the basis of all existence, being original, intangible, and insubstantial. In contrast, material existence came into being at a later moment in cosmic history and characterizes only those creations that the Wise Lord endowed with concrete, embodied being.[16]

Logically, the interaction of these two binaries ought to yield four categories: Good-Spiritual, Evil-Spiritual, Good-Material, and Evil-Material. The relevant texts insist, however, that only the Wise Lord's creatures possess independent material existence. In contrast, the Evil Spirit's existence is defined as spiritual only. Consisting of nothing save darkness and its associated negative qualities (like cold and ignorance), he has no body or material substances that are properly his own.[17] The same is true of the demons he spawned, whose existence is spiritual only.[18] If entities like Appetite, Rage, Sickness, Torpor, and the like are to acquire physical substance and material force, they can do so only by penetrating the bodies of good Ohrmazdian creatures, abiding there in parasitic fashion and manifesting themselves through the kinds of behaviors they encourage in those bodies. As a crucial chapter of the *Dēnkart* explains,

> Spiritual creation is a single, noncompound being. Its character is noncompound, invisible, and intangible. From the Creator's creativity, creation first comes into spiritual being and is noncompound, invisible, and intangible. Then, in the compounding of things that become material, the good creations are changed to be visible and tangible. . . . Spiritual light, by the warm-moist power of its life-essence, is able to change from noncompound being to compound, that is, to material being. Even now, all material things are materially established out of that same warm-moist power. Spiritual darkness, however, is not able to achieve compound material existence because of the cold-dry lying/demonic quality of its death nature. Darkness does not become materially apparent in its own substance, but only when it has clothed itself in a different substance.[19]

Once free in the world, demons thus break into the bodies of living beings, which they corrupt, corruption being understood as a process of both moral and physical decay. Once inside, they distort a person's sentiments, behaviors, and being in ways consistent with their individual nature (Lust, Greed, etc.). This can then spawn new demons,[20] including some that infect previously unafflicted creatures and others that wait to torment their progenitors in hell.[21] Once unleashed, demons multiply and spread, contaminating ever more people, in whom they reproduce, morph, and spread once more. Troubling though it is, this analysis also suggests a solution to the problem it poses—that is, that demons can be defeated on an individual basis by denying them entry into one's body. Further, if all humans can be persuaded to take this step, the triumph of good will necessarily follow.

IV

Turning to individual demons, let us begin with Appetite (Avestan Āzi = Pahlavi Āz), whose name encompasses greed, lust, acquisitiveness, and sensual cravings of every sort.[22] Most important of all, perhaps, is insatiable hunger, as the following description makes clear.

> Appetite [Āz] is the demon that devours things. When it has nothing, due to deprivation, then it eats from its own body. It is that demon that when all the wealth of the material world has been given to it, still it does not become filled and sated.[23]

Appetite is present in all animate beings, and insofar as hunger prompts them to take nutrition, it helps sustain their lives. Yet this need-to-eat is a mark of their fallen state, since the Wise Lord originally intended life to be immortal and perfect, with no need to take food (or anything else).[24] As a result of the Evil Spirit's attack, Appetite is now omnipresent, but constitutes an accidental—that is, nonoriginal and ultimately removable—part of life. Once present in the body, however, it introduces physico-moral corruption, a state—better yet, a process—evidenced by the aggressivity of hungry people and by the odors that accompany eating and digestion. A passage from the *Dēnkart* explains.

> The body has its own perfume inside because of nature, and it has its own stench because of Appetite. . . . Stench, bile [i.e. gastric fluids], and bodily filth are from voracious/demonic devouring.[25]

Consistently, foul smells index demonic presence and activity.[26] Here, they are associated with excrement; elsewhere with pollution of every sort, above all with postmortem putrefaction.[27] Demonic odors also characterize hell, where those whose lives have been corrupted await the end of time.[28] The wait is finite, however, for after a certain number of millennia, their bodies will be resurrected and purged of demonic residues, after which they will enjoy the perfect immortal existence the Wise Lord originally intended.[29]

Before that happy end can be accomplished, all demonic beings and forces must be overcome, and Appetite plays a crucial role in the eschatological drama. Thus, it is foretold that toward the end of this world's last millennium, the Evil Spirit will make Appetite commander-in-chief of the demons.[30] Righteous humans will counterattack by renouncing the practices through which Appetite asserts and gratifies itself in their bodies: sex, eating, and all forms of acquisitive behavior.[31] Starved of its normal sustenance, a ravenous Appetite will then devour the other demons one by one, until only she and Ahreman are left. Some variants imagine that Appetite will eat Ahreman, then herself,[32] while others expect that these two, now hopelessly outnumbered, will be vanquished by the forces of good.[33] In either case, Appetite is the last obstacle, and its defeat ensures that no needs, desires, frustrations, or aggressions will again disrupt the cosmos, whose original perfection is thereby recovered and ensured. Associating non-Aryan enemies with this demon helps explain their apparent greed and aggression and acknowledges the difficulty of overcoming them, but it also construes struggles against such adversaries as a moral project that can—and ultimately will—be won.

Regarding Torpor (Avestan Būšiiạsta = Pahlavi Būšāsp), there is less to say. The term encompasses exhaustion, lassitude, drowsiness, lethargy, and all forms of fatigue or—most basically—an entropic draining away of vital energy as characterized by these states.[34] Different sources describe Torpor as the force that "wants to put all living things to sleep"[35] or "the demon who makes laziness."[36] Regularly, it is included in the set of demons with whom the Evil Spirit first attacked existence,[37] and it is said to come from the north, the direction associated with cold, darkness, and all things demonic.[38] Softly, it whispers in the ears of all creatures, urging them to sleep so deep and long that their slumber approximates death.[39] Some texts treat Torpor as a kind of sloth that compromises one's ability to fulfill the moral and ritual obligations that constitute a good life.[40] Others go further still. Having described the Evil Spirit's decision to afflict humanity with death, the *Dādestān ī Dēnīg* explains how he rendered this operational.

> He assigned the demon Torpor to weaken the breath, and the demon Fever to cause confusion and weaken the intelligence, and the demon Appetite to do away with one's power. He assigned the demon Old Age to spoil the bodily form and to steal its strength; the Wind of expiration to separate life force from the body to produce defeat; the demon Wrath to provoke conflict and to increase killing; the dark vermin in order to make biting and cause damage; the demon Grief to poison foods and to cause death, together with Deprivation and fear-producing Terror, which cools the body's heat, and many destructive powers and very destructive demons, all helpers made for Astwihād [the demon who separates soul and body] for the production of death.[41]

Ultimately, all demons contribute to death in one form or another, and this is among the most essential qualities of the demonic. In describing the process, however, this important passage begins with Torpor, which constitutes the first sign that life force is fading. The struggle between life and death, vitality and entropy, is thus renewed every night in every mortal creature, when the fate of existence is understood to hang by a fragile thread. Quoting from an older, but now lost source, the *Bundahišn* asserts,

This too, it says [in the Avesta]: "Every night, Torpor storms over earth, water, and righteous creatures, just like a pollution. When the sun comes up, it smites the demons over all the earth and makes it pure." This too it says: "If the sun came up one hour late, the demons would destroy all creation."[42]

Consistent with this line of analysis, it would seem that associating one's national enemies with Torpor might have some real attractions. While acknowledging the danger they pose as serious and consonant with other grave threats, it also implicitly characterizes non-Aryans as physically—and militarily—nonformidable and thus relatively easy to conquer. Provided, of course, one first overcomes in one's self any similar (demonically induced) inclination to lassitude, sloth, and torpor.

V

Appetite and Torpor appear together in a few other texts,[43] none more interesting or important than a passage from the *Dēnkart* that ponders the demonic assault each newborn infant suffers.

> The first attacker at the birth of a person is the demon Evil Mind, who causes pain to the child at birth by showing it all the misfortunes that come before death. The sign of this is infantile crying at birth. The opponent of that demon is Good Mind, who shows the good peace and contentment that come at the very end of time with the ever-living resurrected body. And the sign of this is the abiding peace and contentment of infancy. The second attacker is the demon Appetite, which weakens the body by the power of hunger and thirst. That which is necessary to save one from this comes from the Creator's creation of a desire and taste for milk, which holds hunger and thirst at bay. It is the helper of nature, the smiter of Appetite, and protector of the body. The third attacker is the demon immoderate Torpor, who produces lassitude and is a destroyer of the body. That which holds back its harm and soothes the body is moderate activity.[44]

While registering the seriousness of these threats, the passage speaks confidence that the Wise Lord's prescient benevolence has provided defensive measures against all dangers. Thus, however vulnerable and unhappy infants may be, the standard course of existence is for milk to appease appetite and for wakeful activity to increase at the expense of sleep and torpor. Granted that all infants suffer and some actually die, the text takes comfort in the fact that most babies survive, become larger, stronger, more independent, and enjoy ever-more tranquility as they grow. These are the data it organizes in a fairly complex analysis that constitutes these as nothing less than everyday triumphs of salvific divine benevolence over the demonic assault (table 4.1).

As is evident in this passage, the purpose of Mazdaean demonology was

TABLE 4.1 Analysis of infantile vulnerability to demonic threats, as worked out in *Dēnkart* 3.374

	First	Second	Third
Demonic attacker	Evil Mind (*Akōman*)	Appetite (*Āz*)	Torpor (*Būšāsp*)
Nature of assault	Reveals future misfortunes culminating in death	Hunger and thirst	Destroys the body
Sign of demonic presence	Crying from the moment of birth	Weakness	Lassitude, immoderate sleep
Divine defender	Good Mind (*Wahman*)	Milk and desire for it	Moderate activity
Nature of defensive response	Reveals eschatological peace and contentment	Nursing	Periods of wakefulness
Sign the defender has prevailed	Peace and contentment of the infant	Satiety and growth	Increasing physical abilities, decreasing need to sleep

not just to analyze the threats that pervade existence but also to provide reassurance that those threats can be mastered. Success is anticipated, moreover, both in the short term of the individual life and the *très longue durée* of the cosmos, which interact and mirror each other. Thus, the baby attains peace and contentment only when—and because—it is assured the cosmos will attain similar peace and all demonic forces will be overcome at history's end. Conversely, each moment of infantile serenity prefigures this happy final state and provides reassurance of its certain coming. For if every infantile cry reveals the presence and activity of demons, every coo announces the immediate—and ultimate—triumph of powers divine.

VI

The *Dēnkart*'s discussion of infancy displays and depends on some fairly acute empirical observation, following—and reproducing—a well-established theoretical model that had proved its merits by successful application to countless other domains, including the kind of issues we consign to such disciplines as physiology,[45] meteorology,[46] or entomology,[47] to name but a few. This is not "science" as we know it, where empirical observation and experimental method serve continually to test, revise, and refine theory, but a model of "applied theory (or science)" that flourished in many premodern settings. Here, the goal was twofold: first and most explicitly, to gain a new and deeper understanding of a common phenomenon (in this case, the nature of the baby, who represents the quintessential human); second, to confirm the validity of preexisting theory by one more demonstration of its explanatory powers.

The text with which we began (*Yašt* 18.1–2) is probably best understood in similar terms, for all that it elicits a different reaction from modern (or postmodern) readers. Thus, whereas the application of demonological theory to the topic of infancy strikes us as quaint and surprisingly perspicacious, application of the same theories to the topic of international relations offends us deeply for what we recognize as a mix of racism, nationalism, and crudely self-serving propaganda. In large measure, however, this apparent difference reflects a difference in perspective. Thus, the *Dēnkart* passage identifies with the infant it describes—more precisely, with the infant's loving parents—and so do we. When it construes that baby as a battle-field on which the divine struggles against the demonic, we find ourselves sympathizing with parents and child as they confront hunger, exhaustion, and other familiar troubles.

In contrast, when *Yašt* 18 identifies with the Aryan king and construes a more literal battlefield as the site of struggle against some of the very same threats, it fails to enlist our support. Not only do we tend to identify with the non-Aryan others, we find the text's attempt to associate them with demons tendentious and unpersuasive. What we perceive is the sole form of demon-talk with which contemporary readers remain familiar: that which we term "demonization." That is, the rhetorical construction of those from whom one feels radically estranged, not just as different kinds of people, but as outside the pale of the human and the moral: a polemic act of (re-)classification that legitimates subsequent violence against the demonized other.[48]

To be sure, *Yašt* 18 is a prejudicial text that helped cultivate imperialist aggression, and as such I find it abhorrent. That said, it is not "demonizing" in our sense, for it does not dehumanize the non-Aryan others, nor does it recode them as "demons" or anything of the sort. Rather, it states that divinely authorized Aryan kingship overcomes two kinds of adversaries— non-Aryan countries and "evil spirits"—without specifying the nature of the relation between them. The term it uses for the latter, however (Ave-stan *duš-mainiiūm*), reflects the Mazdaean view of demons as spiritual be-ings (Avestan *mainiiava*-, Pahlavi *mēnōg*) who lack material existence. Physi-cal corporeality being restricted to the Wise Lord's creation, demons are obliged to penetrate and corrupt the bodies of good creatures if they are to acquire any physical force, as we have repeatedly seen.

The text thus theorizes the inhabitants of non-Aryan countries in ways that parallel the *Dēnkart*'s analysis of the newborn infant. Both foreign-ers and babies are fully human creatures of the Wise Lord and, as such, entirely good *ab initio*. When they manifest disquieting behaviors—crying or acting aggressive, for example—it is not an evil person who does so but a person whose body has been penetrated and corrupted by demonic forces. Good parents understand this, and such behavior prompts concern for the child's welfare. They comfort the baby, tend its needs, and provide moral guidance as it grows up. Should an older child manifest behaviors that suggest continued demonic presence (e.g. temper tantrums that reveal the presence of Rage, laziness that manifests Torpor), its parents have recourse to discipline. Here, one should note that such a response is not prompted by anger, for that would suggest demonic influence on the parent. Rather, it manifests benevolent (i.e. Ohrmazdian) concern for the safety and welfare of the child, for others endangered by the child, and ultimately for the good of all the good creation. In similar fashion, Persian imperialism experienced itself as paternalistic in the fullest, most flattering sense. The wars it waged were conceived as an attempt, not to exterminate demonic neighbors, but to rescue good people from demonic forces to which they had unfortunately fallen victim.[49] Imperial administration was designed to complete the project of the foreigners' rescue and perfection.[50]

That imperialism should mirror child-rearing is not the result of any influence the one exercised on the other, but follows from the fact that both these—and countless other—domains were informed by Mazdaean demonlogy, which supplied a protocol for consideration of any topic and a template that could be applied to its particular features. One began by perceiving any given material entity as good in its essence, but morally ambiguous in its current state of existence. Next, one sought to identify the accidental evils—the exogenous demonic spiritual powers—that had distorted and corrupted the essential good. Then, one mobilized that which is good to drive out the invasive evil. The operation was to be repeated endlessly and everywhere, until the world's perfection would be restored.

VII

In closing, I would like to attempt a more precise—and more sweeping—description of how Mazdaeans theorized the demonic. Earlier, I provisionally described demonology as "an unflinching attempt to name, comprehend, and defend against all that threatens, frightens, and harms us." Along these lines, Mazdaean demonology identified several-score individually named demons, and several texts provide long lists of same.[51] The longest and most complete of these is found in *Greater Bundahišn* 27.14–50, which describes thirty-six demons, each of which has its own distinguishing characteristics and qualities,[52] but these may be grouped in four general categories. First is the set of demons headed by Appetite. These are the urges and pains that originate in a sense of emptiness, whereby the self feels the lack of something it needs, desires, and/or deserves. This sense compounds itself in feelings of misery as regards the self and resentment of others: resentment that can then prompt violent acts of aggression. In this group one finds Appetite (Āz) herself, along with Envy (Arešk), Rage (Xēšm), Lust (Waran), Deprivation (Niyāz), Distress (Sēj), Miserliness (Penīh), Grief (Bēš), and Sorrow (Zarīg). Second is a group that includes varied forms of ignorance and falsehood. These are the failures of thought and speech that replace an accurate sense of that-which-is with a deceptive image of what-is-not, causing confusion and disorder and providing the basis for all manner of subsequent conflicts. Here one finds the Evil Spirit (Ahreman), Evil Mind (Akōman), Falsehood (Mihōxt), Denial (Akātāš), Deceit (Frēftar), Slander (Spazg), and Untruth (Arāst). The third group includes all those demons concerned with disease, mortality, and decay: the processes whereby life is lost and bodies come undone. This is the group headed by Torpor (Būšāsp), which also includes Fever (Tab), Pain (Dard), the Evil Eye (Aš, and Sūrcašmīh), Sorcery (Kundag), Old Age (Zarmān), Death (Marg), the demon who separates body and soul (Astwihād), the one who drags sinners to hell (Wizarš), Corpse Pollution (Nasu), Rottenness/Pollution (Pudagīh), Stench (Gandagīh), and Vileness (Odag and Wadagīh). A fourth category is much smaller than the others and includes demons who are said to be responsible for the disruptions we nondemonologically inclined moderns are wont to describe as "natural disasters." These include Drought (Apōš); Aspenjarvya, who obstructs the rain in some unspecified way; and Cēšmag, the demon responsible for whirlwinds and earthquakes.[53]

   If demonic multiplicity can be subsumed in these four groups, the groups themselves have a certain coherence that reveals the essence of the demonic as construed in the Mazdaean tradition. For in all these varied demons, one perceives the same underlying menace that haunts the Wise Lord's creation. Most basically, this is the threat of nonbeing itself that manifests itself in anguished awareness of emptiness like appetite and lust; negative entropies like torpor and disease; unreal states like falsehood and ignorance; and finally, in the reeking fluids of bodily decay and the vortex at the center of the whirlwind.[54] These are, in effect, the black holes of a premodern cosmology: terrifying forces of a void that seeks—in myriad forms and by myriad means—to invade good creatures and substances, hollowing them out, infecting them with rot, and turning them to its own infinitely corrupt and corrupting purposes.

Hardly naïve, superstitious, or puerile, this is a profoundly serious and profoundly original vision. Deeply disquieting, it challenges our most fundamental ideas about the nature of being itself, not to mention the smug condescension we commonly harbor toward those who believe in demons.

CHAPTER FIVE

ANOMALY, SCIENCE, AND RELIGION

I

Among the liveliest narratives of emergent modernity is the story of how Tycho Brahe (1546–1601), Imperial Mathematician at the court of Rudolph II, struggled to reconcile his incomparably precise observations of planetary orbits with a geocentric cosmos by producing increasingly complex models of the cosmos, involving epicycles, epicycles-within-epicycles, and other sophisticated mechanisms to account for the peculiarities of planetary motion. For every specific problem that arose, he developed another ingenious solution, and with every solution, there arose further problems. None of these were more intractable than the orbit of Mars, study of which Brahe assigned to his young assistant, Johannes Kepler (1571–1630), who had previously grappled with similar problems as regards Mercury. As Brahe's observations detailed, planets—and no other heavenly bodies—seemed to move forward at some times, then reversed direction for a period, only to move forward again in a "retrograde" pattern incompatible with the Ptolemaic model of the cosmos (which Brahe was working to modify and salvage), but equally incompatible with the rival geocentric model of Copernicus, which Kepler favored. For both models followed Aristotle—and a certain theological sensibility—in maintaining that the motion of all heavenly bodies should be circular, continuous, smooth, and perfect.

Only after Brahe died in 1601 and Kepler succeeded him as Imperial Mathematician (a position he held until 1612) was the latter able to study all his predecessor's detailed records, scrutiny of which led him to realize that to resolve this conundrum, it was necessary to reject both of the available systems and rethink things in radical fashion. Thus, in his *Astronomia Nova* (1609), Kepler first theorized that heavenly orbits were elliptical and not circular, which permitted him to understand their motion as smooth and unidirectional with reference to the sun, and to locate the sun at one focal point of the ellipses, rather than making it the absolute center of perfect circles. Given that the other planets are observed from an earth no longer

taken to be stable, but now understood itself to travel an elliptical course
on the same plane as the others, the motion of the planets thus *seems* to turn
retrograde when the earth passes them—but this illusion is the effect of
the earthbound observer's shifting perspective, and does not accurately
depict the actual pattern of planetary motion.[1]

This is the story that Thomas Kuhn put at the center of his own landmark
contribution, *The Structure of Scientific Revolutions* (1st ed. 1962), where he
developed the notion that "normal science" proceeds by relatively routine
problem solving until such time as research identifies "anomalies"—like the
vagaries of retrograde planets—that cannot be explained on the basis of
extant knowledge and theory. Recognition of such anomalies and repeated
failure to resolve them plunge normal science into a period of "crisis," in
which scientists are obliged to rethink the foundational assumptions Kuhn
called "paradigms." And, as he came to argue, there was nothing inherently
abnormal, unnatural, or monstrous about an anomaly. Rather, anomalies
are constituted as such precisely because they contradict the expecta-
tions of accepted wisdom. Properly understood, anomalies are diagnostic
and useful, for their intractably aberrant features reveal the blind spots
and inadequacies in conventional knowledge, and they serve as signposts
for further inquiry, debate, and progress. Anomalies thus provide impetus
to the whole process, forcing "paradigm shifts" that improve theory and
render the former aberration comprehensible as an orderly, natural part of
a world now more perfectly understood.[2]

In the rest of this chapter, I want to explore how Zoroastrian cosmology responded when it was forced to take account of the same perplexing
aberrations in planetary motion that worried Brahe, Kepler, and others.
This occurred in the latter part of the Sassanian dynasty (226–651 CE),
when Greek and Indian astronomical writings made their way to the Persian court.[3] Newly introduced from outside, these data posed a challenge
to established Persian wisdom no less grave than they did when they were
introduced in Europe a millennium later by way of Islamic sources.[4] What
is more, they did so by striking at much the same vital issues: the relation of
heaven and earth, nature as orderly or chaotic, and the design of the cosmos
as an index of God's plans for his creation. Further, the ways Sassanian intellectuals modified prior cosmological theory in order to take account of the
planets and related phenomena were no less subtle or ingenious than those
of Kepler and his successors, for all that they differed strongly in their style
and content. Ultimately, it is this difference that most intrigues me, for here,
I suggest, we can perceive the categorical divide between the alternative
styles of thought, speech, sentiment, habit, orientation, and purpose that

modernity organized in its binary contrast of religion and science. What
I hope to explore, then, is the relative immunity of certain cosmologies to
a crisis provoked by aberrant data, and the almost limitless capacity of
systems we might call "religious," "prescientific," or "nonscientific" to adduce evidence and arguments that reinforce the system's presuppositions,
recuperating even those phenomena that other (more "scientific") styles
of cosmology will construe as threatening anomalies.

II

Older Iranian cosmology (i.e. that attested in the Avesta) gave a relatively
simple account of the celestial regions, recognizing three different levels
of the heavens, with the stars occupying the lowest position, followed by
the moon and the sun.[5] Occasionally a fourth level, that "of endless lights"
(*anaγranąm raocaŋąm*), is set beyond the sun,[6] and one rather baroque passage
imagines nine different levels, four sub- and four superlunary.[7]

Always, however, the stars are lowest and this is noteworthy, since such
placement contradicts the evidence of eclipses, which reveal the moon
to be nearer the earth than either the sun or stars.[8] Organization of the
system rests, then, not on empirical observation but on a religious homology so powerful as to obviate the need for close reading of the phenomena
themselves. Thus, luminosity and height are imagined to covary, such that
the more light a body possesses (or seems to possess), the loftier it must
be: Sun above Moon, Moon above Stars, Stars above Earth, Earth above
Hell. Celestial light is further correlated with wisdom, virtue, divinity, and
beauty; darkness, with the opposite qualities.

The model is clear, logically consistent, and emotionally satisfying, if a bit
simple and static. In truth, only two Avestan passages show interest in the
motion of heavenly bodies, and the first of these (*Yašt* 13.57–58) asserts that
such motion was not part of the Wise Lord's original plan for creation.

> We sacrifice to the *fravašis* [i.e. preexistent souls] of the righteous,
> who showed their paths
> to the stars, moon, sun,
> and endless lights,
> all of which previously stood in the same place
> for a long time, not moving forward.
> [That was] before the enmity of the demons,
> before the assaults of the demons.
> But now they move forward
> to the distant turning point of the way, arriving at the turning point of the way,
> which is the final Renovation [*frašō.kərəti*].[9]

Elsewhere, Zoroastrian texts narrate in detail how the Evil Spirit (Avestan Aŋra Mainiiu, Pahlavi Ahriman) led a host of demonic powers against the pristine creations of the Wise Lord (Avestan Ahura Mazdā, Pahlavi Ohrmazd), introducing strife, mixture, confusion, mortality, fear, and other hallmarks of existence as we know it. This Assault produced a rupture, not only in the nature of being, but also in the nature of time, replacing an unchanging eternity ("infinite time," *zruuān akarana*) with a period of turbulence and struggle ("long time," *zruuān darəγa*).[10] And in that moment when demonic aggression made the celestial bodies start rotating, history proper began.

History, however, is finite, and some millennia hence the forces of good will vanquish all demonic powers in definitive fashion. At that point, the world's original perfection will be restored in a complex set of events known as the Frašōkərəti ("Renovation" or, more literally, "Wonder-making"), and a final (or eschatological) eternity will begin. The passage just quoted thus organizes time, nature, and morality in a set of binary contrasts (table 5.1).

One other Avestan passage adds a detail to this picture. This is *Yašt* 8.8, which occurs in a hymn devoted to the star Sirius (Tištrya), whom the hymn elsewhere describes as "lord and supervisor of all stars."[11] The verse of interest to us, however, suggests a contrast between the real, proper, good stars, and another, more ominous set of celestial bodies, against which Sirius struggles.

> We sacrifice to Sirius,
> who conquers witches [*pairikās*],
> who subdues witches
> that hover between earth and sky
> in the form of shooting stars [literally "worm stars," *stārō kərəmå*].[12]

As Antonio Panaino has shown, the sinister shooting stars in question are to be understood as the seasonal meteor showers of late summer, associated with the period of drought that normally ends when Sirius gains ascendance and the meteor showers desist.[13] The image thus aligns another set of binary oppositions—Sirius versus the meteors, the moist versus the dry, healthy versus unhealthy times of the year, divine versus demonic forces—giving

TABLE 5.1 Correlated binary oppositions in *Yašt* 13.57–58

Moral and physical state of creation	Perfect	*Mixture of good and evil*
Relations among creatures	Peace, harmony	Conflict
Nature of time	Eternity (primordial and final)	Historic, finite
Nature of celestial bodies	Stable, unmoving	Rotating

TABLE 5.2 Correlated binary oppositions in *Yašt* 8.8

Moral and physical state of creation	Ideal, Ohrmazdian	Troubled, Ahrimanian
Time of year	Rainy season	Dry season
Quality of existence	Moist, conducive to the flourishing of life	Dry, threatening death and sterility
Nature of celestial motion	Regular rotation of sun, moon, and stars	Unpredictable downward motion of shooting stars ("witches")

particular stress to the contrast between two different forms of celestial motion. Thus, where *Yašt* 13.57–58 associates stasis with perfection and rotation with the mixed state, *Yašt* 8.8 contrasts the normal rotation of stars like Sirius, which it takes to be good, and the unpredictable motion of meteors falling from heaven to earth, theorized as decidedly evil (table 5.2).

Of planets, however, the Avesta has nothing to say.

III

Within a Zoroastrian context, the planets first appear in Pahlavi texts that were committed to writing in the ninth century CE, but drew on scientific initiatives of the Sassanian dynasty, particularly those of Xusrōw Anōširwan (r. 531–78 CE), a king who was particularly concerned to acquire Greek and Indian scientific texts.[14] Certain mathematical details make clear the Indic influence on Sassanian astronomy, as David Pingree demonstrated,[15] and some of the Middle Persian technical vocabulary is borrowed from Greek, such as use of Pahlavi *spihr*, derived from Greek *sphairos*, as the name for the celestial firmament.[16] The neologism that was introduced to denote the planets, however, is strictly Iranian in origin, and holds considerable interest.

The word in question is Pahlavi *abāxtarān*, which means most literally "the backward ones."[17] Apparently, this was meant to describe the planets' retrograde motion, which Iranian sages found as profoundly disquieting as did Copernicus, Brahe, and Kepler.

> As for the planets [*abāxtarān*] . . . they disrupt all the arrangement of time, which depends on (the steady rotation of) the zodiacal constellations [*axtarān*], as is apparent to the eye. They invert the relations of up and down, they diminish what is increased, and their motion is not like that of the zodiacal constellations. For sometimes it is quick, sometimes it is slow, sometimes it is backward-motion [*abāz rawišn*], and sometimes it is stationary.[18]

Elsewhere, the planets are said to be deceitful,[19] destructive,[20] demonic,[21] and producers of old age and evil.[22] Sometimes they are accused of stealing light from proper stars.[23] Two forms of action, however, reveal their true nature. First, to describe the motion of planets, the texts consistently employ the verb *dwāristan*, which is used only with reference to demonic creatures, and which suggests a physically and morally defective locomotion that can be awkward, violent, crooked, or suspicious: scuttling, slithering, scurrying, or the like.[24] Second, given a folk-etymological derivation of the word *abāxtarān* ("planet") from the verb *baxtan* ("to distribute") with a negative prefix (*a-*), the planets are described as *nondistributors* or, more precisely, as beings antithetical to proper distribution, insofar as they give only bad things—death, disease, misfortune, etc.[25]—or, alternatively, they steal good things from the signs of the zodiac and give them "not to dutiful worthies, but to evildoers, undutiful persons, prostitutes, whores, and unworthy types."[26] Further wordplay constitutes the planets (*ab-āxtarān*) as the opposite of zodiacal constellations (*nē axtarān*),[27] the latter now being understood as the "goodness-distributor deities."[28] Making matters more complex still, a homonymous noun *abāxtar* denotes the northern direction or quarter, north being perceived as "backward" in Iran because standard orientation was facing the south, the direction of warmth, light, and the gods, while north—the backward direction—was associated with cold, death, and demons.[29]

Here, one perceives the gradual elaboration of a dense and complex symbolic construct, the general nature of which was determined at the start. All begins with the observation of planetary retrograde motion, which is taken to be aberrant and disquieting. This led to a naming operation, as planets were designated *abāxtarān*, "the backward ones." Tendentious rumination on the significance of that name then produced other associations, through which the planets were imagined to be demonic in nature, antidistributors (*a-baxtarān*), and antithetical to the zodiacal constellations (*axtarān*), who, in the most pointed contrast, move only in orderly circles and distribute good things to good people. All these binary contrasts were then brought into alignment with countless others, when the signs of the zodiac were cast as Ohrmazd's heavenly generals, with the planets doing similar service for Ahriman.

> All goodness and its opposite come to people and other creatures via the seven (planets) and the twelve zodiacal constellations. As is said in the Religion, the twelve zodiacal constellations are twelve generals on the Wise Lord's side; the seven planets are seven generals on the side of the Evil Spirit. Those seven planets damage all creatures and creation and consign them to death and every sort of evil, as those twelve zodiacal constellations and seven planets command and arrange the world.[30]

IV

Having arrived at this understanding of what the planets are, Sassanian cosmologists faced the task of explaining how they came to be so. Toward that end, they developed four different theoretical constructs, three of which drew on older Iranian traditions, while the fourth was imported from India. First and simplest was the assertion that Ahriman created the planets, with the possible implication—never rendered fully explicit—that their ominous form of motion is an inheritance from their creator, for whom the verb *dwāristan* is also commonly used.[31] Second was the attempt to build on the analysis of *Yašt* 8.8, which we considered above, and to associate planets with meteors, comets, and other heavenly bodies whose motion is unpredictable, disruptive, or irregular. As we saw, the Avestan passage describes shooting stars as "witches [*pairikās*], who hover between earth and sky,"[32] and the Pahlavi texts expand on this terminology, referring to planets as "sorcerors" (*yadūgān*), the constant companions of "witches" (Pahl. *parīgān* < Av. *pairikā-*), both of whom are given to demonic patterns of movement.[33]

A third line of analysis took its lead from *Yašt* 13.57–58 and its idea that the heavenly bodies were originally motionless until the perfect peace of creation was disrupted by Ahriman's assault. As we saw, that text imagines that the discrete, measured time of history commenced when the sun, moon, and stars started rotating, history being understood as a long but finite era situated between the very different temporality of primordial and final eternities. Going further still, a number of Pahlavi texts add a complementary analysis of spatial categories. Thus, having launched his assault from the lowest depths of "endless darkness," Ahriman is said to have crossed the void and moved toward the heavens that culminate in Ohrmazd's realm of "endless light."[34] At the pinnacle of his success, the Evil Spirit actually invaded the lower portions of the heavens, where he seized some of the stars, and he dragged these down into the void when he was forced to retreat.[35] As a result of this, both void and stars are transformed. The void now receives matter, and becomes a mixture of matter and nothingness, being and nonbeing, light and darkness, a spatial complement to historic time. In similar fashion, the displaced celestial bodies that previously were the lower stars now become planets, which stagger and lurch as they move, having initially been set in motion by the violence of the Evil Spirit. In their new domain, these are entities of decidedly ambiguous character: matter out of place, alternating unpredictably between backward and forward motion (table 5.3).

If this last narrative construed the planets as originally having been Ohrmazdean creations, but regrettably corrupted by Ahriman's acts, a

TABLE 5.3 Parallel analyses of time and space in Avestan and Pahlavi sources

	Yašt 8.8: Analysis of time	*Greater Bundahišn 4.10 et al.:* Analysis of space
Bracketing domains of infinite, but unidirectional extent	Primordial eternity (open to beginnings) and eschatological eternity (open to end)	Endless light (open to the above) and endless darkness (open to the below)
Intermediate zone, bounded in both directions	Historic time, which begins with the demonic assault and ends with the Renovation (*frašō.kərəti*)	Primordial void (*tuhīgīh*), situated beneath the realm of endless light and above that of endless darkness
Definitive role of celestial bodies with regard to the intermediate zone	Historic time begins when sun, moon, and stars begin to rotate, having been set in motion by the demonic assault	The void becomes intermediate space, characterized by mixture, when Ahriman drags the lower stars down from the heavens to this zone, where they become planets

final theory inverted that image. Here, the planets are Ahrimanian in origin, thus intrinsically threatening and evil. Their retrograde orbits, far from being the product of the Evil Spirit's aggression, reflect Ohrmazd's efforts to keep their sinister power under control. Thus, making use of astronomical imagery developed in India, certain Sassanian cosmologists imagined that the Wise Lord used a set of cords to rein in the unruly planets.[36]

> And the Creator, the Wise Lord, in order not to abandon these five planets to their own desires, tied each of them with two cords to the sun and moon, and that is the cause of their forward motion and backward motion. The length of some is longer, like Saturn and Jupiter; that of others lesser, like Mercury and Venus. When they get to the end of the cord, then they are pulled back. They are not permitted to go according to their own desires, so that they do not damage the creation.[37]

V

The Zoroastrian tradition represented in the Pahlavi books apparently saw no need to adjudicate among these theories, which were not rivals in any serious sense, merely alternative ways to explain a phenomenon sufficiently fascinating and troublesome to have stimulated a wide range of speculation. Clearly, when information regarding the retrograde motion of planets was introduced to the Sassanian court, it prompted interest, discussion, and ferment. It did not, however, occasion *crisis* in anything approximating Kuhn's sense. The question is, Why not? At a certain level, this seemingly simple question begs for a general theory of the difference between those styles of cosmology we are inclined to call "religious" and those we regard as "scientific": a topic much too vast for the current context. And yet there are a few observations we can make that offer significant insight into the broader question.

Here, I would begin by observing how a cosmology that includes a robust category of The Demonic is able to treat aberrant phenomena with no apparent sense of crisis and, what is more, can accommodate such data in ways that actually make them ratify its basic assumptions. Confronted with evidence of celestial bodies that moved in a weird, disquieting fashion, Sassanian cosmologists thus explored various explanatory options, all of which constituted the planets' retrograde motion as one more example of the well-known fact that Ahriman's aggression has disrupted the perfect order of Ohrmazd's creation. Rather than challenging or destabilizing this first principle of Zoroastrian orthodoxy, retrograde motion was made to validate and support it. With modest ingenuity, knowledgeable experts can disarm and appropriate virtually any peculiarity by consigning it to the category of The Demonic, just as a robust category of The Miraculous does similar service in other styles of cosmology.

If this is so, one might imagine that it is only among groups within which appeals to the demonic and the miraculous are no longer attractive that aberrant phenomena can be constituted as "anomalies," in Kuhn's sense of the term: phenomena that may seem unnatural only because one's understanding of them—and of nature—is somehow defective and in need of correction. A double restructuring of the category of Nature thus separates Brahe and Kepler from the authors of the *Bundahišn*, *Škēnd Gūmanīg Wizār*, and *Mēnōg ī Xrad* and makes possible the emergence of that which we now call "science." In the first place, the category of Nature expands to encompass all that previously lay outside its grasp in such privileged categories as The Miraculous and The Supernatural. In the second place, this category contracts to deny the reality of all that was previously placed—or place-able—in its own specialized subcategory of The Demonic, and now demands that these phenomena be explained by the same principles that govern the rest of nature.

The shift from a religious to a scientific regime of truth thus involves and depends on revisions in the categories of The Miraculous, The Demonic, and The Natural.[38] Beyond this, one must note the increased importance of empirical observation, mathematical calculation, significant changes in the protocols of research and theory, also in the economy of prestige and politics of reputation within the sciences, such that innovation, discovery, challenges to authority and to tradition, paradigm shift, individual genius, and scientific revolution all came to be positively valorized. What is more, the emergent value of *novelty* in all these forms came to be endowed with a set of mythologies, like the good story of Brahe and Kepler, wherein the great destabilizers are treated as heroic figures who opened the way to better, higher, newer, truer, purer, surer Knowledge. Or, to put it differently, like stories in which the wobbly, anomalous, retrograde planets appear not as demons but as saviors. At the same time, older stories, such as those in which the orderly rotation of the zodiacal constellations figure as signs of divine perfection, benevolence, and harmonious order, now go largely untold. Lacking anomalies, surprise, and novelty, they hold little dramatic interest, and accordingly are consigned to children's literature and the tedium of "normal science."

CHAPTER SIX

BETWEEN HISTORY AND MYTH

I

Theories of myth have a somewhat recursive nature. Like the phenomenon itself, they circle back on themselves and tend to mirror the data they treat. In this vein, most obviously, no one ever theorizes for the first time, much as no one claims originality while narrating a myth, although in both cases one's relation to predecessors—and contemporaries—is always more fraught than one knows or admits. So let me begin with an invocation of mythic ancestors. Although there are others I would and could name—Dumézil, Lévi-Strauss, Malinowski, Frazer, Cristiano Grottanelli, Roland Barthes, and others not normally associated with the study of myth (Gramsci, Bakhtin, Benjamin . . .)—when I think about myth, I almost intuitively begin with Mircea Eliade and Raffaele Pettazzoni, whose tendency to characterize myth as stories of beginnings affords a useful point of departure, whatever else one makes of their work.[1]

Creation and myth were both privileged themes for Eliade and Pettazzoni, who privileged cosmogonic myths above all. In their view, myths are stories that speak of origins, and sacred origins at that. One might, however, productively invert their position by understanding myth as narrative that moves from existence to essence, being to becoming, temporal to primordial, by supplying a (putative) sacred origin for the world and for any worldly items it chooses to legitimate and ennoble. The latter might be physical entities—privileged pieces of the landscape, valued animal and plant species, or culturally significant objects (tools, weapons, special items of clothing, e.g.)—but myth is not reserved for things tangible and concrete. Myths also narrate the origin of existential conditions, cultural norms, ritual and subsistence practices, significant offices and institutions: things such as agriculture, marriage, kingship, priesthood, hospitality, fishing magic, cattle raiding, death, and funerals, to name a few.

Myths also commonly describe how a given people came into being, how they came to be situated in the territory they claim and regard as their own, and/or how they came to enjoy relations of alterity with those whom the story constitutes as their others. Such ethnogonic narratives are a crucial piece of the nationalist imaginary, and the role of myth in nationalism has received considerable comment in recent years,[2] while less attention has gone to narratives that posit the origin of the state. Typically, state-founding narratives represent themselves as historic accounts, but like the heroic tales favored by nationalists, they too can often be easily dismissed as "just a myth." However justified or satisfying such taxonomic demotion might be, more rewarding still is to use such stories to destabilize, challenge, or—best of all—simply to rethink the categorical distinction between history and myth.

II

Before turning to a specific example of state-founding narratives, there is one other characteristic frequently attributed to the category of Myth that requires some attention. This is the impersonal quality mythic discourse assumes in theories that treat it as sacred narrative, timeless truth, deep tradition, cultural product, or the expression of something broad and generically human, such as popular sentiment, the collective unconscious, or, in Clifford Geertz's memorable phrase, "the stories people tell themselves about themselves." To be sure, there are important differences among these views that in another context one would want to tease out. At present, however, my purpose is different: I want to identify what these have in common, describe it in more precise—and more critical—terms, and make it central to our discussion.

    In different ways, and for different reasons, these varied theoretical tendencies all pick up on the fact that mythic narratives typically remain anonymous. Authorship is not announced and claims to originality, invention, and personal responsibility are strikingly absent. Rather, the story presents itself as old, traditional, time-honored, well-known, much-beloved, tested and true, the voice of the people, or—more pretentiously—the voice of sacred reality as it reveals itself. At most, a mythic narrative will acknowledge that it is a variant retelling of an oft-told tale, perhaps differing from other versions a bit in its details, but minimizing such difference and attributing it to regrettable lapses of the narrator. Ultimately, the story is not "his" (or "hers") in any meaningful sense. Rather, the *real* story belongs to all, lasts always, and pervades everywhere. It just happens to pass through this particular conduit on this particular occasion.

    Whether articulated or left implicit, anonymity and all it entails constitute an important part of the way mythic discourse represents and understands itself, so it is no surprise that these issues figure prominently in a wide range of theories. I would gently suggest, however, that instead of reproducing and recoding indigenous ideology, theory ought to accurately report, then actively reflect on it, providing a critical perspective and pointing beyond the most seductive misrepresentations of the phenomenon itself. Toward that end, I would characterize myth as a discourse that consistently denies originality and obscures the identity of its producers and reproducers, thereby concealing their positionality and the interests (material and other) that influence the modifications they introduce in the stories they tell.

In some measure, of course, the narrators are right: they are retelling a well-known tale, and multiple retellings give myth many of its generically distinctive qualities. Audiences have always already heard the story, or at least heard about it, and narrators know this is so. Any variant they offer shuttles between (1) them and their hearers; (2) narrators, audiences, and variants of the past; and (3) rival variants circulating in the present, along with those who tell, hear, remember, and repeat them. Where most variants agree—that is, the commonalities of plot, character, incident, moral, or whatever it is that unites these and makes them variants of a single story (rather than an anthology of different tales)—is the portion that is rightly anonymous, for this shared content is a collective possession and product, also an ancestral heritage that can belong to no individual author.

Where variants differ, however, is in the innovations, modifications, omissions, and fine recalibrations they introduce to the widely known and commonly accepted version. Their own authors' claims notwithstanding, these innovations are not regrettable lapses but the very heart of the matter. For in making such revisions, narrators actively intervene to reshape the story and, through the instrument of the story, to reshape the consciousness of those who hear and retell it. They do so, moreover, not in random, impersonal, or disinterested fashion but from a specific social locus with its own distinctive perspective, representing interests they seek to advance through these variations. Should their variants gain a sufficiently favorable hearing to be repeatedly retold, they can gradually displace the (previous) standard version, transforming the views of the group at large—and those of future generations—on issues of fundamental importance.

Pace Eliade and Pettazzoni, where myths either reveal (Eliade) or constitute "the truth" (Pettazzoni), but also *pace* Lévi-Strauss (where logical structures think themselves until they exhaust their variants) and Dumézil (where myths express "the ideology" of "a people"), I would thus theorize a volatile field of contestation, within which multiple variants jockey for acceptance, each one of them situated, partial, and self-interested. All aspire, however, to the status of unquestioned and unassailable truth.

None ever quite reach that elusive goal, but some get closer than others, winning broad acceptance, frequent repetition, legitimacy, confidence, and an aura of self-evident, taken-for-granted rightness, much like what Gramsci called "hegemony." The question is, Which ones? And also, How do they manage that feat?

III

I cannot imagine what it would take to address these disarmingly simple questions in anything approaching comprehensive fashion, for the subtleties, complexities, and variables are legion, not to speak of the particularities relevant to any concrete situation. So instead of offering a presumptuous and inadequate attempt at sweeping generalization, let me return to the topic at hand and pose a more limited query: In any given historic moment, what narratives about the origin of the state are likely to prevail?

As a starting point, one might hypothesize that the story the state tells of its beginnings will have more currency than any rivals (actual or potential), simply because it is backed by an institution that can—and will—spend more and one that has more channels available to propagate its version. As a corollary, one can also suggest that the more often the state tells its story and the more resources it commits to its telling, the greater will be its hegemony. Further, that the greater the number of media through which that story is told (school textbooks and political oratory of course, but also poetry and fiction, films, TV miniseries, comic books, music, patriotic celebrations, statues, posters, websites, etc.), the more fully the potentials of each medium are exploited (not just the persuasive but the aesthetic and emotional capacities of each), and the more relentlessly the edifying story is repeated, the more dominant the state-sponsored myth of the state will be.

All reasonable enough, but the sorry history of Soviet attempts along just these lines is sufficient to make us rethink these hypotheses, and there is no shortage of other counterexamples. (Seemingly, schoolchildren everywhere learn to resist, if only by inattention.) At a bare minimum, we can say that the state is likely to propagate a version containing an idealized image of its origins and nature, and that it will probably commit more resources to this task than any of its critics and rivals.

These efforts, however, are not enough to secure that version's dominance, for persuasion is not a direct function of budgetary expenditure and message repetition. When the idealized representations embedded in a myth differ sharply from the experience of its hearers, that myth is likely to lose credibility; ditto its narrators and promoters. Critique flourishes in the gap between idealized images and lived realities, taking the form, inter alia, of mythic variants that challenge, mock, corrode, and reconfigure the state-sponsored version of the story.

IV

By way of example, let us consider the story of how Harald Fairhair (r. ca. 858–930) overcame a host of other petty rulers to unify the Norwegian state and establish a national monarchy.[3] The events themselves took place in a preliterate society and were first recorded by poets employed by the royal court. Thereafter, a rich body of oral tradition took shape around Harald, with many legendary accretions. With the conversion of Norway to Christianity toward the end of the tenth century and beginning of the eleventh, literacy entered, first in Latin and used for ecclesiastical purposes, later in the Old Norse vernacular. Beginning in the 1130s or 1140s, historical texts began to be written, first by Icelanders who celebrated their "founding fathers" (*landnámsmenn*) who fled Harald's violence and established a determinedly antimonarchic commonwealth in Iceland (something absolutely unique in medieval Europe). Starting in the 1180s, a genre known as "Kings' Sagas" (Konungasögur) was developed by Norwegians writing in Latin. Over the next half century it came to be written in Old Norse and was ultimately taken over by Icelanders, who were the most active of all Scandinavians in cultivating literary and historical arts.

The culminating work of this genre is the massive volume known as *Heimskringla*, usually attributed to Snorri Sturluson (1178–1241) and written circa 1230–35. So greatly did this text improve on earlier works that its version became definitive, pushing its half-dozen predecessors into obscurity and dominating all subsequent historic discussions.[4]

Some of the Kings' Sagas started their story with Harald Fairhair, some with his father, and some with a euhemerized version of the old pagan gods, from whom the royal lineage claimed descent. All, however, made Harald the founder of the unified state, the national monarchy, and the royal family that continues to this day. Notwithstanding Harald's centrality to the state's origin story, the three earliest Kings' Sagas are relatively brief and reserved in the narratives they offer. As an example, let me cite the variant from the *Epitome of the Sagas of Norway's Kings* (*Ágrip af Nóregskonunga sǫgum*), written by a Norwegian cleric around 1190.

> After Halfdan, Harald took the realm that his father had had and gained for himself more realms than Halfdan had. He grew quickly into a brave and imposing man, so that he made battle against neighboring kings and conquered them all. At twenty years old, he was the first single king to take possession of Norway.[5]

The other two early sources were also written by Norwegian clerics close to the throne, and they bear much the same scant information. Each of them says something in passing, however, that is worth noting. Thus, the *Historia Norwegiae*, possibly written as early as 1150, remarks, "Many things and wondrous ones are remembered of Harald, but now it would take too long to narrate these individually,"[6] suggesting a rich body of oral tradition. Writing around 1180, Theodricus Monachus (Monk Theodore) confessed his difficulty in establishing a firm date for Harald's accession, which took place some two and a half centuries earlier. In attempting to do so, however, he consulted with Icelanders, for "it is known beyond any doubt that they have always been the most curious and best trained of all the northern people in such things."[7]

We are thus reasonably sure there were many legends about Harald circulating through Scandinavia, and that Icelanders were particularly learned about them.[8] One of these stories had it that upon succeeding his father, who ruled a few small districts in southeast Norway, the young Harald swore a great oath that he would neither cut, nor comb his hair until he had conquered all other kings and united the nation, which pledge brought him the nickname "Shaggy Harald" (*Haraldr lúfa*). After ten years of battle, his task was complete, at which point he accepted a haircut and received the epithet by which he has been celebrated ever since, "Harald Fairhair" (*Haraldr hárfagr*). This narrative—let us call it a myth—effectively construes the state-founding hero as one who consecrates himself to a sacred mission and succeeds, not just by his own strength of arm, but as a result of the divine favor that his devotion elicits. It is first recorded in *Fagrskinna*, the last Kings' Saga of Norwegian provenance, a text that survives in two versions, one of about 1225 (the so-called B-Text) and one from a few decades later (the A-Text).[9] This story was also a favorite in Iceland, where four different texts preserve it.[10]

Particularly interesting, however, is that three of the four Icelandic variants add a preliminary episode drawn from oral tradition to their account of Harald's oath, profoundly altering the way one understands both the story and the process of state formation. This episode begins when the young Harald, flush with his first victories, sets his designs on Gyða, the beautiful daughter of a neighboring district king. While marriage to this woman might consolidate a useful alliance, what Harald suggests is, in fact, that she become his concubine, not his wife (Old Norse *frilla*, rather than *kona*). Offended, she refuses and describes Harald's status as beneath her. Were he to conquer all Norway, however, and make himself its sole ruler, then she would consent to be his proper wife (*eigin kona hans*; not only is the adjective added for emphasis, one variant coins the compound *eiginkona*, "proper-wife," to underscore it further still).[11] Hearing this, Harald decides that Gyða has a fine idea, at which point he swears his oath and sets out to create Norway.

These variants undercut Harald's stature in multiple ways. First, he is made dependent on another for the idea of state formation, and on a woman at that. Further, his desire for this woman—which in some ways is a trope of his desires for territory, high office, glory, et cetera—is depicted as morally dubious, at least in its initial phases. To make matters worse, *Heimskringla* reports that among those Harald slew at the battle where he finally won control of the nation after ten years of fighting (Hafrsfjorð, in 872) was none other than Gyða's father, who led the resistance to him.[12] In effect, this man became a victim of the ambitions his daughter unleashed, as did all other district kings and all noble families; for once on the throne, Harald proclaimed laws that stripped the old aristocracy of their autonomy and ancestral lands, converting the latter to crown property.

One could follow the *Heimskringla* variant further, which is extremely complex and has many narrative threads. My research pursues roughly a dozen such leads, each of which resembles the Gyða episode in the way it introduces material that complicates and compromises the way Harald, the monarchy, and the state are represented. As regards Gyða herself, we should also connect her story with Harald's full marital history. Thus,

1. During the time he is waging battles, Harald contracts several marriages, each of which secures him a useful ally. Toward the end of the conquest phase, he begins to have children by these women.
2. Once he has made himself sole king, he remembers Gyða, sends for her, and they are united. The text leaves absolutely ambiguous the question of whether this constitutes a legal marriage or a more informal arrangement. He has five children by her.
3. Some years later, the Danish king offers Harald his daughter in marriage, but demands that Harald first discard his other women. Harald does so without hesitation, and Gyða is among the discarded.
4. Harald's son by the Danish princess becomes his heir, and there is considerable conflict among all his descendants. Gyða's sons do not fare particularly well.[13]

Heimskringla, of course, is an Icelandic text, written at a time when the commonwealth was in sufficient disarray that King Hakon Hakonarson (r. 1204–63) sought to place the island under Norwegian rule, an attempt that succeeded in 1261–62. As *Heimskringla* was being composed, however (ca. 1230–35), this issue hung in the balance, and most Icelanders were bitterly opposed. My research suggests that many of *Heimskringla*'s revisions to Harald's story should be read in this context and should be understood as part of Icelandic resistance to the Norwegian throne.

I could go on at great length about this, but instead of dwelling on *Heimskringla*'s richness and ingenuity, let me simply signal one other datum. First, I mentioned that *Fagrskinna*, the last comprehensive Kings' Saga of Norwegian provenance, exists in two variants. The older of these, written a few years before *Heimskringla*, recounts the story of Harald's oath without the Gyða episode. The younger, apparently written after *Heimskringla*, inserts an alternate version. Here, Harald's object of desire bears the name Ragna, and his intentions toward her are pure from the start. When he professes his love, however, the young lady's response is complex. "I could have no better love than you," she starts, "given your rank and your beauty," but before accepting him, she wants to know what lands he will inherit. Scandalized by her greed, Harald rebukes the girl harshly. "I wanted to have you for love," he says, "but you seem more like a concubine."

The episode is represented as a lover's quarrel. "I was only joking," Ragna answers, "and besides, you shouldn't be fighting with women." Better to fight other kings, she continues, then pledges to marry him once he has conquered them all. Harald agrees and swears his oath, which now includes a clause stipulating he will have no wife save Ragna. And were that not enough, he then proclaims the first laws protecting the rights of women.[14] Clearly, this variant is meant to rebut the insinuations of the *Heimskringla* version, and to restore Harald's good name.[15] *Heimskringla* won the competition, however, becoming the standard version of the Kings' Sagas, relegating *Fagrskinna* (and all others) to relative obscurity. The Ragna episode is more obscure still, surviving as an appendix or footnote in those editions of *Fagrskinna* where it appears at all.

Heimskringla's Gyða story, in contrast, remains much beloved. It is enshrined in Thomas Carlyle's *Early Kings of Norway*,[16] *Bulfinch's Mythology*,[17] influential anthologies of children's literature,[18] and an early suffragist variant.[19] More recently, it has been featured in plays,[20] musical comedies,[21] romance novels,[22] school pageants,[23] museum displays,[24] war-game episodes,[25] radio broadcasts,[26] pop music,[27] and other genres. The Norwegian state regularly tells it to schoolchildren,[28] tourists,[29] and immigrants, and within these contexts it often becomes a paradigmatic story of the mutual love that unites the Norwegian people (as represented by Gyða) and the royal family.[30] Clearly, there is no end to retellings, just as there is no critique so biting it cannot be defanged and recuperated.

V

There is a great deal more one could and ought to say here, but time and patience are finite, so let me briefly engage one issue and then draw things to a close. The one I have in mind is the question of categories and genres: Is the Norwegian story of the state's origins, as preserved in *Heimskringla*, *Fagrskinna*, and the other Kings' Sagas, better regarded as history or as myth? As always, this depends on what one means by these words and how one defines those categories. Experts are reasonably agreed that unification of the Norwegian state did take place in the second half of the ninth century through military force, and that shrewd use of marital alliances also helped advance that project. Those who wrote about these events, beginning in the twelfth century and continuing into the thirteenth, based their accounts on prior sources, differentiating between court poems contemporary to the events and oral traditions that accumulated after the fact, and regarding the former as the best evidence. While their standards and judgment were not identical to ours, they were disciplined, self-conscious, and critical. In these ways, they would seem to be historians by any standard.

Where I see them venturing into myth is not in any tendency to introduce fabulous elements or some sacred aura. There is little of that in the variants considered, and not all that much elsewhere (although admittedly one does find a bit in certain episodes). More important, as I see it, are three tendencies. First, the fact that all the texts we have considered, with the sole exception of Theodricus Monachus, are anonymous in their authorship, obscuring the teller in favor of the tale, and representing the version on offer as simultaneously continuous with and an improvement on all prior versions. Second, there is the tendency of the Norwegian variants (medieval and modern) to represent King Harald, his actions, and the state he founded as paradigmatically admirable and extraordinary. His energy, determination, and vision—like his strength and his beauty—are said to exceed those of all other men, with the implication that these values find continuing embodiment in the Norwegian monarchy and state. Not a sacralizing tale in the strictest and most narrow sense, but one that idealizes and legitimates that of which it speaks by recounting the remarkable deeds of its creation.

Third, as I tried to indicate—and the episode I discussed was only one of many about which one could make similar points—the official version did not go uncontested, and numerous critical variants were put into circulation. Like the story they challenged, these anonymous retellings represented themselves as historical accounts: the real version of what happened (although here, it is the tabloid version of "reality" that is advanced in that they tell an embarassing rather than an ennobling story). What strikes me as particularly mythic here is the way they advance their critique by reworking details of the story and turning the narrative against the purposes of rival narrators. Although their view of the Norwegian state—and, no doubt, of the world in general—differs sharply from that of their adversaries, they feel equally empowered to revise the origin story as they like *and to reshape the world in so doing.*

This is the project—and the ethic—of the mythmaker. That of the historian I take to be different, at least in its ideal-typical form. For the historian's distinctive task is not to remake the world by revising the past in the present. Rather, it is first to recover as much of the past as possible with as much accuracy and interpretive acumen as possible; second, to acknowledge where gaps in the evidence make such recovery difficult, tentative, or even impossible; and third, to challenge those who would fill such gaps with their tendentious inventions. Among the strongest instruments of a historian's critique are doubt, hesitation, reticence, skepticism, and modesty (sincere, and neither affected nor self-deluded)—items generally lacking from the mythmaker's arsenal.

CHAPTER SEVEN

POETIC, ROYAL, AND FEMALE DISCOURSE

I

As an arbitrary point of departure, let me begin with a detail from Hesiod's description of royal discourse that has received rather little attention. This is the "sweet dew" (γλυκερὴν ... ἐέρσην) the Muses are said to
pour (χείουσιν) on the tongue of a newborn king, thereby ensuring that
thereafter, "soothing words flow from his mouth."[1] Most of those who have
commented on this substance ratify the opinion of the ancient scholiasts,
who identified it with honey.[2] Such an interpretation is highly attractive and
should be preserved, but as Deborah Boedeker rightly observes, it ought
not obscure the more specific imagery of dew, for the latter substance has
its own very particular symbolic significance.[3]

Boedeker has shown the strong associations of dew to poetry, song,
and speech, while Marilyn Arthur has discussed the Muses' pouring of this
fluid into the king's mouth as a gender-reversed form of insemination.[4]
Both these lines of interpretation have their value. In addition, I would also
connect this image or trope to a set of mythic traditions widely attested
throughout ancient Eurasia that treat the human body and the cosmos
as parallel, mutually interdependent structures.[5] Sometimes these myths
narrate the creation of the world (or some part thereof) from the bodily
matter of a primordial being. Alternatively, they describe how the first man
was assembled from a mix of worldly substances. But in either case, they
enumerate detailed homologies between the micro- and macrocosm, with
certain details recurring frequently. Thus, flesh regularly appears as the
allomorph of earth, likewise stones and bones, eyes and sun, breath and
wind, hair and vegetation.

One problem that sometimes arises, however, is how to deal with the
multiplicity of bodily fluids, which include blood, tears, sweat, semen,
and others as well. Some texts ignore this diversity and focus on one fluid
only—most often, blood—which they associate with water. Others provide
a more complex analysis, subcategorizing cosmic fluids in ways that suggest
parallels to a corresponding set of bodily fluids. Thus, salt seawater can be

paired with tears, running river water with blood in veins, stagnant swamp water with urine, and so forth.[6]

It is within these more complex discussions that dew emerges as a topic of interest. Sometimes it is homologized to sweat, presumably because drops of both fluids mysteriously appear as relevant surfaces heat up.[7] Alternatively, dew can be homologized to sexual fluids for much the same reason (although the heat in question has a different nature).[8] At times, it is associated with blood,[9] bodily lubricity in general,[10] and even the slaver of mythic horses as they cross the nocturnal sky.[11] Similarly, Hesiod's assertion that the Muses place "sweet dew" on the tongues of baby kings suggests a more specialized homology to nothing other than royal saliva.[12]

Recognizing this has implications for understanding the ways Hesiod theorized the nature and effects of royal speech. Thus, as words pass over a king's tongue, the viscous nature of his saliva (born of dew and similar to honey) is imagined as adhering to their surface. This provides a coating for what now become "sweet, soothing, honeyed words" (ἔπε' . . . μείλιχα)[13] that create sensuous pleasure in the ears of those fortunate enough to hear them. As a result, even angry men locked in contentious disputation are mollified when the king pronounces judgment.[14]

The charm of this mythic image is consistent with the highly positive depiction of kingship found in the *Theogony*. One can, however, note a few subtle points that connect the passage to the more critical treatment of kings in the *Works and Days*.[15] Not only is there a potential gap between the words' underlying content and their sugarcoated surface, but a sweet-talking tongue is reminiscent of the warning issued in the *Works and Days* that one can "tell lies with grace of tongue" (ψεύδεσθαι γλώσσης χάριν).[16] Similarly, when discussing the nature of theft, the latter text distinguishes two forms by their bodily locus. Theft by force employs the hand, while theft by guile is accomplished "by tongue" (ἀπὸ γλώσσης).[17]

II

The *Theogony*'s discussion of royal discourse accompanies its account of poetry, and the two are closely interconnected. A large and excellent literature has already been devoted to this topic, and I will not repeat what is already well known.[18] Rather, pursuing implications of the preceding discussion, I will briefly suggest, inter alia, that the text offers a materialist theory of poetic speech that relates—but also contrasts—the latter to its royal counterpart. Thus, for instance, although the text uses much the same formula to describe that something sweet flows from the mouths of kings, poets, and Muses, it uses subtle distinctions to establish a ranking among the three, for the king utters "words" (ἔπεα), while the others utter the more elevated "speech" (αὐδή, a term to be discussed shortly). The speech of the Muses, moreover, is effortless and inexhaustible (ἀκάματος).[19]

Most specifically, I want to contrast the physical details of the processes through which kings and poets receive certain privileged (and privileging) qualities of speech as gifts from the Muses. With regard to poets, the crucial phrase is Hesiod's assertion that the Muses "breathed divine speech into me,"[20] from which several questions follow. The first is what exactly was the object of this action, and here the text is clear. The answer is αὐδή, which denotes a lofty form of speech that goes beyond mere words, being related to poetry and music.[21] These musical (or "Muse-ical") qualities become clear, for instance, when αὐδή is used to denote the miraculous song of the cicada,[22] or the sound of Odysseus's great bow, which "sang" when he first touched it.[23] Most often, however, the epic reserves this term for acts of speech that mediate the human and divine (23/29 occurrences, 79%), including cases where gods speak to humans, sometimes assuming human voices to do so.[24] Conversely, it covers situations where humans are divinely inspired,[25] speak "like a god,"[26] or address deities in speech and song.[27] And should there be any doubt that the αὐδή Hesiod obtained from the Muses is somehow more than human, its accompanying adjective settles the case, marking it as θέσπις, "divine."[28]

Second, we need to ask how this gift was bestowed, and again the text is clear. The verb employed is ἐμ-πνέω, "to blow or breathe into." Elsewhere in Hesiod, it is used only of Boreas (i.e. the northern wind, personified as a deity),[29] and in Homer it is reserved for the action of gods who breathe some valuable quality into the body of a specially favored recipient.[30] Most often, the quality in question is animating energy (μένος), including the force and determination that permit the aged Laertes to enter the *Odyssey*'s final battle.[31] In another instance, Odysseus had the "daring" (θάρσος) that let him blind the Cyclops blown into him by an unnamed δαίμων.[32] And, on the female side, Penelope had a dazzling idea divinely blown into her, much as we might speak of a "brainstorm."[33] In none of these cases, however, is the metaphor of blowing so perfectly suited to the object of the action as in the case of αὐδή, since the material substance of (literally) in-spired speech is nothing other than air. The air the Muses breathe into the poet—which is, after all, their own exhaled breath—thus becomes the very substance of his verse and song, much as the honeyed dew they pour on a king's tongue becomes the surface of his soothing words, a difference that gently suggests a contrast between the aesthetic concern with surfaces and the ethical concern with substance, content, and depth.

Third, we must ask where the poet's divinely in-spired αὐδή ultimately
came to reside in his body, and here the text is silent. Still, a few inferences
can be drawn, and two viable hypotheses advanced. First, by way of infer-
ence: since his αὐδή is said to flow from the poet's mouth (ἀπὸ στόματος),
it presumably entered through the same orifice.[34] The physiology of the
mouth suggests it then traveled via the throat to one of two possible termini.
First is the lungs (φρένες), and this would be well suited to the imagery of
air and the act of blowing in. Also, as R. B. Onians first demonstrated, the
Greek epic construed the φρένες as a prime seat of intellect, emotion, and
volition, and as such they were considered capable of receiving certain
kinds of inspiration.[35] Only rarely, however, were the φρένες connected to
processes of speech.[36]

There is one atypical scene in the *Odyssey*, however, that has particular
relevance. This is where the poet Phemios begs for his life and conveys
important information about the nature of his art.

"I grasp your knees, Odysseus! Show respect for me and take pity.
Later, there will be woe for you too, should you slay
The poet—I, who sing to gods and men.
Self-taught am I, and a god planted in my lungs [ἐν φρεσίν]
Odes of every sort."[37]

Here, much like Hesiod, Phemios tells how poetry was "implanted" (ἐμ-
φύω) in him: more precisely, in his lungs.[38] With that organ, he absorbed
and incorporated the divine gift, so that subsequently he could produce
poetic speech of his own. The φρένες hypothesis thus seems viable, but it
rests heavily on this one Odyssean passage. Alternatively, one might trace
inspired speech through the mouth and throat to the belly, following a suggestion of Joshua Katz and Katharina Volk.[39] The point of departure for their
argument is *Theogony* 26, where the Muses tell Hesiod that shepherds like
him are "mere bellies" (γαστέρες οἶον).[40] Ever since antiquity, interpreters
of this line have considered it an insult that construes herdsmen as having
no concerns except their next meal.[41] Yet if one takes seriously the charge
that shepherds are *only* bellies (γαστέρες οἶον), then the shepherd Hesiod
has no other organ in which to receive his divinely in-blown αὐδή.

Katz and Volk adduce further evidence of the belly as a site of inspired
speech, including the practices attributed to those specialists whom the
Greeks called "belly-speakers" (ἐγ-γαστρί-μυθοι and ἐγ-γαστρί-μαντεις)
and the Romans *ventri-loqui*.[42] An intriguing idea, and sufficient for us to
treat the γαστήρ hypothesis as viable, alongside that of the φρένες. Among

its other merits, it yields a simple but elegant formula for the making of a poet.

If {Shepherd = Belly}
and {Poet = Shepherd + αὐδή},
then {Poet = αὐδή + Belly}.

III

A somewhat more complex but equally schematic formula is implied in the Homeric passage that describes the automata Hephaistos fashioned to help him deal with his limp.

Handmaidens moved swiftly to support their lord:
Golden ones, resembling living maidens.
There is mind in their lungs [μετά φρεσίν], and speech
And strength, and they know handicrafts from the gods.[43]

Of all the wonders Hephaistos created, these automata are his crowning glory. By placing νόος (mind), αὐδή (speech), and σθένος (strength) in (what became) the maidens' φρένες, he transformed inert gold into living creatures (or the simulacrum thereof).[44] The relevant goddesses then gave these creatures knowledge of handicrafts (ἔργα), which let them put their strength to practical use. Together, these entities constitute a logical set, identifying the capacities for thought (νόος), word (αὐδή), and deed (σθένος + ἔργα) as the hallmarks of life. This same set recurs in Zeus's plan for the creation of Pandora.

[Father Zeus] bade far-famed Hephaistos to moisten earth with water
As quickly as possible, to place human speech [ἀνθρώπου ... αὐδήν] in it,
Also strength [σθένος]; to make her face like the immortal goddesses,
[To make] the maiden's form fair and delightful. Meanwhile, Athene
Should teach her handicrafts [ἔργα], to contrive on the loom many ornamented things.
Golden Aphrodite should pour grace around her head,
Also painful desire and cares that eat at one's limbs.
He commanded Hermes the runner, Argeiphontēs
To place a dog's mind [κύνεόν ... νόον] in her and a wily/thievish character.[45]

This passage presents much the same formula as the story of Hephaistos's automata, which can be summarized as follows:

Automata = Gold + νόος + αὐδή + σθένος + ἔργα
Pandora = Clay + νόος (+ ἦθος) + αὐδή + σθένος + ἔργα

Going further, the Hesiodic text adds several elaborations.

To make her "feminine," add a beautiful face + body + grace (χάρις)
+ desire (πόθος) + cares (μελεδώνας),
+ a "bitchy" (κύνεόν) quality of mind + a "thievish" (ἐπίκλοπον) quality of
character.

IV

Given the clarity and specificity of Zeus's plans (Κρονίδεω . . . βουλάς), it
comes as something of a surprise when the gods fail to carry them out, a
narrative twist that serves to limit his responsibility for the final product.[46]
Still, all the deities failed to do what they were told, in addition to which
some modified their instructions and some innovated (table 7.1).

All the modifications to Zeus's work orders hold interest, but some
concern us more than others. As a general observation, suffice it to say
that the maiden the gods produced was more beautifully ornamented but
less fully human than the initial blueprints envisioned. In his instructions,
Zeus changed the formula used for the automata only in the most minimal

TABLE 7.1 The creation of Pandora; comparison of Zeus's instructions to the actions actually taken by the gods

Relevant deity	Zeus's instructions (*Works and Days* 60-68)	Deity's performance (*Works and Days* 70-82)

Hephaistos	(1) Make maiden from earth and water;
	(2) Place in her
	  (a) speech (αὐδή)
	  (b) strength (σθένος)
	(3) Give her
	  (a) face like the goddesses
	  (b) beautiful body
		(1) Made maiden from earth

Athene	Teach handicrafts (ἔργα)	Girdled and adorned her

Aphrodite	Pour on her head
	  (a) grace (χάρις)
	  (b) desire (πόθος)
	  (c) cares (μελεδῶναι)	

Graces and Seduction		Put golden necklaces on her body
Seasons		Crowned her with flowers

Hermes	Place in her
	  (a) bitchy mind (κύνεόν . . . νόον)
	  (b) thievish character (ἐπίκλοπον ἦθος)
		(1) Shaped for her
		  (a) falsehoods (ψεύδεα)
		  (b) seductive words (αἱμυλίους . . . λόγους)
		  (c) thievish character (ἐπίκλοπον ἦθος)
		(2) Placed in her breast
		  (a) voice (φωνή)

fashion, specifying that the "mind" (νόος) given to Pandora should be "bitchy" (κύνεος) in nature and accompanied by "a thievish character."[47] In the event, however, Hermes omitted mind altogether, delivering only the thievish character (ἐπίκλοπον ἦθος). And this—so the text would have us infer—is why women are unthinking and immoral.

In similar fashion, Hephaistos failed to bestow σθένος, and here again the text advances a misogynist project.[48] Elsewhere in Hesiod, σθένος is used of warriors, mythic heroes, and beasts of burden.[49] To this set, Homer adds wild animals, raging rivers, and Hephaistos's golden automata.[50] As these data make clear, σθένος denotes the physical power necessary for heavy labor and martial combat. If Pandora was meant to receive σθένος, then Zeus intended the female body to be strong, like the male, while also possessing the skill necessary for fine handiwork (ἔργα). Unfortunately, Hephaistos and Athene failed to deliver these gifts. Instead—by way of compensation, perhaps—Athene, the Graces, Seasons, and Lady Seduction (πότνια Πειθώ) gave Pandora the implements and arts of *kosmēsis* that thereafter characterize the "feminine." As a result of these deviations from Zeus's plan, women, now incapable of productive labor and (physical) self-defense, depend on cultivation of their charms to obtain sustenance and protection from hardworking males, who possess the necessary σθένος.

Finally, Hephaistos failed to deliver αὐδή, as ordered by Zeus, in place of which Hermes provided Pandora with φωνή (voice), a distinctly inferior substitute. Thus, the epic only infrequently attributes φωνή to deities, always in the context of battle cries, which are more animal-like than articulate.[51] Humans also use φωναί in battle cries, and in one instance they join their voices with those of dogs to frighten off a raging lion.[52] One person can imitate the voice of another, which involves getting its sound, not its verbal content right,[53] and the nonverbal qualities of music (pitch, timbre, melody, and the like) can also be designated by φωνή.[54] All this suggests that φωνή denotes the sonoric qualities that may be shaped into words, but are themselves prerational and prearticulate. If αὐδή mediates the divine and the human, φωνή does similar service for the human and the bestial. Accordingly, φωναί are attributed to animals,[55] monsters,[56] and a particularly shrill trumpet.[57] This entity—which lies closer to the animal than to the divine, partakes of nature, not culture, and conveys instinct and emotion rather than rational thought—replaces the αὐδή of which Pandora was deprived. And when her φωνή did actually find verbal expression, the latter was not to be trusted, since Hermes placed "falsehoods" (ψεύδεα) and "seductive words" (αἱμυλίους . . . λόγους) in her breast (ἐν στήθεσσι), albeit without Zeus's authorization.⁵⁸

V

If the female voice is negatively marked as lying, mindless, and available for thievish schemes, royal words are treated less harshly. This is not to say they are positively valorized in an ethical sense. Rather, the Hesiodic corpus takes pains to depict them as morally neutral, that is, available for a wide variety of uses. To be sure, *Theogony*, 80–92, offers an ideal picture, in which the king pronounces "straight judgments" (ἰθείῃσι δίκῃσιν).⁵⁹ As the *Works and Days* makes clear however, there is nothing necessary or natural about this conjunction of sweet, soothing speech and a moral purpose. Kings are also capable of delivering "crooked judgments" (σκολιῇσι δίκῃσιν), as the text repeatedly notes. In truth, this theme haunts much of the poem, beginning with Hesiod's assertion that Zeus will straighten out the judgments of crooked men,⁶⁰ then turning personal and poignant in the brief account of how Hesiod's brother Persēs won a disproportionate share of their inheritance by taking the case before "bribe-eating kings" (βασιλῆας δωροφάγους), who failed to give straight judgments.⁶¹ Crooked oaths are a mark of the morally debased Iron Age, but these can be sworn by any dishonest person, not being the particular province of kings.⁶² Crooked judgments, however, are the prerogative of kings, and these are denounced no fewer than five times in the text's discussion of good and evil kingship.⁶³

Straight judgments produce harmony, prosperity, and civic flourishing, we are told,⁶⁴ and Hesiod warns all kings that three thousand deities patrol the earth to guard against those "who trample on others with crooked judgments."⁶⁵ Even so, such offenses occur, and the consequences are dire.

> Justice [Δίκη] is a maiden, born of Zeus,
> Famed and honored by the gods who dwell on Olympus.
> And whenever someone damages her, casting blame crookedly,
> Then straightaway she sits beside Father Zeus, Cronus's son,
> And she decries the mind of unjust men until the people
> Make restitution for the follies and outrages of their kings, who, planning
>   grievous wrongs
> Pervert their judgments, speaking crookedly.
> Guard yourself against these things, O Kings; set your pronouncements straight,
> You bribe-eaters, and forget crooked judgments!⁶⁶

This passage carefully disarticulates the aesthetic and ethical aspects of royal discourse. The former may be given by the Muses, embedded in

TABLE 7.2 System of contrasts drawn between the discourse of poets, kings, and women in the Hesiodic epics

	Poet (*Theogony, 23-34, 94-103*)	King (*Theogony, 81-92, Works and Days, 35-39, 248-64*)	Pandora (*Works and Days, 60-82*)
Divine gift	Speech (αὐδή)	Dew (ἑέρση), which becomes saliva that coats the king's words (ἔπεα)	Voice (φωνή)
Character of gift	Divine (θέσπις)	Dew = sweet (γλυκερή), Words = soothing (μείλιχα)	Lies (ψεύδεα), Seductive words (αἱμυλίους . . . λόγους)
Donor	Muses	Muses	Hermes, in place of Hephaistos
Means of giving	Breathed or blown in (ἐνέπνευσαν)	Poured (χείουσιν)	Placed (θῆκε)
Bodily locus in which the gift is lodged	Lungs (φρένες) or belly (γαστήρ)	Tongue (γλώσση)	Breast (στήθεσσι)
Aesthetic quality	+	+	+
Ethical quality	+	+/−	−
Rank	1	2	3

the king's very body, a fact of nature, eternal and invariable, but the latter remains contingent and variable, dependent on human choices. This is to say that kings may always speak sweetly, but they are equally capable of speaking "straight" and "crooked," with serious consequences for the cases they judge and for the people they rule.

The conjunction of the beautiful with the lying or thievish is precisely that which characterizes Pandora; and when kings produce words of this sort, they approximate the female condition, although in their more ideal speech acts they approach those of poets, even gods. The point is, however, they have the whole range of possibilities available to them. Being morally variable—one might also say, unpredictable and unstable—the king's soothing words (ἔπε' . . . μείλιχα) are thus situated between the divine speech (αὐδή θέσπις) of poets and the debased voice (φωνή) of women, a position that is painstakingly worked out in the texts we have been considering (table 7.2).

CHAPTER EIGHT

ANCIENT AND POST-ANCIENT RELIGIONS

I

In this chapter, I would like to engage two broad sets of questions. First, what do we mean by "the ancient world"? What constitutes the ancient and separates it from that which follows (a category I will, for the sake of convenience and provocation, call the "post-ancient")? Second, what forms does religion take, and what roles does it play in the ancient? In the post-ancient? And how do changes in the religious contribute to the change from one era to the other?

As an initial attempt to engage these questions—one that is admittedly inadequate and destined for further refinement—let me advance the proposition that "the ancient" is that situation in which religion is not one system of culture coexisting among many others; instead, it occupies the central position and plays a unique role, informing, inflecting, integrating, stabilizing, even (at times) controlling and determining all others (a position that has had some currency at least since Fustel de Coulanges [1864]). Such a formulation carries a Hegelian danger, of course, and threatens to turn into its opposite. For were religion to be found everywhere, there would be no borders to delimit and define it. Indeed, its very ubiquity might render it unrecognizable, rather like "culture" or life itself. The fact that many, perhaps most, ancient languages have no term that matches the semantics of English *religion* (Latin is only a partial exception) lends support to this suspicion. It also raises the possibility that the emergence of the term and category "religion" is itself a product of the cultural transformation effected by the Reformation and the Enlightenment, making this concept a particularly anachronistic instrument for understanding the situation of the premodern.[1]

Although this argument has the merit of making us cautious, it errs by way of overstatement. To say that nothing in antiquity was free of religion— not war, disease, erotic love, science, the arts, poetry, or the state; not the landscape, the family, the meat on the table, or the fire on the hearth—is not to say that everything "was" religious, only that religious concerns were *a part* of all else, and a part that remains—to us, at least—analytically recognizable. Proceeding thus, we might theorize "the ancient" as that situation where, to cite just a few examples, one treated toothache by reciting the account of creation,[2] read the organs of sacrificial victims before waging battle,[3] secured the verity of speech acts with sacred oaths,[4] and conducted international diplomacy through appeals to mythic genealogy.[5]

Scholars have often worked with such a model, although frequently it remains subtextual and implicit.[6] Correlated with this (whether as consequence or motive is hard to tell) is an understanding that "the ancient" ended with a "Greek miracle" that anticipated the Enlightenment by breaking with myth, tradition, and puerile superstition to achieve a critical view of religion.[7] Xenophanes, Heraclitus, and Socrates are often singled out in this respect and accorded particular credit. Closer reading, however, makes clear that these thinkers were hardly critics of religion *as such*, but only of specific forms. Thus, for all that Xenophanes criticized Homer and Hesiod for telling scandalous tales about the gods[8] and notwithstanding his sly suggestion that cattle imagined gods in bovine form,[9] he also maintained, a propos of proper etiquette at symposia: "It is fitting, above all, for men of good cheer to hymn the god with well-spoken *mythoi* and pure *logoi*, having poured libations and prayed to be able to accomplish just things."[10] As he made clear in the same passage, which represents the longest excerpt we have of his work, Xenophanes's concern was that religion should promote decorum, well-being, grace, and harmony. As a negative complement, he did maintain that "there is nothing useful" in beliefs that promote violent disorders (*stasias sphedanas*), but this is hardly a critique of religion per se.[11]

Similarly, Socrates claimed to have grounded his incessant critical activity on an oracle received from the Delphic Pythia,[12] and he took pains to assure the jury that tried him for impiety (*asebêia*) that he was incapable of this offense, since a personal *daimôn* supervised his conduct and he always heeded this deity's advice.[13] Plato's valuation of reasoned knowledge (*epistêmê*) over faith (*pistis*) and opinion (*doxa*) also involved less critique of religion than is normally supposed. Thus, he maintained that the philosophical disposition which makes it possible for some—indeed, a very small elite—to acquire such knowledge is itself the product of postmortem experiences before the soul's reincarnation. Only in the great beyond is ultimate reality is revealed to all souls, but the degree to which individuals preserve memory of its true nature in the next life reflects the extent to which they have cultivated control of their base appetites. Those who have accomplished this via prior training and *askêsis* retain the most knowledge of the truth and are thus reborn with a "philosophical disposition" that makes learning (via recollection, or *anamnêsis*) easy for them.[14] Plato's epistemology is thus inseparable from his theory of the soul and its fate (psychology in the most literal sense), also his eschatology, metaphysics, and soteriology. In a word, his philosophy incorporates and depends on religion, albeit a form of religion that tends to eschew civic cult, while drawing on dissident strains of speculation current among Orphics, Pythagoreans, and others.

"The ancient" does break down, of course, but it does so gradually, not through any "miracle" (itself a surprisingly religious trope, as is that of "genius," which often attends it). Earlier, to characterize "the ancient," I cited a set of examples that gestured toward medicine (the Babylonian toothache charm), warfare (Roman divination before battle), law (Greek oaths), and diplomacy (Persian use of genealogies to court potential allies). Change, however, can be seen in all these domains, as when epilepsy ("the sacred disease") is said to derive from natural causes,[15] and when generals repeat divinatory consultations until they get the results they want or proceed in defiance of the readings.[16] The same shift toward a "post-ancient" less thoroughly encompassed by religion can be perceived when one's statements are secured by signing a contract rather than swearing an oath, or when threats and bribes, rather than invocations of shared ancestors, are used to enlist allies.[17] Such changes come piecemeal, however, such that antiquity ends—if the model we are currently entertaining permits one to conclude that it ends at all—only in fits and starts. Indeed, the model permits the view that "the ancient" persists or reasserts itself whenever oaths are sworn in a court of law, wherever prayers are said for the sick or for soldiers in battle, and whenever nations make common cause on the basis of shared ancestry, history, or beliefs.

Our first attempt sought to resolve all problems at once by identifying "the ancient" with the omnipresence of religion, while paying no attention to complexities internal to the latter term. The result was a critical instrument too blunt for our purpose. It is time to back up and seek a sharper blade.

II

Elsewhere, in quite a different context, I have sought to define *religion* as a polythetic entity involving at least four domains. To wit:

1. A discourse whose concerns transcend the human, temporal, and contingent, and that claims for itself a similarly transcendent status;
2. A set of practices whose goal is to produce a proper world and/or proper human subjects, as defined by the religious discourse to which these practices are connected;

3. A community whose members construct their identity with reference to a religious discourse and its attendant practices; and

4. An institution that regulates discourse, practices, and community, reproducing them over time and modifying them as necessary, while asserting their eternal validity and transcendent value.[18]

Accordingly, I would suggest that the transition from ancient to post-ancient might better be studied with reference to these four variables (religious discourse, practice, community, and institutions) rather than to the one that is their sum and product ("religion," *tout court*).

As a starting point, one might observe that the most authoritative discourses of antiquity tended to be acts of speech that understood—and represented—themselves as inspired. Not simply human utterances, these were pronouncements in which some divine agency was felt to be at work, speaking through select human instruments and channels. Mantic, oracular, and prophetic speech regularly enjoyed such status, as did royal proclamations and poetic performance. Poetry, in truth, was extraordinarily important, and the reasons for this must be assessed from two complementary perspectives, technological and ideological.

With regard to the first, prior to the emergence of alphabetic script and the consequent spread of literacy, poetry was by far the most effective technique of memory.[19] Any proposition or narrative that could be put in poetic language was thereby rendered more memorable than in any other linguistic form; therefore, more likely to be disseminated across space and transmitted from one generation to another. Having this precious capacity, such encoding was in high demand and was reserved for those cultural contents that were (better: were judged and became, as a result of this judgment) most important.

Second, reflecting and compounding this practical advantage was the claim of divine status that poets regularly made for themselves and their art. As Hesiod put it, the very breath with which he spoke—that is, the material substance of his speech—was placed in his lungs by the Muses themselves, who were daughters of Zeus and Memory (Mnemosynê).[20] The Delphic Pythia, by contrast, gave oracles only in trance, when putatively possessed by Apollo. The proof that the god spoke through her came not only from the state of her body and visage,[21] but also from the fact that she spoke in perfect hexameters.[22] Similar constructions of poetic discourse as sacred and of poets as "masters of truth"[23] are to be found among the Hebrew prophets, Vedic seers, Roman Sibyls, and the hymns attributed to Zarathustra.[24]

With the spread of literacy and alphabetic script, written prose gradually displaced oral poetry as the most effective mnemonic technique, and widespread cultural changes followed.[25] In the realm of religion, sacred books came to enjoy higher status than did inspired utterances. Growing awareness that the latter might not be what they claimed and were open to manipulation by their human agents also served to undercut their authority. They might be preserved, however, by a process whereby the utterances in question were textualized and reconstituted as revealed scripture, as in the case of the biblical prophets and the Sibylline books.

So bibliocentric (initially in the broad, and later in the narrow sense) did religious discourse become that the danger emerged of excess production and oversupply. To control this threat, priestly bodies assumed the power to impose limits through canon formation and the closure of prophecy, sometimes with the backing of state power, as when Augustus had the Libri Sibyllini collected, purged of suspicious contents, and placed in the temple of his patron deity, where they were kept under lock and key, accessible only to authorized priests.[26] Similar, if less dramatic and less state-controlled processes everywhere produced restricted bodies of scripture that were invested with authoritative status, and a situation in which energies were directed toward the interpretation of these texts rather than the production of new ones. Reading rather than speaking became the privileged moment of religious discourse, and most potential for innovation no longer came through the claim of inspiration, but through the practice of shrewd hermeneutics. To put it in slightly different terms, as Jeremiah yielded to the rabbis, John the Baptist to the church fathers, Muhammad to the *qadis* and *ulama*, one can see not only Weber's routinization of charisma but the historic shift from a prophetic ethos associated with orality to the scholarly ethos of the textual.

III

Religious practices also changed significantly from the ancient to the post-ancient. In specific, two sorts of practices fell into relative desuetude, both of which purported to mediate between the sacred and the profane in direct, material fashion. The first of these was a whole complex of behaviors involving the statues of deities. Most commonly, the presence of such statues in temples constituted the latter as the site of a god's residence on earth and thereby cemented the relation of a specific city and people to a specific deity. Thus, to cite but one example, the statue of Marduk in the temple Esagila at Babylon marked the city as this god's special domain and this god as this city's patron, also the dominant member of the pantheon when Babylon extended its power over others. For as was true with other

Mesopotamian cities, when the Babylonians were victorious in warfare, they often took (the statues of) other cities' deities as token of subordination and risked similar capture of their own god should they in turn be conquered. As long as Babylon remained independent, however, the priests of this temple were charged with the care, feeding, decoration, and worship of Marduk's resident statue, which is to say his virtual, palpable presence.[27] This was not mere servitude, however, since deity and people were engaged in an ongoing process of mutually beneficial exchange. The flow of benefits to humanity was particularly dramatized at the Akitu (New Year) festival, when the king clasped the hands of Marduk's image and thereby had his legitimacy and power renewed by the god himself, with consequences for the prosperity of the land and people.[28]

Other peoples developed practices that differed in their details. Sometimes access to the statues was restricted to the priesthood or its high-ranking members. Sometimes worshippers were permitted to make contact by entering into the temple and being led to an inner sanctum where the statue/deity was housed. In other cases, images were brought forth to outer chambers on festal occasions or even paraded through the streets of the city. Some of the statues represented benevolent, nurturing deities who brought blessings to their people; others were demanding and jealous figures, who threatened those whom they found inadequately devoted or attentive. But in all instances, these blocks of material substance were the site where relations between the human and the divine were transacted, the point of conjuncture between sacred and profane.

At least equal in importance was the practice of sacrifice, the most common and also the most significant form of ritual among virtually all ancient peoples. Countless theories of sacrifice have been offered,[29] and the practice itself could be infinitely varied in its performance. Ordinarily, it involved the immolation of an animal or vegetable victim (much more rarely human), the spiritual portion of which was believed to pass to the divine, while the material portion became the basis of a feast enjoyed by the human performers with the gods as their honored guests, thereby restoring a commensality lost in the mythic primordium. All details of the performance could be invested with symbolic content, such that the division of the victim's body might provide analysis of the categoric distinctions between divine, human, and animal levels of existence;[30] alternatively, they might replicate events recounted in cosmogonic myth that homologize the body to the world as microcosm to macrocosm.[31] Sacrifice also provided a means to invest bloody and violent acts with sacral significance and avoid the charge—also the self-inflicted pangs of conscience—that one killed just to obtain food.

Rather, one assumed the burden and awesome responsibility of caring for the gods and the cosmos, which meant performing each minute part of the action in perfectly controlled, symbolically appropriate fashion. Preparation of the feast and disposal of the remains, no less than actual dispatch of the victim, were subject to the same regulation and scrutiny, since all aspects of sacrificial ritual were "good to think" and therefore subject to symbolic elaboration.

Destruction of the Second Temple in 70 CE made it impossible for the priests of Israel to continue their performance of sacrifice and produced a massive reorganization of cult, thought, and organization that resulted in the emergence of that which we know as Judaism(s). Elsewhere, no such dramatic events were responsible, but in many ways, the results were the same. Sacrifice and the use of statues ceased to form the center of ritual practice, and material mediations of every sort diminished in their import. In large measure—but never completely—they were displaced by very different practices that relocated the prime site of interest and action inside the human subject. Prayer, the cultivation of certain valorized dispositions, sentiments, states of embodied or spiritual being, also the habit of monitoring one's progress toward these ethical and existential ideals, reporting flaws and slips to spiritual advisors while submitting to guidance and discipline from the latter, became privileged parts of religious practice with the move toward the post-ancient.

IV

Clearly, these developments correlated with shifts in the nature of religious community. In the ancient, religion was a shared concern of groups existing at familial, civic, ethnic, and national levels of integration. The collective identity of such groups, moreover, was strongly overdetermined, being based simultaneously on territory, language, polity, kinship, and laws, as well as the religion that members held in common and that, in turn, held them. Within such multistranded formations, one's neighbors were one's fellow citizens and also one's coreligionists, who spoke the same language, shared the same norms, celebrated the same festivals, and worshipped at the same altars, seeking favor of the same gods for the group of which they were all a part. The post-ancient, by contrast, saw the emergence of communities based primarily—also most explicitly and emphatically—on religious considerations, integrating persons who might well be divided by geography, language, culture, and/or citizenship.

Numerous factors contributed to this development, which had already begun as early as the Pythagoreans after their expulsion from Croton.

Among the contributing features, one might mention the formation of great empires that brought disparate populations into a single political entity and tax structure, but left subject peoples only very imperfectly integrated in terms of religion and culture. At the same time, expanded trade and improved communications permitted relatively wide circulation of religious tenets, texts, teachers, all of which gradually refashioned themselves in broader, less localized idioms as they engaged—and absorbed feedback from—a disparate, international audience.[32] At times, imperial powers sought to introduce aspects of their native religion to the provinces, or at least to the elite strata therein (e.g. Seleucid policy at the time of the Maccabean revolt). At other times, the imperial center imported religious forms from the periphery as a conscious part of policy (e.g. the Roman *evocatio*), as a means to indulge growing taste for the exotic (e.g. the introduction of Isis and Cybele at Rome), or as part of the backwash that inevitably accompanies conquest (e.g. Mithraism). The diaspora of various groups (e.g. the Magi and the Jews) and the proselytizing activities of others (e.g. the missions recounted in the Acts of the Apostles and related apocrypha) also contributed to the deterritorialization of religious community characteristic of the post-ancient.

In contrast to older groups focused on a specific temple, city, cult place, or sacred locale, which they served and from which they took their identity, the increasingly international, multiethnic, and geographically disparate population of post-ancient religious communities was held together—often rather loosely—not only by shared symbols, beliefs, and practices but also by itinerant leaders and mobile texts like the Epistles of the New Testament, the polemic exchanges among church fathers, the corpora assembled at Qumran and Nag Hammadi, or the rabbinic responsa.

Inclusion or exclusion in such amorphous communities was not ascribed by birth in a given place, lineage, or social stratum but had an elective quality. One joined by conversion, that is, by accepting the beliefs, practices, texts, and leadership that were constitutive of the group and central to their self-understanding. Regularly, the promise of salvation provided a prime inducement to convert, and the conviction that one's faith offered salvation to others (whose contributions would sustain and renew the group) provided a prime motive to proselytize.[33] Soteriological concerns thus figured prominently in the life of post-ancient religions, whose members sought—and promised others—escape from a world they experienced (and described) as hostile, bewildering and finite to a heavenly alternative of eternal bliss. And on the horizontal plane, such escape was prefigured by the move from one social group, identity, and set of loyalties to another: abandoning one's family, for instance, to join one's new brothers-and-sisters-in-Christ.[34] In a loose fashion, this shift further correlates with a change from "locative" world-views concerned with proper emplacement of all things and persons (since being-in-place is what renders them sacred) to "utopian" orientations that valorize mobility as transcendence and liberation.[35]

One final point about religious community in the post-ancient context: in groups that made shared and adhered-to beliefs and practices their chief criteria of inclusion, deviation from these had serious consequences and could provoke not only debate and discussion but also power struggles and schism. Accordingly, issues of heterodoxy and orthodoxy, hetero-praxy and orthopraxy, heresy and heresiology all rose to prominence, along with the institutional means to frame and resolve them, also to enforce the hierarchic elevation of victors over vanquished.

V

This brings us to institutions. In the ancient, specifically religious institutions—priesthoods, temples, cult sites, and so on—were typically subordinate to institutions of the state, be these civic, national, or impe-rial, democratic, oligarchic, or royal. Smaller and weaker than their po-litical counterparts, they served the latter and were dependent on them for protection, financial support, and personnel. As examples, one may consider Athenian interest in Eleusis, the temples of the Acropolis and the Panathenaea, the haoma sacrifices at Persepolis,[36] or the integration of priestly and magisterial offices in the Roman *cursus honorum*. Only in a very few cases, where the institutions possessed extraordinary prestige and authority such that they attracted an international clientele and rich con-tributions, were they able to sustain themselves and achieve a situation of relative autonomy. Delphi is the paradigm case, alongside which one could list only a handful of others.

In the post-ancient, some religious institutions like the rabbinate attained a certain measure of autonomy from the states to which they were subject, but from which they maintained a cautious distance. In other situations—Byzantium and the Islamic caliphate, in particular—religious and political organs and concerns interpenetrated each other so thoroughly as to become practically merged. The most dramatic development, however, occurred in the West, where historic events beginning with the conversion of Constan-tine and the Edict of Milan (313 CE) produced a centralized, well-staffed and well-funded, hierarchic religious establishment that became senior partner in the collaborations of church and state subsequent to the fall of Rome (476 CE). In all these forms and locales, however, religious bodies secured considerable control over such vital arenas of activity as education (general and professional), social welfare (charity and counseling), record keeping, rites of passage (the crucial moments of subject and family formation), and moral scrutiny and control (through preaching, confession/absolution, and pastoral care). Gradually, they perfected the ability to extract revenue from the faithful through a variety of mechanisms. Thus, in addition to contributions that were often voluntary in name only (tithing, *zakkat*), bequests intended to secure salvation were also an important source of income, as was commerce in spiritual goods and services of varied sorts: blessings, indulgences, relics, charms, mystic knowledge, magic formulae, and so forth.

To summarize, as ancient religion gave way to post-ancient, one could observe a discourse based on canonic corpora of sacred texts displacing inspired performances of sacred verse; practices of prayer, contemplation, and self-perfection displacing material mediations through sacrifice and statues of the deity; deterritorialized elective communities constructed on the basis of religious adherence displacing multistranded groups, within which ties of geography, politics, kinship, culture, and religion were isomorphic and mutually reinforcing; and institutions that, with some exceptions, had better (also more creative and varied) funding, a wider range of activities, and more autonomy from the state displacing their weaker, more localized predecessors.

Although these sweeping generalizations call for extended treatment that would attend to the nuances and particularities of a thousand specific cases, my interests at present point in the opposite direction, toward a summation whose smug oversimplifications serve chiefly to prompt objections, further inquiry, and debate. And so, here it is: the transition yields Christianity. Or, to put things a bit more cautiously, the ancient ends and the post-ancient begins with Christianity(ies), Judaism(s), and Islam(s), with the Westernmost form of Christianity as the extreme case.

CHAPTER NINE

SANCTIFIED VIOLENCE

I

Understanding that the topic is much too vast, I want to discuss several recurrent ways that violence figures in religions of the ancient Mediterranean and will make three approaches to the topic. First, I want to consider the nature of violence and its relation to domination. Second, I will sketch four relatively common ways that acts, campaigns, and systems of violence were "sanctified"—invested with religious significance—in late antiquity, sometimes by their authors and sometimes by their victims, but usually in some relation to the context of empire. Third, I will provide a somewhat more thorough (but still too brief) analysis of one phenomenon that holds particular theoretic interest, historic importance, and contemporary relevance.

II

Taking my lead from Simone Weil's meditation on the *Iliad* as "le poème de la force,"[1] Alexandre Kojève's elaboration of Hegel's master-slave dialectic,[2] and Orlando Patterson's treatment of slavery as a form of social death,[3] let me start by suggesting we can best theorize violence as the deployment of physical force in a manner that tends to convert subjects—individual or collective, but in either case fully human actors—into depersonalized objects. Murder, for instance, transforms a previously living subject into a corpse, an inanimate *thing*. Equally instructive examples include rape, where force is used to make some other person an instrument of the aggressor's sexual pleasure; enslavement, where it reduces human subjects to their labor power, stripped of rights and dignity; and conquest and punitive discipline, where overlords of whatever sort (rulers, jailers, bosses, etc.) attempt to render their charges submissive and compliant.[4]

At the analytic core of violence, then, are not just rough acts but the way such acts mediate relations between an actor (individual or collective) whose power, status, pride, sense of well-being, and control over situations and over others are all enhanced in the process and one for whom these same qualities are diminished, deformed, or extinguished. Such negative effects exist on a cline of increasing intensity, as does violence itself; and one should observe that only the most extreme type of violence—lethal force—physically accomplishes that toward which all other forms gesture, but from which they ultimately retreat: the irreversible transformation of living subject into inert object.[5] Nonlethal force and the credible threat of force may approach this same end, but they stop short of it, and do so by design. For whatever damage these lesser forms of violence may inflict (both physical and psychic), they leave their victims alive, and thus with some measure of personhood, agency, and interiority. Victors, moreover, are ideal-typically concerned that the vanquished retain vital energy in the form of labor-power after they have been forced to surrender the bulk of their autonomy. The image is that of the zombie, a less-than-human creature situated between life and death, stripped of most but not quite *all* subjectivity.

The situation of those who have survived violence is also complex and often contradictory. Thus, to the extent that survivors remain intimidated by the (implicit, explicit, or imagined) threat that violence against them may be renewed, they are likely to participate in their own partial and superficial objectification by *performing* a radically diminished subjectivity. Not zombies but cautious (and skilled) actors who restrict themselves to a zombified public existence, suppressing most signs of autonomous will or desire, for fear that these signs of life might be read as a threat, provocation, or excuse for their enemies to turn violent again.

Having provisionally defined *violence* as the use of force to objectify the other, we are thus led to theorize domination in corollary terms as the cultivation of fear through the threat of violence, thereby producing—and perpetuating—a docile, compliant, and semiobjectified state among the community of the fearful. One can describe that community as having been intimidated: not just bullied, but literally *made timid*. Alternatively, one may speak of them as "cowed," a metaphor that signals the loss (or surrender) of certain human qualities and properties—autonomy, spontaneity, confidence, legal rights and safeguards, territory, patrimony, the products of one's labor, and so on—as the result of fear and a cultivated belief that resistance is futile.

Domination also produces contradictory attitudes in the dominated as regards their own inclination toward and capacity for violence. Surely, fear and memories of past suffering work together to inhibit the defeated from taking arms against their oppressor. But the same memories also stimulate lasting resentment, fantasies of revenge, and hopes for liberation, all of which can inspire bloody acts, should such people overcome their fear.[6]

The preceding discussion helps us understand why violence is regularly condemned on aesthetic and ethical grounds as something both ugly and inhumane. One can also imagine good religious reasons for its condemnation, since it is possible to describe the objectifying effects of violence (in a vocabulary that differs only slightly from that we have adopted) as something akin to the sacrilegious degradation of human subjects, whereby beings who are properly recognized as compounds of matter and spirit are reduced to matter alone.

Commentators of many sorts (politicians, clergy, journalists, e.g.) often voice the opinion that religion stands categorically opposed to violence and necessarily condemns it, but several problems undermine this bromide. First, the straightforward empirical question—How often do religions actually condemn violence, and how often do they adopt other stances?—proves surprisingly difficult to answer, since no representative body of data has been assembled or analyzed, and it is hard to imagine just how this might be done. (Ought one to distinguish, for instance, between statements of general principle ["Thou shalt not kill" {Genesis 20:13}] and casuistic injunctions or judgments ["And the Lord said to him, 'I will be with you, and you shall smite the Midianites'" {Judges 6:16}]? Statements of the latter sort seem to be more numerous in most religious traditions, while the former are decidedly more weighty and emphatic.)

Beyond the strictly empirical issues, one also has to ask what is meant by the term *religion*. The problem is particularly acute in any sentence where this abstract noun appears to govern a transitive verb, since, properly speaking, it is only human subjects who possess agency. Thus, to pursue the example, in order to make sense of the claim that "religion" "opposes" or "condemns" something, one must replace the vague and global abstraction with specific animate actors, such as the official representatives of religious institutions, the authors of canonical texts, or persons who represent and experience their views not as idiosyncratic opinions but as founded on sacred truths and transcendent principles to which they have either direct or mediated access. Once this is done, counterexamples are all too readily available, for—as everyone knows—religious authorities, texts, and communities have frequently reacted to incidents, campaigns, and systems of violence not just with condemnation but also by ignoring, condoning, mitigating, even encouraging and rewarding them, according to circumstances.

Of course, it is possible to dismiss such episodes as embarrassing aberrations: moments when flawed people misinterpreted what "true religion" *really* had to say. As a historian and a realist, I am inclined to dismiss such a view as naïve, for history contains only flawed human actors and no true religion. But those considerably more pious than I also reject attempts to constitute the religious as categorically opposed to the violent, as witness, for example, St. Augustine's theory of Just War,[7] or Kierkegaard's characterization of the most profound faith (typified by Abraham's willingness to sacrifice Isaac) as requiring a "religious suspension of the ethical."[8]

In the face of these difficulties, let me advance three propositions that, I hope, all but the most doctrinaire can accept. First, the relation between "religion" and violence takes many forms, being contingent and variable rather than categorical, fixed, and absolute. Second, it is the norm for "religion" to condemn acts of violence, so much so that this is often taken for granted and need not be rendered explicit.[9] Third, there are countless cases in which interested actors seek—and find—reasons for investing specific violent episodes with religious value, adopting attitudes that can range from sorrowful, world-weary acceptance to eager incitement and celebration. The question then arises: Under what kinds of circumstances might acts of violence, which by definition dehumanize and objectify their victims, be positively valorized *on religious grounds?* I can think of five general patterns that recur with some frequency in late antiquity, but the list is by no means exhaustive.[10] Let me treat four of them briefly, holding the fifth for somewhat fuller discussion when other pieces of the argument are in place.

(1) *Conquest as divinely sanctioned.* Here, a group that enjoys certain material and sociopolitical advantages (superior numbers, wealth, weaponry, organization, etc.) sheds whatever moral inhibitions previously kept it from using force against neighbors and rivals by defining itself as more righteous, pure, or divinely favored than those who, in that moment, begin to become its prey. Insofar as incipient aggressors persuade themselves that their victims are morally and spiritually defective, the use of violence against them becomes more acceptable, since it only dehumanizes that which was already somewhat less than fully human. Such a perspective also permits victors to narrate their campaigns of conquest as a form of religious generosity and noblesse-oblige, through which they bear priceless gifts—nonmaterial goods like law, order, morality, enlightenment, even salvation—to the conquered: gifts that promise to raise the benighted closer to the conqueror's higher, more blessed level. (Material goods flow in the opposite direction, of course, bringing wealth, glory, and compensation that can be construed as confirmation of divine favor). Recently, I have

studied the way ideas of this sort animated the Achaemenian kings, who represented themselves as God's chosen instruments to establish paradisal perfection throughout the world,[11] but similar themes also attend Roman imperialism (as theorized in pagan terms under Augustus,[12] and in Christian terms under Constantine[13]), Zoroastrian imperialism in Sassanian Iran,[14] and that of the Islamic caliphate.[15]

(2) *Defeat as humiliation.* If conquerors can justify aggression by demeaning their enemies and arguing, in effect, "They deserved what they got and in the long run they were better for it," the same logic permits victims to make sense of the violence they suffer by a simple substitution of *we* for *they*. Such a construction avoids dwelling on the superiority of the enemy's armies and steadfastly refuses to entertain the superiority—or existence—of their gods. Instead, it locates responsibility for historic trauma in one's own (real or imagined) cultic and moral failings or, more often perhaps, in the failings of one's wayward countrymen, whom earlier polemics and cleavages had identified as somehow inadequate in their observances, devotion, loyalty, or commitment.[16] In a theodicy of great daring and originality, these offenses are construed as having prompted chastisement by one's own god, who is thus permitted to retain all his power and benevolence as the sole causal agent of importance. From this perspective, conquest and domination are represented, also experienced, as salutary humiliations: harsh reminders that prompt a wayward people to restore their proper relation to a god from whom they had previously estranged themselves. Such an analysis posits five distinct stages to a process simultaneously historic and religious: (a) an initial ideal; (b) a state of gradual fall, during which the people in question lost their proper piety and humanity while becoming rich, lazy, deluded, and decadent; (c) the dis-illusioning experience of defeat and foreign domination, which forced them to realize their failings; (d) a process of repentance, through which they gradually recover their moral and religious bearing; (e) escape from bondage, restoration of political independence, moral righteousness, and proper relation to god: a step normally set in the future. The scenario I have sketched most closely follows the interpretation Israel's exilic prophets gave to military defeat by Assyria and Babylon,[17] but similar (if less elaborate) strains of self-chastising discourse are attested in Babylonian responses to defeat by Persians,[18] Persian responses to defeat by Greeks and Arabs,[19] and certain Roman responses to sufferings during the Civil Wars.[20]

(3) *Millenarian revolt.* When defeat is construed as divine humiliation, what happens when the cathartic process of repentance has been completed? Or, to put the problem in its most acute form: when a conquered

people feels it has recovered its proper moral and religious status, its full measure of humanity, subjectivity, and agency, also its ideal relation with the divine, but still remains oppressed and exploited, what then is to be done? Foreign conquerors are not easily persuaded to depart, nor is it easy to drive them out. Straightforward calculations of a military and political sort would lead one to judge most attempts at insurrection against more powerful overlords as ill advised, even suicidal. And yet such insurrections do occur, and sometimes even succeed, fueled by a conviction that supernatural assistance is available, either by virtue of the completion of some cosmic cycle (typically, a period of 1,000 years) or through the miraculous appearance of a charismatic hero (in both theological and Weberian senses). Such salvific figures take many forms: angelic beings, sons of a god, inspired prophets or their descendants, revivified mythic heroes, and pretenders in royal lines dethroned by imperial conquest. In all cases, however, messianic figures of this sort embody the conviction that there are forms of power superior to those of brute force, through which the Evil Empire can be defeated. Whether such heroes exist only in popular fantasy or are instantiated in the human actors who claim these roles, they can inspire a dominated people to rise up, believing that divine favor and superior moral/religious status (as embodied in such figures) will ensure victory over oppressors and a salvation simultaneously this- and other-worldly. Further, perception of their overlords as more corrupt, more debased, more impious—indeed, less fully human—than themselves also helps rebels justify their own violent means. Such situations are well attested in Roman Israel[21] and Zoroastrian Iran,[22] but one can also perceive similar dynamics in the rebellions of Spartacus, Vercingetorix, Civilis, and others,[23] as well as—with important modifications—in the emergence of Shi'a Islam.[24]

The three types we have considered strike me as particularly characteristic of late antiquity, where most collective violence—and most attempts to provide religious valorization for violence—occurred in the context of empire. Thus, divinely sanctioned conquest is the mode that best serves those who would pursue imperial projects, imbuing them with the requisite moral confidence. Conversely, defeat as humiliation is the theme best suited to provide solace for empire's victims as they struggle to endure. Finally, millenarian revolt is the type that emerges when endurance gives way to anti-imperial activism and movements of national liberation. These three types can be conveniently (if a bit roughly) schematized in the form of graphs, where the X-axis represents the religious and human status attributed to the people concerned, while the Y-axis represents time and historic process (figs. 9.1–9.3).

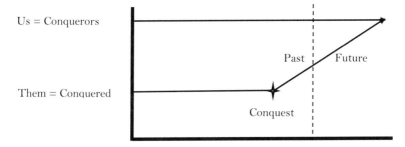

FIGURE 9.1 Conquest as divinely sanctioned. The aggressor justifies his violence, first by believing it falls on victims of deficient religious and human status, second by suggesting that the long-term result will be elevation of the other.

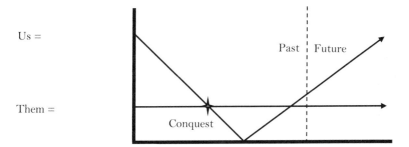

FIGURE 9.2 Defeat as humiliation. The conquered justifies the violence he has suffered by interpreting it as the result of his own prior failings. The experience of captivity and domination then spurs repentance and recovery of proper religious and human status.

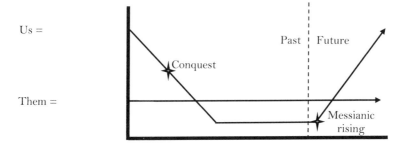

FIGURE 9.3 Millenarian revolt. The conquered experiences himself as trapped in a demeaning domination. To recover proper human and religious status requires not only violent action but also divine assistance and sanction, which take the form of a salvific hero.

IV

In addition to these three types, religious valorization is also available for certain kinds of violence less directly connected to sociopolitical considerations. I would note one such form here, before moving to the last and most complex type of all.

(4) *Mortification of the flesh.* Second only to lethal violence, ascetic rigors offer the clearest example of violent practices that reduce a human subject to an inert object. The chief difference, however, is that two actors are involved in lethal violence, one of whom is left standing when the deed is done. In mortification, by contrast, the same person performs violence on him- (or her-) self, although the actor in question is hardly a unified subject. Rather, ascetics work across a division they take to be internal to themselves, construing subjectivity proper as a dimension of spiritual being, while regarding the body as degraded (and degrading) matter. Consistent with this view, that part of the person associated with will and spirit uses physical force against his (or her) flesh, while withdrawing as far as possible into the nonmaterial realm of the sacred. Implicitly, this process leads to death, theorized as the liberation of the spirit from its bodily prison, after which the corpse-object can be discarded. The liberation in question is less political and this-worldly than is that pursued in millenarian revolt, just as the self-abnegation is less collective and historical than that of those who interpret defeat as humiliation; but all three types represent attempts to endure the pains of a difficult world while cultivating hopes of escape. The process of mortification can be graphed, as in figure 9.4. Examples include not only Christian ascetics[25] but Manichaeans,[26] Gnostics,[27] the Phrygian

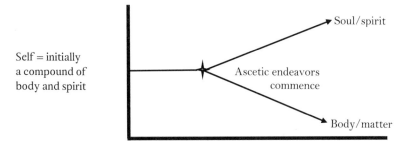

FIGURE 9.4 Mortification of the flesh. Understanding the person to be a compound of base matter and divine spirit, the agentive will, which associates itself with spirit, uses violence to separate itself from the body, construing this as an act of liberation.

Galli,[28] certain strains of Islam[29] and Rabbinic Judaism,[30] and also, perhaps, the Stoics, who pursued the less radical goal of disciplining rather than mortifying the body.[31]

V

In the preceding discussion, we considered four styles of providing religious valorization for violent acts. Of these, two are used by aggressors to justify what they did to their enemies (conquest as divinely sanctioned and millenarian revolt); one by victims to justify what was done to them (defeat as humiliation); and one by people who are simultaneously aggressors and victims to justify the violence one part of a divided self practiced against the other (mortification of the flesh). There is, however, one last type that has certain continuities with all the above, while differing sharply from them. This is martyrdom, a phenomenon that occurs when groups who suffer imperial violence respond, not with self-blame or acts of insurrectionary violence, but by embracing the violence done to them in a way that discredits and delegitimates their adversaries while elevating their own moral, religious, and ontological status above that of all other humans.

Make no mistake: these are jujitsu tactics of paramount skill, whereby the intended victim captures his enemy's violence, then redirects it to fall back on the original aggressor with potentially devastating effect. I will not attempt to summarize or amplify what authors as varied and distinguished as Elizabeth Castelli, Daniel Boyarin, Glenn Bowersock, and G. E. M. de Ste. Croix have written concerning the history of martyrdom, or the way Jewish, Roman, and Christian traditions influenced each other.[32] Rather, let me limit myself to some more general observations consistent with the broader lines of analysis explored in this chapter.

First, however, one must say a few things about imperial religious policies and episodes of persecution. Although there are some noteworthy partial exceptions (Sassanian Iran and Christian Rome chief among them), few empires aspire to achieve religious unity or to convert the peoples they conquer. These tasks are simply too daunting and the benefits are normally considered too slim to justify the effort. Rather, rulers usually understand that in an imperial context, stability is secured by political and military control, economic integration, maintenance of extractive taxation at tolerable levels, impressive public works, and reasonable tolerance of the multiple languages, cultures, and religions that flourish in the provinces. Accordingly, the goal toward which most empires labor is not assimilation, homogeneity, or orthodoxy (i.e. the production of religious uniformity in one fashion or another) but encompassment. That is to say, conquered peoples are permitted to keep their own gods, cults, temples, and the like, so long as they make certain requisite gestures of deference to those of the imperial power. From the ruler's perspective, such gestures acknowledge his hierarchic supremacy and that of his gods, but it may look and feel different to others. In practice, all sorts of compromises get struck (via syncretism, deliberate ambiguity, and the like) that preserve the dignity of all who cooperate in the bargain.[33]

Only when subordinate populations bluntly refuse such intentionally modest demands do the authorities become exercised. Normally, they will settle for select symbolic concessions from elite strata of provincial populations (even if these were disingenuous, bribed, or coerced). And normally, that is what they get. Occasionally, however, certain groups are so exclusive as regards the object and nature of their devotion that they adamantly refuse to compromise, viewing such accommodation as anathema and apostasy.

In a stable imperial order, credible threats are normally enough to produce compliance, but in the face of sustained defiance, rulers may (feel forced to) employ violence itself. When they do so in public, however—even more so, when they do this in spectacular ways—one should distinguish the immediate use-value of the violence employed (i.e. physical elimination of intransigents) from its much more diffuse, but much more important sign-value (i.e. an object lesson designed to dis-courage others of like persuasion).[34]

All signs being reversible, however, Christian martyrs managed to turn the drama in the arena upside down.[35] Where the Romans meant to cast them as incorrigible fanatics who had brought just punishment on their own heads, martyrs constituted themselves as the most devoted servants of the one true God: as such, figures deserving veneration and emulation. The extraordinary courage and calm they displayed in extremis was meant—and understood—to testify on behalf of their faith and its saving power (such is the literal meaning of Greek μάρτυς = "one who bears witness"). More broadly, they disarticulated might and right, and asked their immediate audience (also that which would later hear of their deeds at second hand) to judge who really was the victor in these encounters between an impious, violent state and its righteous, unflinching victims.

The practice of martyrdom thus redefined what the imperial state understood as exemplary punishment, transforming this into a contest between adversaries of radically different nature (might vs. right), the outcome of which hung in the balance. Martyrological discourse went further still, crafting narratives in which the victory won by the martyrs is unmistakable and unambiguous.[36] In these stories, imperial violence does not reduce living persons to inert objects, but has quite the opposite effect. As in the case of mortification, martyr's death served to liberate immortal spirit from base matter, winning sainthood and heavenly reward for the soul thus freed, while creating a name and reputation that would endure forever and provide inspiration to others. Such stories not only cast agents of the empire as villains; sometimes they went so far as to treat them as demonically inspired. In this and other ways, they radically questioned the nature of power, arguing that the physical might of the state, being exclusively material in nature, was inferior to the spiritual power of the martyrs (and the discursive power of those who told their story). Lacking sacred sanction, the "power" in which rulers naïvely put their trust is a lesser form of power, and a self-deluded one at that, marked by arrogance and brutality. It is not the martyr whose humanity is diminished by the encounter in the arena but the emperor, whose callous use of violence reveals him to be no better than the lion. The extraordinary inversions accomplished by the practice of martyrdom and the discourse of martyrology are not easily graphed, but they may be summarized, as in table 9.1.

TABLE 9.1 Martyrological inversion of imperial narratives. *Note*: A spectacle in which the state understands itself to be using just punishment on those who defy its rightful authority and enlightened policies is transformed into a narrative that shows worldly power to be inferior in every way to power of a spiritual nature.

	Subjects of violent acts	Objects of violent acts	Victor
Imperial spectacle of exemplary punishment	Hero of story: Legitimate rulers +Might +Right	Villain of story: Intransigent fanatics −Might −Right	State authorities
Practice of martyrdom	Villain of story: Tyrants +Might −Right	Hero of story: The faithful −Might +Right	Open to interpretation of spectators
Discourse of martyrology	Villain of story: Tyrants and devils −True might (≠ Physical force) −Right	Hero of story: Sainted martyrs +True might (= Spiritual force) +Right	Martyrs, their church, and their god

VI

As a general principle, scholarly discourse ought not uncritically reproduce the self-representations and self-perceptions of those it purports to study. In the case of martyrs and martyrology, it is easy enough to introduce other explanatory frameworks—masochism, self-righteousness, *ressentiment*, passive aggression, for example—and to note the unfortunate tendency of those who have suffered violence, persecution, and domination to turn violent, dominating, and vengeful, when given the opportunity.[37]

Even granting the validity of these revisionist critiques, as one must, it is hard (for me, at least) not to harbor some admiration for the martyrs, and this for two reasons. First is the way martyrdom responds to the objectifying effects of violence. For when rulers use force to make inert things of those who dare resist, and stage this as a spectacle of intimidating power, martyrs fight with the only weapons at their disposal. These consist chiefly of language and a dignified bodily comportment: subjective qualities, through which they assert their ineradicable humanity, even in extremis.

Second, I am struck by the way martyrdom responds to intimidation. For if violence is the use of force so as to objectify the other, and domination is the cultivation of fear (through the threat of violence) so as to keep that other in a docile, compliant, and semiobjectified state, then the reversal of domination begins with the victory of fearlessness over fear. Or, to put it differently, it begins with the discovery of an alternative form of power with which to challenge those whose power is based on violence and threats. This alternative form of power can be theorized—and experienced—as something spiritual, moral, religious, psychological, discursive, rhetorical, or semiotic in nature, and it may be all the above. Regardless of how one conceives it, martyrs (and the martyrologists who tell their tales) provide one of the clearest and most extreme examples of just how potent this power can be. Such phenomena are not limited to late antiquity, moreover, as contemporary imperialists are learning, even those who try to manage this threat by denying the title of "martyr" to those who style themselves as *shahideen*.[38] But that is another story.

CHAPTER TEN

RELIGIOUS AND OTHER CONFLICTS IN TWENTIETH-CENTURY GUATEMALA

I

If by "indigenous religions" we mean to denote religious traditions that have not (yet) been influenced or colonized by the global "isms," such are notoriously difficult to locate, since most of our evidence is not the autonomous self-expression of an ab-original entity but a product of contact between indigenous cultures and encroaching others. Indeed, the very mediations that make these data available to anyone other than indigenes also render them most problematic (travelers' accounts, colonial archives, missionary reports, ethnographies, coauthored autobiographies, and studies by those educated in mission schools or Euramerican universities). As a result, our view of the "indigenous" per se is always refracted, if not obstructed: what we observe most clearly is not "the other" but the situation of encounter between that other and an exogenous intruder. This, however, need occasion no regret, for it provides the stimulus and opportunity to transform our understanding of "indigenous" and "world" religions alike.

Thus, the encounter situation reveals the methodological and moral fallacy of treating "world religions" in ahistorical fashion, and forces one to recognize these as emergent phenomena that expanded their territory, numbers, and power always at the expense of others. Here, one needs to inquire about the extradoctrinal factors that facilitated their expansion by asking, for example, When and how were specific areas and populations identified as targets of opportunity for missionizing and conversion? Who made these determinations, and in consultation with what other interests (the state, the military, chartered monopolies, or venture capital, e.g.)? Whence came the personnel and material support for such ventures? How were these resources deployed, and what returns were expected on the investment? Perhaps most important, What kind of subjects did missions seek to constitute, and how did they pursue this project? (Proletarianization is likely to be a key issue). Further, Which portions of prior doctrine, canon, ethical and ritual practice were emphasized, and which ones reinterpreted or occluded for local consumption?

Conversely, focusing on the encounter situation also helps us avoid theorizing an unrealistically pristine "indigenous" and lets us appreciate that local traditions meet advancing world religions in situations of vastly unequal power, within which they mount certain kinds of resistance, while also making strategic accommodation at points they consider less than vital. At the points of most serious contention, one can observe the crudest shows of force, the most audacious bluffs, the subtlest jockeying for position, and the most complex negotiations. Such points are many and varied, and they shift in locus, nature, and intensity as the engagement continues. Over the course of that engagement, the strategic and tactical sense, cultural and material resources, determination and endurance of the contending parties are constantly put to the test. At any given moment and in any given locale, the details of religious discourse and practice reflect the extant balance of power between indigenous and exogenous populations, traditions, and values. What is more, they provide the means through which interested parties comment on, maneuver within, and seek to revise that same balance of power.

II

I would like to illustrate these points by treating a few incidents drawn from the history of Guatemala, where for the last half millennium Spaniard has struggled against Maya, *ladino* against Indian, the cosmopolitan against the local, the intrusive against the enduring.[1] The first is a story Charles Wagley collected in 1937, as part of his work in Santiago Chimaltenango, a Mam-speaking village of the western highlands.

> Before, the earth was flat, and there were no mountains or barrancas (canyons). Father José and Mother María Santissima were the first naturales (Indians) to live on the earth. The first man was José and he made the earth, and then came María, his wife. José then made men. At that time their burdens were light because there were no hills or barrancas to tire them. The world was puro plano (perfectly flat). When Father José first made the earth, neither he nor other men could see what they were doing. Then it was always night and people did not know when to sleep and when to work. Then, so he could see men as they went about, Father José made a great machine, the sun, and then, later, he made the moon so people would have some light as they slept. He made the moon so it would follow the sun and made it strong part of the time and weak other nights. But then the sun and the moon were not regular; they did not appear at the same time every day. Then, Jesús Cristo, the first son of José and María, was born. While María was pregnant the Devil came to José and told him that he was not the father of the child. He said that María had many lovers. José did not believe

the Devil and sent him away. On the first day after Jesús Cristo was born, he sat up and talked, and in four days he grew to full size. He told Father José that his name was Jesús Cristo and told him that he would not work on this earth, for he had houses and land above. Jesús told his father, "Do not be troubled, Father, for I am going to make another world and you will be able to help me." Then, day by day, the mountains began to appear on the earth and he (Jesús) began to make valleys and barrancas for the rivers. He made the moon weaker [than the sun] so there would be night and day. He set three times a day for people to eat and told people when they should sleep. Now a man watches the sun and eats when it is at regular places [in the sky] and sleeps when the sun is gone. Jesús made roads over these mountains for the Indians to travel. The naturales were happy but the people of the Devil, when they saw these mountains appear, were angry and said, "We are not accustomed to these hills. It is the work of that man José and his son. It is better that we kill them."[2]

Wagley described this text as a "combined Chimalteco Genesis-Crucifixion story," and he used it to illustrate the ways orthodox doctrines had been reworked by local traditions and orientations. Although Chimaltecos understood themselves as extremely faithful Catholics, they had little contact with the priest whose service to their community consisted of a brief visit every year or two. In the interim, religion was in the hands of local officials, some of them attached to the church (*cantores, sacristanes, mayordomos*) and some not (diviners and healers, Mam *chimanes*).[3] Within these circumstances, as he observed, the Christian savior came to be portrayed as a culture hero and trickster who was born as an Indian in absolutely human fashion, and whose life was lived on local terrain.[4] I think, however, one can go further.

Through his creative acts, the Jesús of this story introduces valorized dichotomies at the level of heaven, earth, and society. Thus, he made the sun shine brighter than the moon and brought mountains and valleys into a previously flat earth, an act which also divided humanity into two types.[5] One group of people lives and works happily in the highland terrain, and these are said to be "Indians," or *naturales* (as are Jesús, José, and María). Others find it onerous to trek up and down, and presumably prefer life on the coastal plain or in urban centers.

In the next phase of the plot, the mountain-haters set out to kill Jesús, the maker of mountains. Initially, the text calls this murderous band "the people of the Devil," thereby associating them with the malicious spirit who earlier tried to destroy the love of José and María by labeling Jesús a bastard. Later, it shifts nomenclature and calls them "Jews," a term missionaries in New Spain borrowed from the Inquisition for use against adherents of indigenous religion, whom they constituted in this fashion as enemies, not just of imperial conquest and colonial domination, but of the church and Christ himself.⁶

This text, however, reworks the conquerors' favored analogic construct—{Spaniard : Indian :: Christian : Jew}—in daring fashion, first by associating Indians with the Christians (rather than with Jews), and second by subtextually identifying "Jews" with that group most antithetical to the Indian community: the Europeanized ladino elite who have dominated Guatemalan politics and economy since independence.⁷ This is skillfully suggested—without being openly or bluntly asserted—in the story's dénouement.⁸ Thus, several episodes describe how Jesús evaded these "Jews" for forty days, deceiving them with one hilarious ruse after another, until finally they caught and crucified him.

> Then the Jews placed Jesús' body at the edge of the pueblo. Late that night a burro came along and breathed over the body of Jesús. The breath of the burro made the marks of the nails disappear at once. That same night Jesús went to heaven and has never returned. When the Jews returned next day for the body, they were angry and frightened to find that it had gone. Then, they were afraid and went to many people and asked where Jesús Cristo had gone. They were told that he had gone to heaven. Then the Jews hid behind trees and in the brush in fear, but a great storm came with thunder and lightning and with each flash a Jew was killed. Now only those who live beneath the ground where Jesús placed them are alive.⁹

Here, Jesús transforms the "Jews" into Guardians of the mountains (Spanish Guardias de los Cerros, Mam *taajwa witz*): rich, powerful spirits of the wilderness who are as remote as they are capricious. Capable of helping Chimaltecos should they wish, they more frequently lure naïve Indians into Faustian bargains, as in the following example:

> Two men, Juan Martín and Pascal Hernandez, both of whom died many years ago, were walking near the summit of Pichon [the mountain which towers over Chimaltenango], when they met a strange ladino. The ladino "had long blond hair, wore a shiny coat and a hat with long feathers on it." The ladino warned them to stay away from the summit. Both men were afraid, but one asked if he were the Guardian of Pichon. The ladino at first said "No," but when one of the Chimaltecos asked if the ladino might possibly lend them money, he admitted his identity as the Guardian, and lent them money. The Guardian told them to close their eyes, and when they opened them, they were inside the mountain, inside a huge house. "There was a large coffee plantation inside the mountain. Many animals were inside the house; large ferocious dogs were chained to the walls." The Guardian gave them money—"who knows how much." He asked

them to repay it after some days and told them to make costumbre to him every four days. After the two men had shut and opened their eyes again, they found themselves back at the same spot where they met the Guardian. But after returning to the village, they did not even once make costumbre to the Guardian, nor did they make any effort to repay the money. At the same time they were sleeping with each other's wives; "these good friends cheated each other." After several months, both men and their wives died and "all the people knew why." Now the Guardian is punishing them; "they are working inside Pichon for the Guardian to repay the money and as a punishment. They will work there for many years on the plantation of the Guardian."[10]

In relatively open fashion, this passage offers a telling critique of money, debt, wage labor, consumption of luxuries, illicit sexuality, and abandonment of traditional religious practice (*costumbre*). Particularly striking is the resemblance of these Guardians of the mountains—who are repeatedly identified as ladinos—to the three labor recruiters who visited Chimaltenango each year and used loans, drink, and other stratagems to entrap Chimaltecos in seasonal labor contracts, committing them to work under truly appalling conditions on the large coffee plantations of the western coast.[11] Mirroring the relation of exploitive ladinos to vulnerable Indians, the Guardians of the mountains are also regularly contrasted to the protective and usually benevolent saints (*santos*), who reside in the church at the village center, dress in traditional Chimalteco costume, and receive their prayers in Mam rather than Spanish.[12]

The text with which we began encodes a set of oppositions between the groups and values listed below. Within the episodes of the narrative, victories alternate between the contrasted groups, but no outcome is ever conclusive. Each escape is followed by capture, and capture by escape. Crucifixion leads to resurrection, and lightning-blast death only occasions metamorphosis into spirits of the mountains. Down to the present, the struggle continues.

CONTRAST	EPISODE
José and María [= *naturales*] : The Devil ::	(1)
Faith, love, trust : Gossip, suspicion, troublemaking ::	
Mountains : Valleys ::	(2)
Sun : Moon ::	
Day : Night ::	
Work : Rest ::	
Those who like Mountains : Those who like Plains ::	(3)
Naturales : "People of the Devil"	
Contentment, labor : Anger, indolence ::	

CONTRAST	EPISODE
Jesús & Christians : The Devil & Jews ::	(4)
Indians : Ladinos ::	
Ingenious survivors : Persistent persecutors ::	
Santos : Guardians of the mountains ::	(5)
Village center [= culture] : Outlying wilderness [= nature] ::	
Healers, protectors : Exploiters, enslavers	

Understanding the immediate context in which this text was collected helps refine our interpretation. Although the ladino population of Chimaltenango was relatively small (six families in a population of 1,500), ladinos controlled disproportionate shares of land and wealth while also monopolizing top political offices, with the support of the Guatemalan state. Moreover, in 1934, the dictatorship of Jorge Ubico (r. 1931–44) introduced measures devastating to Indian interests.[13] Most sweeping in their import were the notorious "Vagrancy Laws" that obliged men with landholdings below a certain level (and this included 43% of Chimaltecos) to work on ladino coffee plantations for a minimum of one hundred days each year. Of more immediate local concern was a December 1935 ruling that reduced Chimaltenango from a *municipio* to a subordinate hamlet (*aldea*) of San Pedro Necta, a village whose large ladino population Chimaltecos viewed with fear and suspicion. In particular, Chimaltecos worried that their loss of legal status and autonomy would leave them unable to protect their ownership of land and leave them no options but wage labor. Faced with this crisis, the ranking elders (*principales*) of the village decided to contest the novel arrangements, and they chose a relatively young man, Diego Martín, to represent them, because he spoke fluent Spanish, had some experience of government, and was known as a man "who was not afraid of *ladinos*."[14]

After eight days' journey on foot, Martín and four companions reached the capital, where he met with the Minister of the Interior and negotiated a compromise in which Chimaltenango retained its foremost emblems of municipal status, including the title to its lands,[15] while remaining, for the record, an *aldea* of San Pedro (a status it retained until 1948). Chimaltecos hailed this as a victory, and celebrated their delegates' return with a lavish impromptu fiesta. Sixteen months later, Diego Martín became Wagley's most valued informant and recited for him the story of Jesús and the "Jews."[16]

III

Diego Martín gave this account in the wake of a limited and local, but materially and symbolically significant victory, won in a difficult period.

Within the genres of mythic narrative and theological speculation, he offered his reflections, as of that precise moment, on the nature of Indians, ladinos, and struggles between the two. Now I would like to move from the western to the eastern highlands, from the 1930s to the following decade, from a village with relatively few ladinos to one where they accounted for 35% of the population and owned 70% of the land, from one where a priest went unseen for years at a time to one with monthly clerical visits, and from an instance of mythic discourse to one of ritual practice.

The case I have in mind is the healing ceremony performed in the Pokomám village of San Luis Jilotepeque in the summer of 1946 that provided the basis for John Gillin's classic article titled "Magical Fright."[17] At the center of these events was an elderly woman whom Gillin gave the pseudonym "Alicia." One day, while walking along the river outside the village, she and her husband, Fernando, quarreled badly, dredging up a long and bitter history that involved episodes of drunkenness, poverty, illness, infidelity, financial irresponsibility, and physical cruelty.[18] Words were exchanged. Tempers flared. Then Fernando picked up a rock, struck Alicia with it, and afterward she fell ill. Her symptoms included aches, pains, listlessness, fatigue, diarrhea, loss of appetite, insomnia, depression, and an inability to work or carry out household tasks. Untreated, they were utterly debilitating and posed a serious threat to her life, but help was sought from an accomplished *curandero*.

In the quarrel that prompted the illness, one can perceive two different, but interrelated sets of tensions. At one level, Alicia and her husband fought about land, money, and standing in the community: resources that were scarce and becoming scarcer as the Indians of San Luis lost ground (literally and figuratively) to their ladino rivals. In addition, the couple fought about sex, drink, and domestic violence: issues of love, respect, pleasure, pain, intimacy, dignity, fear, and betrayal, where the lines of cleavage were male and female rather than Indian-ladino. These issues were largely relegated to the background by the *curandero* who treated Alicia and the researchers who reported the case, all of whom focused on the former set of difficulties, each for their own reasons and each in their own idiom.[19]

According to the *curandero*, whom Gillin called "Manuel," the quarrel caused a condition of "Fright" (*espanto* or *susto*), in which Alicia's soul was dislodged from her body and stolen by spirits.[20] To effect a cure, it was necessary to recover her soul from those who now held it, and toward this end he assembled the couple's friends, neighbors, relations, and one of the village's *principales* for a grueling nightlong ceremony, culminating in two

expeditions. The first of these led from the patient's home to the church in
the central plaza, where the *santos* were asked to give their assistance and
to sanction the second, more dangerous journey.

> The curer and the principal, together with two male helpers, now went to the
> place where the precipitating fright of the present espanto occurred. They car-
> ried with them in a gourd the four eggs just used to draw the aires out of the
> patient, digging sticks, pine splinters for light, two candles, and a collection of
> gifts to be offered to the evil spirits. These gifts included a cigar, a bunch of hand-
> made cigarettes, an earthen pitcher of chilate (a maize gruel used as ceremonial
> drink among the Pokomám), four cacao seeds, some sweet biscuits, and a small
> bottle of drinking alcohol. Davidson [Gillin's field assistant] and I accompanied
> the party. We walked in single file through the darkness, following a dim path
> among the bushes upstream along the river. Finally, we came to a spot about ten
> feet above the river which the curer announced was the place where Alicia had
> lost her soul. A pine splinter was lighted. While the two helpers started digging
> a hole in the ground, the curer and the principal turned their backs and faced
> across the river to the west. All previous prayers had been in Pokomám but now
> the curer spoke in Spanish and in familiar, man-to-man terms. He addressed
> five spirits, calling them by name and addressing them as compadres (a form of
> ceremonial kinship). The names of the five were "Avelín Caballero Sombrerón,
> Señor Don Justo Juez, Doña María Diego, Don Manuel Urrutia, and San Graviel
> [Gabriel]." After saluting the others, he directed his remarks to Don Avelín. He
> explained in detail that he had brought them a feast to eat and alcohol to drink.
> He explained that here Alicia had lost her soul through a susto. He dwelt upon
> her symptoms and said that the eggs would bear him out. He said that he knew
> that his compadres knew where her soul was hidden and that they had it in their
> power to return it to her. As a favor to him, the curer, would they not help him
> to secure the lost soul? And so on.[21]

Leaving the security of the village, Manuel and the others ventured by
night to a place of fear: the spot where the patient had lost her soul. There,
they hoped to find the forces responsible and to secure their cooperation
in restoring Alicia's balance, energy, self-confidence, and sense of purpose,
without which she could not survive. Their concern, however, went beyond
her condition to that of the community as a whole, for which she served as
synecdoche. The wild terrain they entered was not just a physical space
but also a space of their collective imaginary, within which they explored
and addressed their communal troubles, especially their relations with
ladino neighbors.

In terms reminiscent of Chimalteco descriptions of Guardians of the
mountains, the San Luiseños voiced their direst fears and entertained a

radical critique, depicting ladinos as devils (Pokomám *tiéwu*, Spanish *diablos*) who threatened to steal their very souls.[22] Numerous details establish this identification. First, whereas all other ritual proceedings were conducted in Pokomám, these spirits alone were addressed in Spanish. Second, they bore the names and titles of historic ladinos well known in San Luis.[23] Third, they dressed in ladino fashion, their leader being particularly known for his large sombrero and blond hair. Finally, the gifts they received include cigars and cookies: luxury items favored by ladinos but not *naturales*.[24]

Over the course of the ritual, however, the *curandero* revised this narrative of diabolism and guided it toward a satisfying dénouement, revealing in the process that however alien these spirits might be, negotiation with them was both possible and productive. Toward this end, he put on display a repertoire of techniques for success in dealing with powerful others: a repertoire that included flattery, cajolery, and bribery (i.e. the use of gifts to call forth reciprocity) as well as extreme politesse (espcially the euphemistic coding of demands as requests—*por favor*).

Most important, Manuel addressed these spirits as *compadres* (literally "co-fathers," i.e. the godparents of one's children), thereby constituting them as his ritual kin and invoking an institution of extraordinary importance. *Compadrazgo* is one of the few instruments that serve to integrate Indian and ladino into a single civic and moral community, and one of the few means through which an Indian can make legitimate demands on a ladino that obligate him to respond with benevolence.[25] The relation, however, is asymmetric, and as such, fraught with perils and uncertainties.

> The important point is that Indians frequently secure ladino compadres, whereas ladinos never ask an Indian to serve as padrino. Thus a bridge of ceremonial kinship is built across caste lines, although a rather patronizing attitude colors the ladino view of the relationship, and the Indian compadre and godchild are in a subordinate and semi-dependent status, rather than in a position of equality with the ladinos involved. One result is that the term "compadre" is not much used between Indians and ladinos, because it implies an equality which the ladinos will not admit. On the other hand, ladinos do recognize obligations toward Indian godchildren. I have found no cases or complaints of ladinos failing to "do something" for an Indian godchild in case of emergency.[26]

To call on a ladino as "compadre" was thus an operation that could bring desired results, but one that could backfire, should it be considered an unwarranted presumption. In order to succeed, this maneuver had to be carried out with considerable tact, in a voice that conveyed both respect and confidence, without signaling anything that could be read as audacity or fear. Like Diego Martín, Manuel was known as a man very little intimidated by ladinos.[27] Moreover, at the time Gillin watched him bargain with the spirits, the ladinos of San Luis had never seemed so approachable.

This was the local result of national events. Roughly two years earlier, on October 20, 1944, Jorge Ubico was driven from the Guatemalan presidency, ushering in a revolutionary government under Juan José Arévalo that was committed to improving the lives of Indians and peasants. In San Luis, this news catalyzed a latent cleavage between the wealthiest ladinos and those less well situated, who had been disgruntled in the past and were sympathetic to the incoming Arévalistas. When a Pokomám-speaking leader of the latter faction (one of the two ladinos—out of 5,500—who had such competence) spoke to the Indian population about these events, they rallied enthusiastically to the cause, chased the older leaders from the village, and elected a new government in which a ladino of the revolutionary faction became mayor and Indians, for the first time, held a majority in the municipal council.

In his account of these events, Gillin lists seven reforms that were rapidly introduced, consistent with trends throughout the nation. All of these were important, and they cover such areas as land ownership, education, and participation in politics and commerce, as well as an end to all forms of legal discrimination. Two items, however, are particularly helpful in establishing the context within which Manuel negotiated with soul-stealing ladino spirits, whom he addressed as compadres.

1. It was one of the stated goals of the revolution that the Indians should be incorporated into the national culture. The local ladino democrats spoke of this frequently and in public, and made a point of fraternizing with Indians up to a point, arranging favors for them, etc.

5. Indian curing ceremonies, which had formerly been a favorite target for police when they had nothing else to do, were tolerated without interference.[28]

IV

From 1944 to 1954, reforms of this sort were pursued with ever-greater determination, until a coup organized by the CIA at the urging of the United Fruit Co. toppled Arévalo's successor, Jacobo Arbenz Gúzman, and brought an abrupt end to Guatemala's experiment with popular democracy.[29] Since that time, the Guatemalan state and army, with significant (if inconsistent) US backing, have carried out the Western Hemisphere's most savage campaign of repression against intellectuals, opposition politicians, organized labor, and, above all, the nation's peasant and Indian population. Reliable estimates number those killed by the army and death squads in the hundreds of thousands, not to speak of those imprisoned, tortured, and driven into exile.[30] The absolute height of that campaign came during the military dictatorship of Efraím Rios Montt (1982–83), when "counterinsurgency" policies were unconstrained by democratic institutions, international pressure, or any rule of law.[31] Some religious establishments—particularly the evangelical Protestant groups to which Rios Montt belonged and conservative fractions of the Catholic church—have aligned themselves with the killers; others, with the victims, Maryknoll missions and proponents of liberation theology being noteworthy in this regard. All, however, have pressed—often with considerable success—for what they view as a purer and more proper Christianity: that is, one more consistent with that practiced in Europe and North America, and one less accommodating toward local traditions.[32]

When John Watanabe began fieldwork in Santiago Chimaltenango, more than forty years after Wagley had been there, he found that since the early 1950s, Maryknoll missionaries based in San Pedro Necta had been active in the village. Funded from overseas and independent of the Archdiocese of Santiago de Guatemala, they had earned the respect and gratitude of Chimaltecos with medical, agricultural, and educational reforms they introduced, and their concern for the well-being of the community. At the same time, they had established a cadre of catechists who took control of the church in Chimaltenango from the traditional authorities and instituted what they considered more "orthodox" patterns of worship. In the course of so doing, they also undertook what a Maryknoll priest termed a "holy war" against traditional healers and diviners (*chimanes*), whom they derided as charlatans whose cures were inferior to those of Western medicine and whose *costumbre* was a waste of money. At times, they spoke more stridently still, depicting their adversaries as "murderers" (*choolil*) who covertly collaborated with the demonic Guardians of the mountains—spirits whom, at other times, they dismissed as figments of a superstitious imagination.

As a result of their successes—material and polemic—when Watanabe was present in the mid-1980s, there were no more *chimanes* in Chimaltenango. In addition, *costumbre* for healing was no longer practiced and the Guardians of the mountains figured in tales for children, but not as objects of adult belief.[33] Still, traditional understandings remained operative in many contexts, as in the stories Chimaltecos told about events of 1983. Although Chimaltenango escaped the worst excesses of this period, the dangers were very real, particularly when local residents were forced to serve in civil patrols in which their military commanders pressured them to identify and eliminate all "subversives" in their village.[34]

> One night, a civil patrol on the San Pedro road met an imposing figure on a white horse who told them to turn back. When the Chimalteco [members of the squad] told him that they were under pain of death to carry out their patrol, he led them back to town himself. When the soldiers tried to shoot him, their rifles misfired, and the horseman rode up the steps of the church and disappeared inside. The next night, the army commander, "a hot-headed man," led the patrol himself, and they again encountered the man on the white horse, this time at the edge of town just above the cemetery. The commander tried to shoot him, but the horse reared and knocked him down the hill into the cemetery, and again the horseman rode into town and entered the church. The horseman returned a final time to confront the army commander, warning that if any Chimaltecos were killed, he would kill the soldiers: he, not they, best protected the village. The next day, according to the story, the army withdrew.[35]

As Watanabe observes, all understood this horseman to be Santiago, patron saint of Chimaltenango and protector of its Indian population. Ordinarily, the equestrian image of Santiago resides in the church at the village center, from which it emerges on his fiesta to dance and celebrate with his people. In this narrative, however, the saint makes a different, more aggressive sally to confront and repel a dangerous outsider who cast himself as an alternate protector for the village: the "hot-headed" army commander. Conceivably, this character may be implicitly connected to General Rios Montt, that is, the commander's commander, the man ultimately responsible for the campaign of terror, and someone whose evangelical commitments made him particularly hostile to the cult of the *santos*.

Many of the contrasts that structure this account resemble those in the other examples considered above: Indian/ladino, saint/devil, threatened harmony/intruding violence, urban center/wild periphery. To these are added some novel but parallel pairs: church/cemetery, resident/soldier, possibly also Catholic/Protestant. Above all, the narrative contrasts one form of protection that is true, dependable, rooted in local tradition and in the church with another that comes from powerful interests outside (the army and the state), and is, in fact, the opposite of what it claims to be: a threat, not a protection. Implicit throughout is a contrast of "the indigenous" and "the intrusive," but Santiago's origins ought to caution us against too simplistic an understanding of these categories. For the figure who serves as protector and collective representation of the Chimaltecos was imported by earlier intruders, and serves as patron not only of Chimaltenango but also of Spain.

V

These three examples—a creation account, a healing ceremony, and a vision of a *santo*—are small episodes in a much larger history. The first comes from a period of severe economic exploitation (1937); the second, a time of political reform (1946); the third, at the height of military repression (1983). Notwithstanding their individual differences (and they are many), in each instance those whom we have considered addressed their immediate situation with a narrative or performance in which they represented themselves as "good Christians," while depicting adversaries as their religious and moral antitheses: Christ-killing "Jews" and labor-recruiting "Guardians of the mountains" in the first instance; soul-stealing ladino devils in the second; (Protestant?) enemies of the saints in the third.

In all three cases, one could probably determine whether elements traceable to Maya origins preponderate over those derived from the Catholic tradition, or vice versa. Thus, the Pokomam *curandero* might seem to continue Maya practices beneath a Catholic veneer, while the vision of Santiago could be understood as a piece of "folk Catholicism" with a few Maya vestiges. But such a crude analytic, which characterized much of the pioneering ethnography, yields little of value, for the critical issue is not the classification of given items as "indigenous" or "exogenous," or establishing the relative balance between them, but understanding the uses to which such items are put, regardless of their ultimate derivation. Models of "syncretism" that blur the distinction of indigene and intruder are also potentially quite misleading, particularly when they create the impression that either people or religions have melded in anything that approximates a stable or peaceful synthesis.[36]

Preferable, I think, is a dialectic model that acknowledges the extent to which both parties have been transformed by their encounter, while also recognizing that even as all else changes, their opposition remains and their struggle continues. As a result of the Spanish imperial adventure, two different groups first confronted each other in the early sixteenth century, and among their defining differences were those of religion. Since then, the sacred practices, discourses, and institutions of Mayans and Spaniards, ladinos and *naturales* have served as battlefields, instruments, and stakes of a struggle, the results of which are anything but conclusive. Indeed, it is hard to imagine how a conclusion could ever be reached, for with every religious utterance or performance, relations between the contending parties—who began their marathon match as "the indigenous" and "the invader"—are ever so subtly revised and their balance of power ever so slightly recalibrated.

CHAPTER ELEVEN

IN PRAISE OF THE CHAOTIC

I

When historians of religions take up the theme of chaos, they usually begin with the earliest Greek evidence, that of Hesiod's *Theogony*. Typically, discussion then heads north to note how similar is the Old Norse Ginnungagap, as described in Snorri's *Edda*. After these almost-obligatory opening moves, virtually anything is fair game, it being understood that a general category has been established. All that remains is to build as long a list as possible, mixing new and exotic examples in with the familiar chestnuts.[1]

Although I will follow this same pattern to a certain extent, I do so not from idle habit but for a critical purpose. At the outset, let me dissociate myself from any suggestion of universal patterns, for I doubt that "chaos" or something translatable as such is to be found everywhere. At best, there are concepts with family resemblances to the primordial situation described in some myths, which we might term "the chaotic," reserving "Chaos" (with the majuscule) for the Greek datum and "chaos" (with the minuscule) for a term used more broadly to describe—often, with pejorative connotation—a state of ferment, turbulence, and disorder. All examples that might be cited, moreover, have their own context-specific particular features that complicate—which is to say, enrich and modify—the discussion.

Progress comes from identifying these particularities and probing their significance, then revising our general model to take account of them. Toward that end, the strategy I will follow is relatively straightforward. Beginning where everyone else begins—τό χάος in Hesiod, followed by Snorri's Ginnunga-gap—I will adduce one more example: the Void (*tuhīgīh*) of Zoroastrian cosmogonies, as found in Middle Persian (Pahlavi) texts. Not only does this last datum differ from both the Greek and the Old Norse in important ways, the mythic narrative also moves the Void from the chaotic to chaos.

Having recognized this, we will revisit the Greek and Old Norse materials to note similar developments there. And once that portion of the inquiry is complete, I will venture some conclusions while recalling an argument between two legendary figures of our discipline that took place *in illo tempore* (as one of them would have said). Thirty-six years later, their disagreement continues to haunt me, and the way they resolved it still strikes me as wrong. Using the materials just described, I hope to advance their discussion.

II

Directly following the *Theogony*'s proem and its invocation of the Muses, Hesiod announces the theme of his work.

> Hail, daughters of Zeus! Give [me] a delightful song.
> Celebrate the holy race of immortals, who are eternal,
> *Born from Earth and starry Sky,*
> *From dark Night, and those whom the salty Sea nourished.*
> Tell how the gods and earth first came into being. . . .
> Tell these things to me, O Muses, who dwell on Olympus,
> From the beginning, *and tell me which of them first came into being.*[2]

In this passage, the poet suggests that all divine beings descend from four parents—Earth (Gaia), Sky (Ouranos), Sea (Pontos), and Night (Nyx)—a claim borne out by the rest of the poem. Yet when the question of primacy is posed ("Which of them first came into being?" at line 115), the response is surprising. Rather than naming any of the entities just identified, the text states in effect "(e) None of the above," then introduces another set of four *truly* primordial beings, only one of which—Earth—recurs from the first-named tetrad.[3] She, moreover, is relegated to second place, absolute primacy being granted to a previously unmentioned figure.[4]

> Tell these things to me, O Muses, who dwell on Olympos,
> From the beginning, and tell me which of them first came into being.
> *Truly, Chaos was born first; next*
> *Wide-breasted Earth,* forever the unmovable seat of all
> The immortals who possess the summit of snowy Olympos;
> [*Then*] *misty Tartaros*, in the furthest depths of wide-stretching earth,
> *And Desire (Eros)*, who is fairest among the immortal gods.[5]

The text then connects the two tetrads genealogically, establishing that the four entities it introduced first are, for the most part, children of those it introduced second. The latter actually constitute the first generation of the cosmos (fig. 11.1).[6] Beyond this, a subtle distinction is drawn, which helps explain why the two tetrads were presented in inverse order of their births. Thus, the first-named tetrad includes beings who are much more

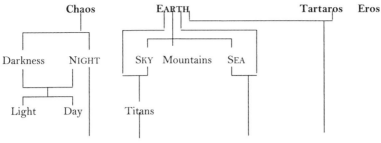

FIGURE 11.1 First generations of existence according to Hesiod's *Theogony*. The four entities that appear in small capital letters figure in the first-named tetrad, introduced at lines 104–7. Those that appear in boldface type figure in the second-named tetrad, introduced at lines 116–20. Note that Earth (Gaia) appears in both groups.

easily perceived and recognized, since their existence is fully material (Earth, Sky, and Sea; in this regard, Night—the daughter of Chaos—is a mediating figure). By contrast, the firstborn (but second-named) tetrad includes beings whose existence tends toward abstraction and nonmateriality: at best, they find only minimal realization in concrete substance (Chaos, Desire, and Tartaros; here, it is Earth who mediates). More elusive, mysterious, and subtle than the second-born tetrad, it is thus more difficult to know. As a result, members of this group are revealed to us only after we have made the acquaintance of their children, for knowledge of the first generation's nature—indeed, of their very existence—is constituted as a higher level of understanding, which comes only with reflection and not from immediate sensory perception.

The contrast of abstract and concrete is most clearly drawn, perhaps, between the first-named members of each tetrad: Chaos and Earth. From these two, all other beings descend, but their lineages remain forever distinct, there being no sexual connection between any of their progeny, no matter how temporally distant. All the descendants of Chaos come via Night, and all (save Day and Light) are the products of parthenogenesis. As a result, they—like their ancestors—share an abstract, indistinct, nonmaterial nature.[7] Initially, Earth also reproduces asexually, giving birth to Sky, Mountains, and Sea. Thereafter, she mates with two of her sons (Sky and Sea), and from these unions descend all (save one) of her offspring.[8]

Of all the primordial beings, Earth is not only the most fertile, but also the most substantial. Thus, within the second tetrad, one can observe a cline from Night (daughter of Chaos and least material of the four) through the sequence Sky-Sea-Earth; in other words a gas, a liquid, and a solid. Earth is the most concrete, the most stable, and the most tangible of the four or, to put it differently, the most fully realized in matter.

Chaos stands at the opposite extreme. Of all that exists, it is most unformed and inchoate in its material existence. This conclusion is consistent with the etymological significance of the term, for most precisely τό χάος denotes a gaping space: "void, chasm, abyss."[9] Insubstantiality as yet without bounds, Chaos stands just a half step removed from Nonbeing. As Hermann Fränkel aptly put it, "nicht ein rein privatives Nicht, sondern ein negatives Etwas."[10] Even so, it is the condition of possibility for all else. Initially, Chaos may then be understood as existence in its zero grade, coupled with potentiality at the maximum: the point of departure for all subsequent creation and creativity.

III

Another classic instance of the chaotic is found in Old Norse traditions that situate the first acts of cosmic history at a place called Ginnunga-gap.[11] The word is a compound, whose second element denotes an empty space (ON *gap*, cognate to English *gap* and derived from the verb *gapa*, "to gape, open wide").[12] The compound's first element, however, is an adjective of less certain meaning. Most experts relate *ginnunga* to Old Norse *ginn-*, itself a prefix that can mean "vast, wide," also "great," and perhaps also "powerful" (in the view of some, magically so).[13] Also tempting are connections to Old High German *ginunga* (with single *n*), "opening, cleft, *rictus*,"[14] and Anglo-Saxon *be-ginnan, on-ginnan*, "to begin, commence, endeavor" (conceivably, "to open a space in which things can happen").[15] All these comparisons are semantically appropriate and phonologically possible, if strained in some particulars.

In contrast to Chaos, however, Ginnungagap was not theorized as first of all beings or the parent of any others. Rather, according to Snorri's *Edda*, it was an emptiness that lay between two already extant realms of more positive character: Niflheim to the north and Muspellheim to the south. Notwithstanding the initially static nature of this situation, the gap provided possibilities.

> Just as cold and all grim things come from Niflheim, so that which is near to Muspell was hot and bright. But Ginnungagap was as mild as windless air. And when the icy rime and the warm breeze met, it melted and dripped, and from these living drops, life quickened with the strength of that which sent the heat. It had the bodily form of a man and he was named Ymir.[16]

We will have more to say about Ymir, but at present let us simply observe that Ginnungagap, unlike Chaos, is not a first half step toward being but an (almost)[17] empty space of encounter: the crucible in which two other entities could meet and transform each other. The two, in fact, are inverse images, for Niflheim and Muspell each possess one positive, life-sustaining quality (Niflheim's moisture, Muspellheim's heat), but lack precisely that quality the other possesses (cold being the absence of heat and dryness the absence of moisture). The dialectic interaction of these two contraries thus yielded a synthesis of cosmic importance.[18]

Niflheim + Muspellheim → Drops of water that become Life
(–Heat/+Moisture) + (+Heat/-Moisture) → (+Heat/+Moisture)

Like Chaos, Ginnungagap mediates Being and Nonbeing. It is not, however, the first principle in any absolute sense, and its role is more catalytic than foundational, for it provides other, already existing entities a fertile, if nondescript space where they can meet and interact in dynamic fashion. This being accomplished, Ginnungagap disappears from the story, except for one last, reprise appearance, which we will consider later. The same is true of Chaos.

IV

Unfortunately, there is no canonic version of the Zoroastrian cosmogony, and we will have to draw on several sources. One of the most thorough, the *Greater Bundahišn*, begins its account as follows:

1.1 It is revealed thus in the good religion: Ohrmazd is highest in omniscience and goodness, for infinite time always exists in the light. That light is the seat and place of Ohrmazd, which one calls "Endless Light." 2. Omniscience and goodness exist in infinite time, just as Ohrmazd, his place and religion exist in the time of Ohrmazd.

3. Ahriman exists in darkness, with total ignorance and love of destruction, in the depths. 4. His crude love of destruction and that place of darkness are what one calls "Endless Darkness."

5. *Between them a Void existed*—the wind, in which is a state of mixture.

6. Both realms have the quality of finitude and infinitude, 7. since the height one calls "Endless Light" has no end, and the depths known as "Endless Darkness" are without limit.

8. At their border, the realms of "Endless Light" and of "Endless Darkness" are both finite, *since there is a Void between them* and they are not connected to each other.[19]

As with Snorri's narrative, the Zoroastrian cosmogony begins with certain entities already well established: the deity Ohrmazd ("Wise Lord"), who inhabits the realm of "Endless Light," and his demonic counterpart Ahriman ("Evil Spirit"), who resides in "Endless Darkness." Initially, the chief difference between Ginnungagap and the "Void" (Pahlavi *tuhīgīh*)[20] seems to be their spatial orientation. While the former is located on a horizontal plane (mediating north and south), the latter is set on the vertical (mediating heaven and the infernal depths).

There are, however, other important distinctions to be drawn. Thus, if Chaos is a space of emergence and Ginnungagap a space of productive encounter, the primordial Void of Zoroastrianism is a tense no-man's land: a buffer between potential adversaries. To make war against Ohrmazd, then, the hyperaggressive Ahriman first had to cross the Void, as is narrated in *Dēnkart* 5.24.

> *The Adversary's movement went from place to place in the Void.* From the beginning, the Adversary scurried about without reason, and he came to the border of the light-substance by a motion toward power that was not particularly well-considered. That Adversary was also unreasoning, foolish and evil. Since he came witless and combative, he was perceived as being of an oppositional nature.[21]

Directly Ahriman entered the Void, it ceased to be a neutral border zone and became contested territory, just as he ceased to be a distant threat and became an active invader. As the open space offered him little resistance, the Evil Spirit rapidly reached the lowest heavens, where his attack was checked, as is recounted in several sources.[22] Falling back, he dragged some of the lower stars with him, creating a mixture of light (from the stars) and darkness (from himself) in what previously was the Void.[23]

No longer empty, this space now became the battleground in which good and evil struggle. Inside this intermediate zone, nothing is pure and all is a mixture. Thus, differing proportions of light and darkness, wisdom and ignorance, benevolence and aggression, self-control and impetuosity, creativity and destructiveness are present in all living beings, such that some incline more toward Ohrmazd and some toward Ahriman, but none are entirely one way or the other. As a result, until the end of history all beings suffer a certain measure of doubt, division, and internal conflict as they are called to take sides in the cosmic struggle.

However ferocious that struggle might be, the Pahlavi scriptures show confidence in its outcome. After a finite period of combat (most texts stipulate 6,000 or 9,000 years), Ohrmazd's forces will rout their adversaries and restore primordial perfection. Most texts suggest that Ahriman will then be consigned to the endless darkness from which he came,[24] but *Dēnkart* 5.24 has a different version.

He was thrown and fell back into the Void, having been thoroughly tested, utterly defeated, impotent, completely deformed, his abilities destroyed, sickly-faced, anguished, heavily oppressed, clothed in fear, consigned to the prison called "Victory that is [really] Non-Victory," deprived of his capacity for battle, and rendered hopeless by the power of God.[25]

Continuation of this text makes it clear that Ohrmazd's triumph is definitive and total. Never again will Ahriman rise to threaten the peace and perfection of the good creation.[26] In this moment, the (former) Void is once more transformed as it receives the vanquished Evil Spirit. In so doing, that which was once a borderland, then a battleground, now becomes a graveyard or prison, also a monument to the victor and a reminder—if any were needed—of what happens to those who oppose him.

V

This image—the Void as final resting place of the vanquished—prompts a return to the Old Norse and Greek texts we considered earlier, for they both contain something similar that makes us rethink the chaotic.

Thus, we left Snorri's account of Ginnungagap at the point where life first appeared in drops of moisture (born of fire and ice), and these coalesced to form the body of a being known as Ymir. In the continuation of his narrative, Snorri goes on to tell that Ymir was a frost giant, the first of this race,[27] and that another race known as the Æsir later came into being independent of Ymir. Conflict followed and a struggle for power, in the course of which the Æsir, led by Óðinn, killed the giant and made use of his body.

They took Ymir *and brought him to Ginnungagap* and made the earth of him; of his blood, the sea and waters; of his flesh, the earth was made; and mountains of bones. They made rocks and stones of his teeth and jawbones, and of the bones that were broken. . . . On the edge of the sea they gave land for dwelling to the race of giants, and inland they made a stronghold around that region, because of the hostility of the giants. For this stronghold, they used the brows of the giant Ymir, and they called that stronghold Miðgarð.[28]

In this way, the gap was filled with material substance taken from Ymir's corpse and became the world over which Óðinn then came to rule as king. The cosmos itself is thus a monument to his victory, but that monument can be read in alternative fashion. From the perspective of the marginal territories to which they are relegated—alongside the sea, which is, in fact, their ancestor's blood—the surviving frost giants regard Miðgarð as the site of not a glorious triumph but a primordial crime. Their resentment of the Æsir, their invasions of Miðgarð, and their continued attempts to disrupt Óðinn's kingdom are all grounded in their desire to set things right by avenging Ymir.[29]

VI

Much as the Void was modified by Ohrmazd's victory over Ahriman, and Ginnungagap transformed when Óðinn killed Ymir, something similar happened to Chaos when Zeus struggled with the Titans for the kingship in heaven. At the height of the battle, according to Hesiod,

> Zeus no longer restrained his spirit, but straightaway his
> Lungs were filled with power and he revealed
> All his violent force. He strode forth from the sky and from Olympos,
> Hurling incessant lightning, and the thunderbolts
> Flew fast from his strong hand, spinning out holy flame.
> All around, life-bearing Earth cried out,
> And her vast woodlands crackled as they burned.
> The earth boiled, as did all the streams of Okeanos,
> And boundless Sea. Hot wind surrounded
> The chthonian Titans, flames reached the vast aithêr
> Above, and the flash of the lightning
> Blinded the eyes of these powerful beings.
> *The fierce divine heat overpowered Chaos.*[30]

This passage is often taken to be an account of Zeus's *aristeia*, his glorious deeds in the heat of that battle in which he overthrew Ouranos and established himself as lord of creation.[31] More precisely, it describes how his violent power reached and shook all regions of the cosmos: land (Gaia, line 693, and Chthōn, 695), sea (Okeanos, 695, and Pontos, 696), air (Autmē, 696, and Aithēr, 697), and the below, here represented by Chaos (line 700), which was effectively invaded and captured (*katekhen*) by the god's fiery blast.[32] This assault opened up a new phase in the struggle, followed by quite horrific violence on all sides, with Zeus ultimately triumphant, after which he consigned the defeated Titans to Tartaros, lowest and bleakest of all cosmic realms.

At this point in his narrative, Hesiod pauses to provide a long description of Tartaros, complete with all its personnel and landmarks.[33] One phrase above all concerns us, however, where he says: "apart from all the gods the Titans dwell, *beyond misty Chaos.*"[34] Which is to say that the primal near-emptiness has been annexed, repositioned, and put to new use. Now situated between the above and the below, the emptiness of Chaos constitutes an uncrossable barrier that will keep the vanquished in their prison and Zeus on his throne.

(1)

Archer on skis from the Böksta Rune Stone (Balingsta Parish, Uppland Province, Sweden, ca. 1050 CE), often taken to be Ullr on the basis of Snorri's testimony. Photograph courtesy of the photographer, Gaylon Polatti.

(2)

Ullr, as depicted in the *Edda oblongata* of 1680; manuscript AM 738 4to, Árni Magnússon Institute, Reykjavik, Iceland. Photograph courtesy of the Árni Magnússon Institute.

(3)

Ullr, as depicted by Ólafur Brynjúlfsson, who provided sixteen illustrations for the 1760 Icelandic manuscript titled "Sæmundar og Snorra *Edda*." The inscription in the upper right reads: "Ullr, Odin's son, with his bow, striding on his skis." NKS 1867 4to, Danish Royal Library, Copenhagen. Photograph courtesy of the Danish Royal Library.

(4)

Ullr, as depicted in an Icelandic manuscript compiled in 1765–66, patterned after Brynjúlfsson's version of 1760 (cf. plate 3). SÁM 66, Árni Magnússon Institute, Reykjavik, Iceland. The text states, "He was the best skier of all" (han var best skyðfar af öllumm). Photograph courtesy of the Árni Magnússon Institute.

(5)

Etching of Ollerus by Friedrich Wilhelm Heine; from Wilhelm Wägner and Jakob Rover, *Nordisch-germanische Götter
und Heldensagen für Schule und Volk* (Leipzig: Otto Spamer,
1908), p. 103.

(6)

Figure of Ullr by W. Meyer; from Fredrik Sander, trans., *"Edda," Sämund den Vises: Skaldeverk av Fornnordiska Myt-och Hjältesänger om de Götiska eller Germanska Folkens Gamla Gudatro, Sagominnen och Vandringar* (Stockholm: P. A. Norstedt & Söner, 1893), p. 161.

(7)

Ullr by Voenix (www.voenix.de), 1994; from Power of the Runes, a deck of divination cards (© AGM AGMüller Urania). The runic inscription reads "Eihwaz" (yew), the name of the rune that appears in the diamond-shaped medallion in the bottom border, which occultists and neopagans commonly associate with the god "Ullr," based in part on the yew wood of which his bow is made. Photograph courtesy of the artist and the publisher.

(8)

Pyrograph of Ullr by Debra Arnold (2008).
While the image foregrounds Ullr's bow, the
runic text in the serpentine figure surrounding the god, which was added by the artist,
gestures toward his skis. Transcription of it
yields the text: "Hail Ullr, god of hunting and
skiing!" Photograph courtesy of the artist.

(9)

Ullr by Agnes Olson, www.Agnes.Olson.com. The runic inscriptions on the armbands contain the artist's signature and the date when the work was executed (Agnes Olson on the left arm, September 2003 on the right). Photograph courtesy of the artist.

(10)

Protective medallion for skiers, with image of Ullr (ca. 1965–70). Photograph courtesy of the Shire Post Mint. Design by Maya Heath / Dragonscale Jewelry.

(11)

Poster for Ullr peppermint-cinnamon schnapps liqueur (2007). Design by
Leopold Ketel & Partners. Photograph courtesy of Hood River Distillers, Inc.

(12)

Brent Nielson's poster for the 2007 Ullr Chase, a 40K, cross-country ski race.
Photograph courtesy of the artist.

(13)

Statue of Ullr by Richard Jagoda (2001), located at 500 South Park Ave, Breckenridge, Colorado, site of the annual Ullr Fest. Photograph courtesy of the Town of Breckenridge.

(14)

Float at the 2009 Ullr Fest of Breckenridge, Colorado. Photograph courtesy of Timothy Faust, Altitude Stock Photography.

(15)

Ullr by Juan Vazquez (2002). Photograph courtesy of the artist.

(16)

Ullr by Anna Känkänen/Zardra (2004). Photograph courtesy of the artist.

VII

In the Fall of 1971, I was fortunate to begin my graduate studies with a class offered by Jonathan Z. Smith as an introduction to the history of religions. At the time, Smith was locked in a personal and intellectual struggle with Mircea Eliade, then the dominant figure in the discipline.[35] At that point, the nature of this struggle was not as clear as it would later become, nor did entering students realize how high were the stakes; but it was hard not to feel the tension and excitement of the moment.

Several episodes from that era remain indelible, but none more so than a day when Smith entered class late, visibly shaking with frustration and nervous energy. He had just left Eliade—whom I had not yet met—and they had been forced to break off an important conversation. "We were arguing about which came first," he explained, "order or disorder." Predictably, Eliade favored order and Smith the reverse, and their exchange produced only partial agreement. "He forced me to acknowledge," Smith went on, "that disorder can only exist in contrast to a prior order. I don't know if that's just a sly debater's point, but I have to take it seriously. So I'm prepared to concede that order came first, *but only by one half-second!* After that, I insist there was always disorder."

At the time, I was impressed by both men, by the intelligence—also the integrity—of the positions they articulated, and the importance of their disagreement. I wasn't sure who had gotten the better of the debate, but I could see that astute and principled arguments had been made on both sides. I knew enough to understand that Hesiod's notion of Chaos was a crucial datum for the discussion, and that other myths of the chaotic also figured implicitly, but most of the subtleties were quite lost on me. It was clear, however, that giants were throwing thunderbolts, and worlds could turn on the outcome.

Having now had forty years to reflect, I am inclined to think that both Eliade and Smith got things wrong, as becomes clear from the mythic narratives we have considered. Thus, all three cosmogonic accounts (those of Hesiod, Snorri, and the Pahlavi texts) begin by positing a primordial situation that includes—either alone or as part of a relatively small set—a vague, murky, unformed, decidedly insubstantial entity, rich in potential and neutral, even benign, in its disposition. This image represents neither "order," "disorder," nor anything of the sort: not yet, at any rate. Rather, it is simply "the chaotic," that is, the nebulous *Etwas* that mediates Nonbeing and Being as the precondition of all subsequent creation. The situation is precosmic and thus, a fortiori, premoral and prepolitical.

Gradually, however, each text introduces new characters, who become adversaries in a struggle for rulership over the emergent cosmos: Zeus and the Olympians versus Ouranos and the Titans, Óðinn and the Æsir versus Ymir and the frost giants, Ohrmazd and the gods versus Ahriman and the demons.[36] In the course of these struggles, the relatively peaceful and egalitarian situation of primordial anarchy ends, violent conflict erupts, one party wins, and one party loses, after which a monarchic regime of cosmic dimensions is established. What is more, as a crucial part of consolidating his power, the new world ruler appropriates, transforms, and redeploys "the chaotic," which now becomes a more specific, more limited, and more tendentious *something* rather than remaining the nebulous reservoir of all potentials. In this new context, it becomes an instrument for exercising power over the vanquished, as when Chaos becomes part of the apparatus locking the Titans in a subterranean prison; when the Zoroastrian Void becomes a battleground, a trap, and a tomb; or when Ginnungagap becomes Miðgarð, fortress of the Æsir and monument to Óðinn's victory.

Something similar can be observed at the level of discourse when newly emergent regimes of power develop the habit of describing their predecessors and adversaries (also their victims and, in truth, everyone and everything that threatens, questions, or eludes their grasp) as manifestations of "chaos," by which they now mean "disorder." In effect, what they have done is to capture an older discourse of primordial potentiality and absolute freedom ("the chaotic"), which they tendentiously remodel for use as a weapon with which to stigmatize opponents and foreclose all unwanted possibilities: above all, any challenges to their power.

Returning to the disagreement of Smith and Eliade, let me suggest that neither "order" nor "disorder" came first, but the two came forth as a pair. What is more, these fraternal twins were born well after other entities, under the influence of other forces. Were I Hesiod, writing a theogony, I would thus place "the chaotic"—which is to say, sheer potentiality and absolute freedom—at the very dawn of creation. In the second or third generation, then, I would introduce a character named "Power," whose abilities were martial in the first instance and political in the second, including all the subtle arts of propaganda. The subsequent narrative would describe how Power captured the chaotic and worked to make it his servant.

The story would have many episodes, but ultimately, as a sort of test, Power would offer his prisoner a new suit of clothes, encouraging him to choose a wardrobe that suited his nature: something, moreover, that contrasted sharply with the drab business suits and stiff military uniforms that Power himself favored. And when the chaotic chose a Harlequin costume, a riot of colors, soft fabrics, and exotic, exuberant, playful design, Power was delighted. The time had come to set his captive free, he said; and to help forget all their past troubles, he suggested they take new names. And so, exercising the prerogatives of his office, he called himself "Order" and his new servant "Chaos," and he advised the public to choose very, very carefully between them.

CHAPTER TWELVE

THESES ON COMPARISON

*« with Cristiano Grottanelli * »*

I

Let us begin with a few schematic observations concerning the goals, logic, and continuing appeal of comparatism, the very formidable obstacles it faces, its sorry historical record, and the reasons for its many failures.

(1) As both Heraclitus and Saussure observed, meaning is constructed through contrast. All knowledge, indeed all intelligibility, thus derives from consideration of data whose differences become instructive and revealing when set against the similarities that render them comparable.

(2) It is also the case that the same exercise supports errors and misconstructions of every sort, there being no guarantees. At best, comparison yields not knowledge but that which provisionally passes for knowledge while inviting falsification or revision as further examples are considered and familiar examples receive fuller study. This process of testing, amplification, and rectification is interminable.

(3) All generalization depends on comparison, although the latter is usually pursued in ways inadequate to the task. Still, the only alternatives are (a) a discourse whose generalizations remain intuitive, unreflective, and commonsensical, that is without basis, rigor, or merit; and (b) a parochialism that dares speak nothing beyond the petty and the particular.

(4) Comparison is never innocent but is always interested, and the interests of the researcher (which are never arbitrary, exclusively intellectual, or fully conscious) inevitably condition (a) definition of the issues and categories to be considered, (b) selection of the examples judged relevant, (c) evaluation of these data (including the relative dignity and importance accorded to each), and (d) the ultimate conclusions.

---

* I take the liberty of adding the name of my late friend and colleague, Cristiano Grottanelli, who so deeply influenced my thought on these issues as to have virtually been my coauthor. Alas, he did not have the opportunity to review the manuscript and refine its discussion: it would have been far better had it benefited from his direct rather than his sedimented input. I alone remain responsible for its errors and inadequacies. Citation of Grottanelli is meant to let him rightfully share whatever credit there may be, not to shift blame on him.

(5) Whether acknowledged or not, the researcher's world (nation, culture, religion, politics, e.g.) and his/her attitudes toward it enter and inflect all comparative projects, most often providing the implicit point of reference against which other data are measured. The only check on this tendency is collegial criticism.

(6) Wide-ranging comparison—comparatism of the strong sort—has consistently disappointed. The books of Lévi-Strauss, Dumézil, and Eliade now sit beside those of Max Müller and Frazer as cautionary examples. Although one can admire the energy, intelligence, and dedication of all these scholars, they consistently misrecognized products of their own imagination and desire ("the human mind," "tripartite ideology," "homo religiosus") for objects having historic, prehistoric, and/or transhistoric actuality. Others made the same mistake regarding such fictive entities as "totemism," "Urmonotheismus," "la mentalité primitive," and "the collective unconscious."

(7) The more examples compared, the more superficial and peremptory is the analysis of each. In such cases, researchers regularly turn their understanding of a few key data into a template for treating less familiar examples. The deception and self-deception involved in such ventures is of the same sort that typifies all ideology: misrepresenting a part for the whole.

(8) Comparative endeavors of the strong sort fall into one of three types, based on the horizon of their ambitions: (a) those that claim to reveal universal patterns (Tylor, Jung, Lévi-Strauss, Lévy-Bruhl, Eliade, Girard, e.g.); (b) those that claim to demonstrate a genetic relation among specific peoples and phenomena (Jacob Grimm, Max Müller, Robertson Smith, Dumézil, Gimbutas, e.g.); (c) those that claim to trace diffusion of certain traits from one group to others over the course of history (Reitzenstein, Widengren, Burkert, Bernal, e.g.). All three types constitute similarity as the fact of primary interest and regard difference as a complicating development of considerably lesser importance.

(9) With regard to the universalizing type: there are no true universals, save at a level of generalization so high as to yield only banalities. Thus, while it is true that all humans have bodies, the way they theorize their bodies and the ways they use and experience them vary with history, class, and culture (as Mauss was first to observe). Real interest emerges only as one pays attention to these differences.[1]

(10) With regard to the genetic type: use of comparison to reconstruct (i.e. hypothesize) a remote past era for which no direct evidence survives is an invitation to project one's favored fantasies onto a relatively blank screen. That screen, moreover, is distorting and prejudicial, as it invests such projections with the prestige of "origins" (e.g. "our most ancient traditions," "the world of our ancestors," "the archaic," "the primordial").

(11) With regard to the diffusionist type: the attempt to show transmission of culture traits always advances—if only subtextually—a tendentious ranking of the peoples involved, constituting temporal primacy ("originality," "invention," "authenticity") as the sign of superior status, while conversely treating reception as a mark of relative backwardness, need, and submission.

(12) These strong forms of comparatism having failed, it is time we entertained comparatism of weaker and more modest sorts that (a) focus on a relatively small number of comparanda that the researcher can study closely; (b) are equally attentive to relations of similarity and those of difference; (c) grant equal dignity and intelligence to all parties considered; and (d) are attentive to the social, historical, and political contexts and subtexts of religious and literary texts. As precedents, one might invoke the examples of Fustel de Coulanges, Geoffrey Lloyd, and Eric Havelock or—should one stray beyond classical antiquity—those of Marc Bloch, Max Gluckman, Norbert Elias, and Marshall Sahlins.

II

As an example of the weak kind of comparatism we take to be both defensible and productive, let us offer a case involving two data only: a classic scene from Middle Persian myth and one from Anglo-Saxon epic. The first is taken from the *Greater Bundahišn*, a priestly compendium committed to writing in the ninth century CE.[2]

Chapter 1 of that text opens with two antithetical beings: the Wise Lord (Ohrmazd), possessed of omniscience and benevolence, and the Evil Spirit (Ahriman), characterized by a spiteful, destructive stupidity. Neither is omnipotent and each has to confront the other's power. Still, their initial situation is a stability born of separation, with Ohrmazd dwelling in endless light above, Ahriman in infinite darkness below.[3] Still, the Wise Lord anticipates conflict, understanding that Ahriman's innate disposition to envy (Pahlavi *arešk*) will make him turn aggressive.[4] In contrast, the Evil Spirit understands nothing. Wandering idly, he encounters light for the first time, and his reaction—one of aggression prompted by envy, just as the Wise Lord foresaw—sets all subsequent history in motion.

> Because he possessed (only) knowledge-after-the-fact, the Foul Spirit was unaware of the Wise Lord's existence. Then he rose from the depth and he came

to the boundary of the visible lights. When he saw the Wise Lord and the light of ungraspable brightness, because of his aggressivity and his envious nature [arēšk-gōhrīh], he launched an attack in order to destroy it.[5]

Most broadly, the text identifies Ohrmazd as a plenum, characterized by the possession of goodness, wisdom, and light, while Ahriman is an absence of these same qualities. Zoroastrian theory associates him with nonbeing in general, as recent research has shown, and the primordial assault represents his attempt to replace Ohrmazd's something with nothing.[6] Another Zoroastrian text develops this point, once again stressing Ahriman's envy of creation.

> The Creator of the world made the spiritual creation pure and undefiled. He made the material creation immortal, unaging, without hunger, without bondage, without sorrow, and without pain. . . . In envy [pad arešk], full of vengeance, perfect in deceit, [the Evil Spirit] rushed to seize, destroy, smash, and ruin this well-made creation of the gods.[7]

Ahriman's envy thus involves bitterness at his absolute deprivation, an anguished sense of emptiness, and wild indignation at his deficiencies vis-à-vis Ohrmazd. Jealousy, resentment, and wounded pride are all involved, as are frustration, self-pity, and a self-righteous sense of cosmic injustice. All these give rise to an infantile destructive rage, motivating his assault.[8] Zoroastrian theology understands the world's woes as having originated with that assault, and looks forward to the day when Ahriman will be overcome, at which point history will end and the world's perfection will be established.[9]

In its treatment of Ahriman, the *Bundahišn* passage is not concerned to provide nuance, sympathy, or psychological depth in the mode of a modern novel. Rather, as a religious text it integrates ethics and cosmology, tracing all violence and destructivity to that which it identifies as the primordial vice of envy, which will manifest itself in humans throughout history and against which moral agents must constantly struggle, as the fate of the cosmos hangs in the balance.

III

Similar themes and images are found in a passage from *Beowulf* (a text whose dating remains controversial), where Grendel shows intriguing similarities to Ahriman, as well as important differences.[10] To appreciate the significance of the monster, it is useful to start with his lineage and descent.

                                          In the abode of the race of
                                          monsters,
An unhappy man   long dwelt
Since the Creator   had banished him.
The eternal Lord   avenged that murder
On the race of Cain,   the one who slew Abel.
The Judge did not rejoice at that   but for that crime,
feud,
He banished Cain far   from the race of man.
From him all   misbegotten creatures arose:
Giants and elves,   and infernal beasts,
Likewise giants   Who have struggled against God
For a long time.[11]

This passage works with traditions well attested in Anglo-Saxon literature, in which Cain—who committed the first homicide and did so out of envy—was theorized as primordial ancestor to a race of miscreants, spawned in the barrens, who became ever more bestial with each generation.[12] Cursed by God, cast out from human society, they sunk ever further into a state of sin and savagery, becoming monsters (*fifel-cyn*), misbegotten things (*untȳdras*), infernal creatures (*orcnēas*), and giants (*eotenas, gigantas*), constantly battling against the deity (*wið Gode wunnon*).

This passage says nothing explicit about the emotions and motives that prompt such aggression, for all that it suggests a bitterness cultivated over many generations. The immediately preceding lines, which introduce Grendel as he lurks outside King Hrothgar's mead hall, are less coy on this question.[13]

Then a powerful spirit   suffered
Miserably while   lingering in the shadows,
As every day   he heard rejoicing
Resound through the hall.   There was the sound of the harp
And the sweet song of the poet,   who told
The well-known ancient story   of mankind's creation.
He said that the Almighty   made the earth
A magnificent plain   ringed by water.
Triumphant, he established   sun and moon,
Luminaries to provide light   for land-dwellers
And he adorned   the quarters of the earth
With limbs and leaves.   Also life he created

For each type	of living beings who move about.
So then Hrothgar's retainers	lived in rejoicing,
Happily, until	that one began
To commit terrible sins,	a fiend from hell.
He was a grim spirit	named Grendel,
Famed waste-wanderer,	he who occupied the moors,
Fens and fastnesses.[14]	

Grendel's sins and crimes (*fyrene*) that he commits thus originate in his suffering, more precisely in the pain he experiences upon perceiving the pleasure (*drēam*) enjoyed by the hall's inhabitants. Above all, he is anguished to hear the sweet song of the poet (*swutol sang scopes*) recounting how God Almighty—the ancestral enemy of Cain's race—created heaven and earth, bringing light, life, and splendor into material existence.[15] To this, Grendel reacts first with agony, then with rage, for the song conjures up everything he is not and has not: beauty, grace, harmony, sociability, goodness, and above all the creative power enjoyed by God, the poet, and the king, but which he is utterly lacking.

This scene thus resembles the episode from the *Bundahišn* in many ways, as both identify envy—and more precisely, envy at creation—as the motive behind a malevolent being's violent attack, which sets all subsequent action in motion. There are, however, significant differences between the two narratives. Whereas Ahriman is a demon (and the arch-demon at that), Grendel is a monster or, more precisely, the last, most degenerate descendant in the line of the most sinful human. And whereas Ahriman's envy sets him against Ohrmazd and creation, Grendel's assault is directed not against God but against King Hrothgar and his mead hall.

The two narratives thus differ in structure. That of the *Bundahišn* is dyadic and is set at the level of the supernatural (fig. 12.1). In contrast, the

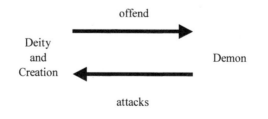

FIGURE 12.1 Dyadic structure of *Greater Bundahišn* 1.14–15.

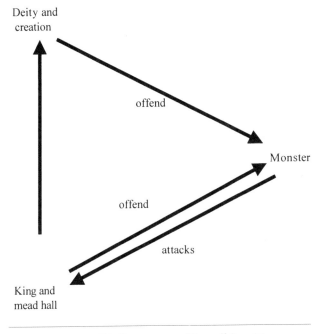

FIGURE 12.2 Triadic structure of *Beowulf*, lines 86–114.

episode in *Beowulf* has a triadic structure, connecting human and divine levels via the mediation of the monstrous (fig. 12.2).

IV

There is, however, more to this story. Immediately before introducing Grendel, the epic describes how Hrothgar's mead hall was built.

Then was success in war   granted to Hrothgar,
Glory in battle,   so that his friends and kinsmen
Eagerly obeyed him.   until the youths around him increased
To form a mighty band.   It came into his mind
That he wanted to order   the building of a hall,
A great mead-hall   for men to make
So that men and children   would ever hear of it.
And inside there   to young and old
He would distribute   such as God gave him
Except for the land itself   and peoples' lives.

Then I heard from all over:	Many men
Were ordered to work	throughout this middle earth.
To adorn this place of the folk.	In due time
The work was done quickly	and it was all ready,
The greatest of halls. . . .	
Not leaving his boast unfulfilled,	Hrothgar distributed rings
And treasure at banquets.[16]	

In marked contrast to the argument of the *Bundahišn*, this passage makes clear that violence began not with the forces of evil but rather with Hrothgar, and it is his violence of primitive accumulation that makes possible the construction of his hall, which is, in effect, the material manifestation of his military, political, and economic success, a structure whose magnificence announces his wealth and power. It also serves as a theater for displays of royal generosity,[17] in which the king defined his troop-won booty as the product (and proof) of God's grace (*eall . . . swylc him God sealde*), a portion of which he redistributed to secure the loyalty of those troops, doing so in a way designed to win the admiration of all who witnessed—or heard about—these transactions.

Beyond God's creation and the poet's song, Grendel's envy is thus occasioned by the more immediate—and more human—fact of Hrothgar's hall. Huddled outside its warmth and splendor, he resents the wealth, power, and prestige that find expression in the hall's grandeur and adornments, also the ceremonies and festivities staged therein. Surely, if he understood how the hall functions as an apparatus for the legitimation, naturalization, reproduction, and enhancement of royal privilege—something the text lets readers perceive—he would resent that also. One way or another, his envy is bitter and violent, but not demonic or anticosmic. It is a human—all too human—envy: the kind those with far too little harbor toward those with far too much.

The triadic structure of *Beowulf* sutures together different types, causes, and objects of envy, creating the impression that when outcasts envy kings, they also resent God and threaten the very cosmos. As a priestly rather than a courtly work, the *Bundahišn* is less concerned to protect the position of kings per se, but it does defend privilege in general by construing human envy as a local manifestation of Ahrimanian evil.

Although the two narratives differ in their details and structure, they treat the same themes, advance similar projects of persuasion, and protect the interests of similar social institutions and strata. Ultimately, both are concerned to stigmatize certain kinds of feelings and action, although

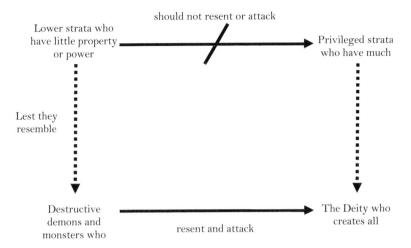

FIGURE 12.3 Implicit quadratic structure underlying both *Bundahišn* 1.14–15 and Beowulf, lines 86–114.

they do this indirectly, speaking more of gods, demons, and monsters than of fully human subjects. If one restores the primacy of the human, what emerges is a quadratic structure (fig. 12.3).

V

The weak form of comparison refrains from imagining that universal themes, a shared prehistory, or a process of diffusion are responsible for the similarities between mythic narratives, nor does it constitute their similarities as evidence for same. Rather, we take these stories to have arisen independent of each other in very different times, places, and cultural milieux. Such common features as they share are not accidental, however. Rather, they reflect similar points of tension in the social structure of the peoples among whom these stories circulated. The stories address these problems and seek to resolve them, not by modifying social structure itself, but by reshaping the consciousness of the audiences they reach and influence.

Most immediately, our two examples are concerned with something commonly called "envy," and they show the point of departure for this discourse to be a situation in which certain desirable goods (light, wisdom, goodness itself in the first case; wealth, power, prestige in the second) are inequitably distributed. Seen from below, such inequality appears as injustice and maldistribution; in pointed—and far from innocent—contrast, from above inequity seems the just and proper result of meritocratic distribution. Have-nots then charge those who have most with greed, and the latter reciprocate by accusing their critics of envy (also: "jealousy," "*ressentiment*," "ingratitude," and "Communism," for the surplus enjoyed by the rich extends to the lexicography of invective).

The texts we have considered intervene in this dispute in multiple ways, but always to the same purpose. Thus, they treat the possessions of Ohrmazd and Hrothgar as unproblematic expressions of their innate excellence and nobility: something they have created and something they richly deserve. Accordingly, they ignore the issue of greed while amplifying the charge of envy by (a) attributing it to demons and monsters; (b) making it culminate in mindless destructive violence without exploring any other means of redress; and (c) representing it in its most extreme form: envy at creation, thereby casting it as a cardinal sin, an offense against God, and a threat to the order of the cosmos.

Although apparently simple, recoding of this sort involves three correlated operations. First there is an ethical inversion as moral condemnation shifts its object from the disproportionate assets of the dominant to the "envy" of subalterns. Second is a political reversal as a call for change is transmuted into a defense of the status quo. Third is an ontological displacement as a critique of social, political, and property relations is relocated from the human to the divine level, where the order of things is no longer contingent or negotiable.

These three levels do not always covary precisely as they do in the texts we have studied. Deprivileged strata can frame their critique as an expression of God's judgment on the arrogant, for instance, as often happens in millenarian movements, apocalyptic texts, and prophetic discourses. The alignment we have observed, however, is probably the most common, not because "God" favors kings and big battalions—however much it may seem that way—but because a religious coding offers the best protection for systems, structures, privileges, and inequities that are otherwise very difficult to defend.

In closing, I cannot take sole credit for the above discussion, least of all the initial theses. Most of my views on comparison took shape in prolonged epistolary exchanges with Cristiano Grottanelli. On most points, it is difficult, if not impossible, to separate my ideas from his, for they are the product not of one person but of a friendship and a sustained conversation. I remain deeply indebted to Grottanelli, and his death was a terrible loss. This chapter is dedicated to his memory.[18]

CHAPTER THIRTEEN

THE (UN)DISCIPLINE OF RELIGIOUS STUDIES

As we all know, the modern university—with reason (not faith) as its core principle, under patronage of the state (not the church), with arts and sciences (not theology) at the center of its curriculum, designed to produce civil servants and citizens (not priests)—emerged in the nineteenth century and replaced an older institution of the same name, which had taken shape in the Middle Ages.

It's surely an oversimplification to see this as a direct effect or straightforward extension of Enlightenment values, for other trends (romanticism, nationalism, idealism, capitalism, e.g.) also contributed. But it is certainly the case that religion occupied a very different place in the nineteenth-century university than it did in its predecessor. Rather than being central to the institution's mission, raison d'être, and organizing apparatus, "religion"—whatever that means—increasingly became available as an object of study and, as such, excited considerable interest.

Virtually all the novel disciplines that came to flourish in this setting cut their teeth on critical interrogation of religion and things religious. It is probably anachronistic to include philosophy in this set, since such critique already thrived in the seventeenth and eighteenth centuries (not to speak of the longer trajectory that leads from Xenophanes through Spinoza). More characteristic of nineteenth-century developments is the introduction of a critical perspective on religion in older disciplines such as philology (as in the "higher criticism" of biblical scholars like F. C. Baur and Julius Wellhausen, not to speak of Friedrich Max Müller or the early Nietzsche); history (already in Gibbon's *Decline and Fall of the Roman Empire*, then in Leopold von Ranke's *History of the Popes*, also David Friedrich Strauss and Ernst Renan on the historical Jesus); and classics (Sir James George Frazer, Jane Ellen Harrison); but above all in the emergent disciplines of the social sciences, such as anthropology (E. B. Tylor's theory of animism, J. F. MacLennan on totemism); folklore (Andrew Lang, Wilhelm Mannhardt); sociology (Durkheim, Mauss, Weber); and psychology (Freud and Jung, of course, but also Wilhelm Wundt and William James).

Although some lines of inquiry were openly hostile, considerations of job security spawned a certain restraint or discretion, with the result that the most aggressive approaches came from authors situated outside the university (Freud and the later Nietzsche) or those whose writings had cost them any hopes of a university career (Feuerbach, Marx; the case of W. Robertson Smith is also relevant). Others practiced a less agonistic style of critique that refused to reproduce the idealized self-understanding of the religious, in favor of novel perspectives that could be warmly appreciative of religion, if demystifying (Durkheim, James, Max Müller, also others like Malinowski).

Such approaches flourish from the 1820s (Baur) through the 1930s (Freud), after which the critical impulse faded as many concluded its work was done. By the end, the topic of religion had lost its novelty, and the frisson of first critical engagement with the previously sacrosanct was long since exhausted. In addition, insofar as many were persuaded that secularization had become a hallmark of modernity and progress, there seemed little need to flail at religion now that it had slid into irreversible decline. Whatever the reason, virtually all the disciplines turned their attention to other issues, and few scholars saw any need to develop a field specifically devoted to the study of religion. An early expression of this attitude was Marx's pronouncement of 1844 (only half correct): "For Germany, the critique of religion is essentially completed; and the critique of religion is the prerequisite of every critique."[1]

In point of fact, a full quarter century elapsed after the final blast of the critical era (Freud's *Moses and Monotheism*, 1939) before a discipline of religious studies took shape; and when this did finally happen, it occurred not in Europe, where critical approaches had originated and flourished, but in the United States, where attitudes toward religion consistently were—and remain—kinder, gentler, more cautious, and more reverent.

The circumstances in which this discipline emerged are significant and revealing, for immediately precipitating that development was a specific text and event: to wit, a paragraph Associate Justice Tom Clark inserted into the majority opinion he delivered in *Abington School District v. Schempp*, the case that ruled Bible readings in public schools to be a violation of the First Amendment. The passage in question reads:

> It is insisted that unless these religious exercises are permitted a "religion of secularism" is established in the schools. We agree of course that the State may not establish a "religion of secularism" in the sense of affirmatively opposing or showing hostility to religion, thus "preferring those who believe in no religion

over those who do believe." (Zorach v. Clauson, supra, at 314). We do not agree, however, that this decision in any sense has that effect. *In addition, it might well be said that one's education is not complete without a study of comparative religion or the history of religion and its relationship to the advancement of civilization. It certainly may be said that the Bible is worthy of study for its literary and historic qualities. Nothing we have said here indicates that such study of the Bible or of religion, when presented objectively as part of a secular program of education, may not be effected consistently with the First Amendment.* But the exercises here do not fall into those categories. They are religious exercises, required by the States in violation of the command of the First Amendment that the Government maintain strict neutrality, neither aiding nor opposing religion.[2]

The *Schempp* decision was handed down on June 17, 1963. Before the year was out, leading figures in the National Association of Bible Instructors (founded 1909) took dramatic action designed to exploit the opportunities they perceived in Mr. Justice Clark's opinion. To appreciate their boldness and strategic acumen, one must understand that NABI (as the group styled itself, having deliberately chosen a name that yielded as acronym the Hebrew term for "prophet") was one of two American societies devoted to promote study of the Bible in higher education. Most of its members were committed Protestants who taught in seminaries, Bible colleges, divinity schools, and strongly sectarian institutions, and of the two organizations, NABI was decidedly more conservative and confessional than its rival (the Society for Biblical Literature). Its goals were summarized in the group's motto: "To Foster Religion in Education," the Bible here being understood as the foundation of (proper) religion.[3] Within months, this group renamed itself the American Academy of Religion, in which guise it played the formative role in creating the discipline known as "religious studies." Today it boasts "over 10,000 members, who teach in some 1,000 colleges, universities, seminaries, and schools in North America and abroad." Its mission statement is deliberately bland and inclusive, accurately reflecting the nature of the field that NABI helped to invent and foster, in which affection for religion in general replaces fervor for the Bible.[4]

What the NABI/AAR group recognized was that given a superficial makeover—one that would make it a bit less exclusive, sectarian, and scripturally grounded, a bit more tolerant, ecumenical, and open—it could move from its institutional backwaters to leading state universities, research centers, and elite colleges, where it could establish a friendly haven for religion (and for the religious) in the previously heartless academy while also gaining access to state and foundation funding. Working within the parameters established by the *Schempp* case, it founded a discipline that was deliberately ambiguous in its dispositions, neither explicitly confessional nor—in the words of Justice Clark—"showing hostility to religion."

I am inclined to distinguish a weaker and a stronger variant of the model AAR developed, although the two resemble each other in most fashions. Still, the weaker form aspired to a certain tact, discretion, and modesty in its treatment of religious concerns and phenomena, with the result that it cultivated an ethos of inoffensiveness and a general intellectual timidity. The stronger form advanced an approach that was not just respectful of all things religious but actively sympathetic, thereby reversing the critical trend that had characterized academic discussions of religion from the inception of the modern university. The distinction between the weaker and the stronger form has some importance, but one ought not stress it unduly, for both produce the same anomaly: a field of "religious studies" that is virtually unique, in others words a discipline consciously designed to shield its object of study against critical interrogation. (The closest analogues of which I can think are "art [also music] appreciation," topics that never achieved academic respectability or disciplinary status; the case of economics, however, is worth consideration.)

When religious studies took shape in the mid-1960s on campuses beyond NABI's prior clientele and orbit, its students quickly came to include many who were curious and/or conflicted about their own religious commitments and longings, which is to say, starry-eyed seekers of all sorts (this was, after all, the 1960s!), and the standard introductory course on "world religions" was designed to offer a veritable mall of attractive and exotic goods to the would-be consumers. Buddhism, Sufism, shamanism, and Tantra were all given sympathetic if superficial treatment, alongside Gnosticism, Kabbalah, and more staid—but profoundly *spiritual* exemplars of the Judeo-Christian tradition. Little attention was devoted to the institutional side of religion that so many found alienating or offensive, or to potentially embarrassing details of the historical record. Rather, discussion tended to dwell on the eternal search for meaning: a *meaning* simultaneously transcendent and most profoundly human, and a search troped as most often successful.

To be sure, some of the classic critical theories—Freud, Marx, Nietzsche, for example—remained in the curriculum, but always buffered and offset by the much more edifying (i.e. supportive, even celebratory) approaches of, inter alia, Kierkegaard, Martin Buber, Paul Tillich, T. S. Eliot, Clifford Geertz, Huston Smith, Joseph Campbell, and Mircea Eliade, whose superior sensitivity and depth could be used to rebuke the critics as providing smug but shallow forms of reductionism associated with materialism, the social sciences, and the ills of a fallen modernity.

All that played fairly well for some decades, and in terms of institutional acceptance, departmental growth, student enrollment, AAR membership, and the like, the discipline certainly thrived, for all that it remained intellectually vapid. Apparently, many people—students and faculty alike—were happy to hear, tell, re-hear, and re-tell the eminently reassuring story that *au fond*, religion is a very good thing (notwithstanding occasional lapses that, if acknowledged, can be dismissed as anomalies: not "real" religion but perversions thereof).

Over time, there have been some changes, of course, as the academic rehabilitation of religion and religion's resurgence in other spheres have continued and to some extent interacted. On many campuses, the friendly haven now welcomes not only vague and amiable seekers but those of firmer convictions, who expect—and sometimes demand—confirmation of the truths they bring into the classroom. In certain circles, it has also become fashionable to turn criticism against the critics and to insist that secular reason, far from being an alternative to faith, is simply a different form of faith (i.e., faith in reason), and as such no less narrow or intolerant than those it constructs as its other. Rather than providing a privileged position from which to carry out critical inquiry, it needs now to defend itself and its claim to authority.

Countervailing such developments, there has been some renewal of critical approaches, now inside the discipline. Where these exist, however, they remain a minority and must struggle to preserve their hard-won footholds. Most students and scholars in the field, as well as its journals, favored books, and syllabi, reflect the national mood regarding religion. As such, they remain committed to a validating, feel-good perspective, and do not welcome interventions that disrupt the serene, benign, and eirenic ethos they have fostered.

This is a pity, for the continued importance of religious identities, loyalties, commitments, aspirations, and passions throughout the world has never been clearer: ditto the need for a rigorous, uninhibited, unintimidated, theoretically and empirically informed, wide-ranging, irreverent, and appropriately critical study of same. It is thus time to rethink the phenomena in question—starting with the simple question of what it is that we are accustomed to call "religion," and whether that entity is to be regarded as something divine, something human, or something that somehow mediates the two. This implies, of course, that the time has also come to rethink the nature, goals, methods, and habituated dispositions of the discipline that claims religious phenomena as its own: a discipline, I submit, that has sought to straddle the interests of religion and the values of the academy, overtly denying the possibility of contradiction between them while consistently tilting to defend the former (which it implicitly loves) against threats posed by the latter (which it implicitly fears). Really, it is time to do better.

NOTES

PREFACE

1. The Theses have been reprinted on numerous occasions, appear on many graduate and undergraduate syllabi, and prompted a sharp challenge from Tim Fitzgerald
in "Bruce Lincoln's 'Theses on Method': Antitheses," *Method and Theory in the Study of
Religion* 18 (2006): 392–423, which I answered in "Concessions, Confessions, Clarifications, Ripostes: By Way of Response to Tim Fitzgerald," *Method and Theory in the
Study of Religion* 19 (2007): 163–68.

CHAPTER ONE

"Theses on Method" was originally presented at the annual meeting of the American
Academy of Religion (November 1995), and first published in *Method and Theory in
the Study of Religions* 8 (1996): 225–27. Reprinted by permission.

CHAPTER TWO

"How to Read a Religious Text" was originally presented at a conference hosted by the
University of Copenhagen's Institute of History of Religions (November 2003), and
first published in *History of Religions* 46 (2006): 127–39. Reprinted by permission.

    1. For a good general introduction, see Patrick Olivelle, ed. and trans., *The Early
Upanisads* (New York: Oxford University Press, 1998), pp. 3–27 and 166–69. Still useful
are A. B. Keith, *The Religion and Philosophy of the Veda and Upanishads* (Cambridge, MA:
Harvard University Press, 1925); Louis Renou, "Remarques sur la *Chāndogya-Upaniṣ
ad*," in his *Études védiques et pāṇinéennes* 1 (Paris: E. De Boccard, 1955), pp. 91–102; and
Henry Falk, "Vedisch *upaniṣad*," *Zeitschrift der deutschen morgenlandischen Gesellschaft* 136
(1986): 80–97.

    2. Bruce Lincoln, *Discourse and the Construction of Society* (New York: Oxford Uni-
versity Press, 1989), pp. 136–41. See also the splendid discussion of Brian K. Smith,
Classifying the Universe: The Ancient Indian Varṇa System and the Origins of Caste (New York:
Oxford University Press, 1994), which expands the analysis far beyond the givens
of the *Chandogya Upaniṣad*.

    3. On the place of this chant in the Sāman performance and the mystical signifi-
cance attributed to it, see Otto Strauss, "Udgīthavidyā," *Sitzungsberichte der preussischen
Akademie der Wissenschaften* 13 (1931): 243–310.

    4. *Chandogya Upaniṣad* 1.3.6–7:

> atha khalūdgīthākṣarāṇy upāsītodgītha iti. prāṇa evotprāṇena hy uttiṣṭhati; vāg
> gīr vāco ha gira ity ācakṣate 'nnaṃ tham anne hīdam sarvaṃ sthitam. dyaur evot,

antarikṣaṃ gīḥ, pṛthivī tham; āditya evot, vāyur gīr, agnis tham; sāmaveda evot, yajurvedo gīr, ṛgvedas thām.

This and all subsequent Upaniṣadic extracts are taken from S. Radhakrishnan, ed., *The Principal Upaniṣads* (London: George Allen & Unwin, 1953). All translations are original.

5. Thus, for instance, *Bṛhadāraṇyaka Upaniṣad* 1.3.11–13, 1.3.25–27, 1.4.17, 3.1.3–5, 5.8.1, 6.2.12; *Chandogya Upaniṣad* 1.7.1, 6.5.2–4, 6.6.3–5, 6.7.6. Certain passages do have the relations reversed, however. Thus: *Bṛhadāraṇyaka Upaniṣad* 1.3.24, 1.5.4–7, 6.1.1–14, 6.3.2; *Chandogya Upaniṣad* 5.1.1–15.

6. See, for instance, *Aitareya Upaniṣad* 1.1–2.

7. Bruce Lincoln, *Theorizing Myth* (Chicago: University of Chicago Press, 1999), pp. 150–51.

8. *Chandogya Upaniṣad* 1.10.1: "uṣatir ha cākrāyaṇa ibhyagrāme pradrāṇaka uvāsa."

9. Ibid., *maṭacīhateṣu*. The term *maṭaci* is rare, and some commentaries have suggested that the village was devastated by locusts rather than hail. The situation of need remains the same in either event.

10. Ibid., 1.10.2–5. According to Sir Monier Monier-Williams, *Sanskrit-English Dictionary* (Oxford: Clarendon Press, 1899), p. 296, *kulmāṣa* is "an inferior kind of grain, half-ripe barley" or a sour gruel made from same. Hardly what a rich man (*ibhya*) would eat, except in times of privation; yet the text has him assert that he has no other food. 1.10.2: "sa hebhyaṃ kulmāṣān khādantam bibhikṣe, taṃ hovāca, neto 'nye vidyante yac ca ye ma ima upanihitā iti."

11. *Chandogya Upaniṣad* 1.10.5. The text comments on the shameful nature of leftovers at 1.10.3–4. On this point, see Charles Malamoud, "Observations sur la notion de 'reste' dans le brâhmanisme," *Wiener Zeitschrift für die Kunde Südasiens* (1972): 5–26, esp. p. 20.

12. *Chandogya Upaniṣad* 1.10.6: "sa ha prātaḥ saṃjihāna uvāca, yad batānnasya labhemahi, labhemahi dhanamātrām: rājāsau yakṣyate, sa mā sarvair ārtvijyair vṛṇīteti."

13. Ibid., 1.10.7–8.

14. Ibid., 1.10.8–11.

15. Ibid., 1.11.1–3.

16. Ibid., 1.11.4–5: "na svid ete 'py ucchiṣṭhāḥ iti, na vā ajīviṣyam imān akhādann iti hovāca, kāmo ma udakapānam iti. sa ha khāditvā 'tiśeṣān jāyāyā ājahāra, sāgra eva subhikṣā babhūva, tān pratigṛhya nidadhau."

17. Ibid., 1.11.9: "annam iti hovāca, sarvāṇi ha vā imāni bhūtāny annam eva pratiharamāṇāni jīvanti." The homology of the Udgītha, Udgātṛ, and Sun (*āditya*) occurs at 1.11.6–7.

18. Cf., for example, *Bṛhadāraṇyaka Upaniṣad* 1.5.3–13 (Sun/Fire/Moon); *Chandogya Upaniṣad* 3.15.6 and 4.17.1 (Sun/Wind/Fire); *Taittirīya Upaniṣad* 1.5.2 and 1.7.1 (Sun/Wind/Fire).

19. *Bṛhadāraṇyaka Upaniṣad* 3.4.1–2.

20. To gain an initial hearing and not be rejected outright, such a simulacrum needs to meet two conditions: (1) in form, it should resemble other, more orthodox doctrines sufficiently closely that a knowledgeable audience should find it plausible;

(2) in content, it should be sufficiently different from others that the same audience would find it novel and intriguing, thereby entertaining the possibility it is an esoteric teaching, previously held secret by a spiritual elite. Should it become widely accepted, it loses its nature as simulacrum and becomes a doctrine proper.

21. *Chandogya Upaniṣad* 1.10.6.

22. Thus, for instance, *Chandogya Upaniṣad* 1.3.6 (quoted above), 1.8.4, 1.11.5–9 (quoted above), 5.2.1, 6.5.4, 6.6.5, 6.7.6, 7.4.2, 7.9.1. Numerous like statements are found in the other Upaniṣads. On the importance of Food (*annam*) in Vedic speculative thought, see R. Geib, "Food and Eater in Natural Philosophy of Early India," *Journal of the Oriental Institute, Baroda* 25 (1976): 223–35; Bernhard Weber-Brosamer, *Annam: Untersuchungen zur Bedeutung des Essens und der Speise im vedischen Ritual* (Rheinfelden: Schauble, 1988); Brian K. Smith, "Eaters, Food, and Social Hierarchy in Ancient India: A Dietary Guide to a Revolution in Values," *Journal of the American Academy of Religion* 58 (1990): 177–205; and Carlos Lopez, "Food and Immortality in the Veda: A Gastronomic Theology?," *Electronic Journal of Vedic Studies* 3 (1997), online at http://www.ejvs.laurasianacademy.com/ejvs0303/ejvs0303.txt (accessed June 6, 2011).

23. One of Kafka's finest stories, "Researches of a Dog," seems to have been inspired by this chapter of the *Chandogya*. Consider, for instance, the following passage:

> I began to enquire into the question: What the canine race nourished itself upon. Now that is, if you like, by no means a simple question, of course; it has occupied us since the dawn of time, it is the chief object of all our meditation.... In this connection, the essence of all knowledge is enough for me, the simple rule with which the mother weans her young ones from her teats and sends them out into the world: "Water the ground as much as you can." And in this sentence is not almost everything contained? What has scientific enquiry, ever since our first fathers inaugurated it, of decisive importance to add to this? Mere details, mere details, and how uncertain they are: but this rule will remain as long as we are dogs. It concerns our main staple of food: true, we have also other resources, but only at a pinch, and if the year is not too bad we could live on this main staple of our food; this food we find on the earth, but the earth needs our water to nourish it and only at that price provides us with our food, the emergence of which, however, *and this should not be forgotten, can also be hastened by certain spells, songs, and ritual movements.*

Franz Kafka, "Researches of a Dog," in *The Great Wall of China: Stories and Reflections* (New York: Schocken Books, 1937), pp. 20–22 (emphasis added). Translation by Willa Muir and Edwin Muir.

24. *Chandogya Upaniṣad* 1.12.1–5:

> athātaḥ śauva udgīthaḥ. tad ha bako dālbhyo glāvo vā maitreyaḥ svādhyāyam udvavrāja. tasmai śvā śvetaḥ prādur babhūva: tam anye śvāna upasametyo-cur annaṃ no bhagavān āgāyatv aśanāyāma vā iti. tān hovācehaiva mā prātar upasamīyāteti; tad ha bako dālbhyo glāvo vā maitreyaḥ pratipālayāṃ cakāra. te ha yathaivedam bahiṣpavamānena stoṣyamāṇāḥ saṃrabdhāḥ, sarpantīty evam āsasṛpus te ha samupaviśya hiṃ cakruḥ. aum adāma, aum pibāma, aum devo varuṇ aḥ prajāpatiḥ savitānnam ihāharat. annapate annam ihāhara, aum iti.

25. Ibid., 1.2.13–14: "tena taṃ ha bako dālbhyo vidāṃ cakāra. sa ha naimiṣ-īyānāmudgātā babhuva. sa ha smaibhyaḥ kāmān āgāyati. āgātā ha vai kāmānām bhavati ya etadevaṃ vidvān akṣaram udgītham upāste." Baka (or Vaka) Dālbhya

consistently appears as an Udgātṛ priest of great stature and a sage whose deep learning is rooted in his mastery of the Udgītha chant (*Kāṭhaka Saṃhitā* 10.6; *Jaiminiya Upaniṣad Brāhmaṇa* 1.9.3 and 4.6–8; and the *Chandogya* passages cited here). The fullest discussion to date is Petteri Koskikallio, "Baka Dalbhya: A Complex Character in Vedic Ritual Texts, Epics and Puranas," *Electronic Journal of Vedic Studies* 1, no. 3 (November 1995), esp. pp. 11–13, online at http://www.ejvs.laurasianacademy.com/ejvs0302/ ejvs0302.txt (accessed June 6, 2011).

26. Glāva Maitreya is usually regarded as an alternate name of Baka Dālbhya, but may be another Udgātṛ priest of mythic stature. He appears at *Pañcaviṃśa Brāhmāṇa* 25.15.3; *Ṣadviṃśa Brāhmaṇa* 1.4.6; and *Gopathabrāhmaṇa* 1.1.31.

27. *Chandogya Upaniṣad* 1.12.5: "aum adāma, aum pibāma."

CHAPTER THREE

"Nature and Genesis of Pantheons" was originally presented at the annual meeting of the Atelier Chicago-Paris sur les religions anciennes, Paris (September 2009).

1. A rough survey of the pages Jan de Vries devoted to "die Götter" in the third edition of his *Altgermanische Religionsgeschichte* (Berlin: Walter de Gruyter, 1970) 2: 1–358 yields ninety-eight different names, some of which represent individual gods, and others groups of deities (e.g. Matronae, Alagabiae).

2. Caesar, *De Bello Gallico* 6.21.2: "Deorum numero eos solos ducunt, quos cernunt et quorum aperte opibus iuvantur, Solem et Vulcanum et Lunam, reliquos ne fama quidem acceperunt." Text is taken from H. J. Edwards, ed., *Caesar, The Gallic War* (London: William Heinemann, 1919). Translation is original.

3. Tacitus, *Germania* 9: "Deorum maxime Mercurium colunt, cui certis diebus humanis quoque hostiis litare fas habent. Herculem et Martem concessis animalibus placant. pars Sueborum et Isidi sacrificat." Text is taken from Rudolf Much, ed., *Die Germania des Tacitus*, 3rd ed., revised by Herbert Jankuhn (Heidelberg: Carl Winter, 1976). Translation is original.

4. Cf. some of the better commentaries on the *Germania*, including Much, pp. 171–79; and J. B. Rives, *Tacitus, Germania* (Oxford: Clarendon Press, 1999), pp. 156–62.

5. *CIL* XIII 7789. The XXXth Legion (Ulpia Victrix) was first levied by Trajan in 105 CE for the Dacian Wars. Its base was relocated to Castra Vetera (modern Xanten), near the confluence of the Rhine and the Lippe, in 122 and remained there until early in the fifth century. Other inscriptions show that German soldiers served in this legion (see esp. *CIL* VI 3360, *CIL* XIII 1847, 8292, and 8633). The bulk of the legion was Roman, however, with Belgians, Britons, Dalmatians, and Thracians also attested. Further information is available online at http://www.livius.org/le-lh/legio/ xxx_ulpia_victrix.html and http://www.romanarmy.com/cms/content/view/25/114 (accessed June 6, 2011). The names of the individuals included in the inscription— M[arcus] Ulp[ius] Panno, T[itus] Mans[uetius] Marcu[s], M[arcus] Ulp[ius] Lellavu[s], and T[itus] Aur[clius] Lavinus—suggest that two of them belonged to families that achieved citizenship under Trajan, when this legion was founded (this is the significance of their bearing that emperor's gentilician name, Ulpius); their nomina (Panno and Lellavus) look neither particularly Roman nor Germanic, and it is quite hard to say how the ethnic mix in the human personnel of the legion affected the mix of deities mentioned in the inscription. Mention of the genius loci makes clear there was

some concern to appease local divinities, as does the inclusion of Ambiomarcis. The others, however (Jupiter, Mars, Hercules, and Mercury), may be Roman gods, the *interpretatio romana* of German and/or Celtic gods, or some deliberately ambiguous formation meant to encompass them all.

6. On Ambiomarcis, see K. H. Schmidt, *Die Komposition in gallischen Personennamen* (Tübingen, Germany: Max Niemeyer, 1957), p. 123, and Alfred Holder, *Altceltischer Sprachschatz* (Graz: Akademische Druck, 1961–62), 1:121. This deity also appears in an inscription from Cologne listed as number 005413 in the Epigraphic Databank Heidelberg, which is similar to that from Remagen, but includes the tetrad of Mars, Mercury, Nepture, and Ceres, along with the genius loci, two Celtic gods, and unnamed gods and goddesses (Roman? German? Other?). The text reads as follows:

> In [h(onorem)] d(omus) d(ivinae) / et Genio lo[ci] // Ambiamarcis / *Ambio*renesibus / Marti Victori Mer / curio Neptuno / Cereri diis deabusq(ue) / omnibus Primini / Octavius Ver(us) Felic(issimus?) / Quartius Vetus / et Mi[nius? Vi?]talis v(otum) s(olverunt) 1(ibentes) m(erito) / Imp(eratoribus) d[d(ominis) nn(ostris) Ga]llo / [I]I et V[olus]iano Aug(ustis) / [c]o(n)s(ulibus).

I am grateful to Clifford Ando for this reference and for other helpful comments.

7. Biblioteca Apostolica Vaticana, Codex Palatinus Latinus 577: "end ec forsacho allum dioboles uuercum and uuordum, Thunaer ende Uuoden ende Saxnote ende allum them unholdum, the hira genotas sint." Translation is original.

8. Beyond the abjuration formula discussed above, Wodan is attested in no other Old Saxon or Old High German text, with the sole exception of the Second Merseburg Charm, where he appears alongside Balder, Sinthgunt, and Friia, with Fol, Folla, and Sunna also being named. Attempts to trace the origin and diffusion of this deity—whose popularity in Scandinavia may derive from his close associations with poetic inspiration—are numerous and the topic remains contentious. Inter alia, see Karl Helm, *Wodan: Ausbreitung und Wanderung seines Kultes* (Giesen, Germany: W. Schmitz, 1946), in contrast to the excessive enthusiasms of Martin Ninck, *Wodan und germanischer Schicksalsglaube* (Jena, Germany: Eugen Diederich, 1935), and Otto Höfler, *Kultische Geheimbünde der Germanen* (Frankfurt: Moritz Diesterweg, 1934), or more recent reaffirmations of the same dubious theories, like Priscilla Kershaw, *The One-eyed God: Odin and the (Indo-)Germanic Männerbünde* (Washington: Journal of Indo-European Studies, 2000).

9. The name Saxnōt means "Need of the Saxons" or "Companion of the Saxons," and the variant Saxneat appears in the genealogy of the Anglo-Saxon kings of Essex. On his place in Saxon religion, see, most recently, Philipp vom Stein, *"Entsagst du, glaubst du?" Die Religion der Sachsen vor der Christianisierung: Das altsächsische Taufgelöbnis* (Wuppertal, Germany: Bergische Universität, 2006).

10. Adam of Bremen, *History of the Archbishops of Hamburg and Bremen* 4.26:

> In hoc templo, quod totum ex auro paratum est, statuas trium deorum veneratur populus, ita ut potentissimus eorum Thor in medio solium habeat triclinio; hinc et inde locum possident Wodan et Fricco.

This and subsequent texts are taken from Bernhard Schmeidler, ed., *Adam von Bremen, Hamburgische Kirchengeschichte*, 3rd ed. (Hannover: Hahn, 1917).

11. Ibid.: "Wodanem vero sculpunt armatum, sicut nostri Martem solent; Thor autem cum sceptro Iovem simulare videtur."

12. Ibid., 4.26–27:

Tertius est Fricco, pacem voluptatemque largiens mortalibus. Cuius etiam simulacrum fingunt cum ingenti priapo.... Omnibus itaque diis suis attributos habent sac-
erdotes, qui sacrificia populi offerant. Si pestis et famis imminet, Thor ydolo lybatur,
si bellum, Wodani, si nuptiae celebrandae sunt, Fricconi.

On Freyr as the apical ancestor of Uppsala's Yngling dynasty, see Walter Baetke,
*Yngvi und die Ynglinger: Eine quellenkritische Untersuchung über das nordische "Sakralkönig-
tum"* (Berlin: Akademie Verlag, 1964), and Olof Sundqvist, *Freyr's Offspring: Rulers
and Religion in Ancient Svea Society* (Uppsala: Acta Universitatis Uppsaliensis. Historia
Religionum, 2002).

13. Among these are Tuisto, described as *deum terra editum*, and his son, Mannus
(*Germania* 2); *Ingwaz and *Irminaz, referenced in the ethnonyms Ingaevones and
Hermiones (chap. 2); the Alci, twin deities worshipped by the Naharvali, compared
to Castor and Pollux (chap. 43); the goddess Nerthus worshipped by the Reudigni,
Aviones, Anglii, Varini, Eudoses, Suardones, and Nuithones, equated with "Mother
Earth" (*id est Terram matrem*, chap. 40); the unnamed "mother god" (*matrem deum*)
worshipped in boar form by the Aestii (chap. 45); and the unnamed *regnator omnium
deus* of the Semnones (chap. 39).

14. Regarding Snorri's motives and methods, see now Kevin Wanner, *Snorri Sturluson
and the Edda: The Conversion of Cultural Capital in Medieval Scandinavia* (Toronto: University
of Toronto Press, 2008); Heinz Klingenberg, *Heidnisches Altertum und nordisches Mittelalter: Strukturbildende Perspektiven des Snorri Sturluson* (Freiberg: Hochschul Verlag,
1999); and Hans Fix, ed., *Snorri Sturluson: Beiträge zu Werk und Rezeption* (Berlin: De
Gruyter, 1998).

15. At certain points in his text, Snorri makes explicit attempts to identify the
northern deities with Greco-Roman counterparts, as when he traces their origins to
Troy, makes Thor an eponymous Trojan hero, equates Sif with the Sibyl, etc. Above
all, see the Prologue to his *Edda* 3–4, 9–10; *Gylfaginning* 9, 54; and Epilogue. Secondary
literature on the topic of Snorri's knowledge of Latin literature in the original or in
some mediated form includes Valeria Micillo, "The Latin Tradition and Icelandic," in
History of the Language Sciences (Berlin: de Gruyter, 2000), pp. 617–25; Anthony Faulkes,
"The Sources of Skáldskaparmál: Snorri's Intellectual Background," in *Snorri Sturluson*,
ed. Alois Wolf (Tübingen, Germany: Gunter Narr, 1993), pp. 59–76; and Ursula and
Peter Dronke, "The Prologue of the *Prose Edda*: Explorations of a Latin Background,"
in *Sjötiu ritgerðir helgaðar Jakobi Benediktssyni*, ed. Einar Petursson and Jonas Kristjansson
(Reykjavik: Stofnun Arna Magnussonar, 1977), pp. 153–76.

16. The numbers of the deities are stipulated at *Gylfaginning* 20 (Tólf eru Æsir
guðkunnigir) and 35 (Þá mælir Gangleri: 'Hverjar eru Ásynjurnar?' Hár segir: 'Frigg
er œzt ... Önnur er Sága ... Þriðja er Eir ... Fjórtánda Gná'). The gods are described
at considerable length from *Gylfaginning* 20 through 34, while the goddesses receive
briefer explication in chapter 35.

17. Typically, the toponyms name the deity and describe the nature of his place.
Thus: Ullarhaug ("Ull's Barrow"); Ullarvin, Ullarin, and Ulleren ("Ull's Meadow");
Ullarøy ("Ull's Island"); Ullavi, Ullevi, Ullervi, and Ullvi ("Ull's Sacred Precinct");
Ulledalen ("The Valley of Ull"); Ulleland and Ullinsland ("Ull's Land"); Ullenes

("Ull's Headland"); Ulleråker, Ullensaker, Ulsaaker, and Ullinsakr ("Ull's Field"); Ullevaal ("Ull's Hill"); Ullevík ("Ull's Bay"); Ullinhof, Ullinshof, and Ullershov ("Ull's Temple"); Ullunda ("Ull's Grove"); Ullsjö and Ullasjö ("Ull's Sea"); Ultuna and Ullentuna ("Ull's Courtyard").

18. The so-called Thorsburg Chape bears a runic inscription in the elder Futhark alphabet, which includes the compound *wlþuþewaR*, "servant of Ulþuz" (= Old Norse Ullr).

19. Old Norse *Ullr* is cognate to Anglo-Saxon *wuldor*, "glory," and to Gothic *wulþus*, which Ulfila used to translate δόξα ("glory, majesty") at Matthew 6:29, John 11:40 and 12:41, and elsewhere. See Jan de Vries, *Altnordische etymologisches Wörterbuch* (Leiden: E. J. Brill, 1977), p. 633.

20. The fullest discussion of Ullr is that of de Vries, *Altgermanische Religionsgeschichte* 2:153–63, where all the relevant evidence is presented and discussed.

21. The full set of skaldic references to Ullr is listed in Sveinbjörn Egilsson, *Lexicon Poeticum Septentrionalis: Ordbog over det Norsk-Islandske Skjaldesprog*, 2nd ed., revised by Finnur Jónsson (Copenhagen: S. L. Møller, 1931), pp. 578–79.

22. *Atlakviða* 30: "eiða opt um svarða / oc ár of nefnda . . . / at hringi Ullar." All translations from Old Norse are original. Texts from the *Elder Edda* are taken from Gustav Neckel, ed., *Edda: Die Lieder des Codex Regius* (Heidelberg: Carl Winter, 1962).

23. *Grímnismál* 5: "Ýdalir heita, / þar er Ullr hefir / sér um gorva sali."

24. *Grímnismál* 42: "Ullar hylli hefr / . . . / hverr er tecr fyrstr á funa."

25. Saxo Grammaticus, *Gesta Danorum* 3.81:

> Hunc itaque, ne publicam religionem exulare cogeret, exilio mulctantes, Ollerum quondam non solum in regni, sed etiam in divinitatis infulas subrogavere, tanquam deos ac reges creare in æquo positum foret. Quem licet perfunctor flaminem creavissent, integro rerum honore donabant, ne alieni officii procurator, sed legitimus dignitatis advereteretur esse successor. Et ne quid amplitudinis deesset, Othini quoque ei nomen imponunt, vocabuli favore invidiam novitatis exclusuri. Quo denis ferme annis divini senatus magistratum gerente, tandem Othinus, diis atrocitatem exilii miserantibus, satis jam graves pœnas dedisse visus, squaloris deformitatem pristine fulgoris habitu permutavit. . . . Igitur Ollerus, ab Othino Byzantio pulsus, in Svetiam concessit, ubi, veluti novo quodam orbe, opinionis suæ monumenta restaurare connisus, a Danis interfectus est.

This and subsequent text are taken from Hilda Ellis Davidson, ed., *Saxo Grammaticus, The History of the Danes, Books I–IX* (Suffolk: D. S. Brewer, 1998).

26. Ibid., 3.82: "Fama est, illum adeo præstigiarum usu calluisse, ut ad trajicienda maria osse, quod diris carminibus obsignavisset, navigii loco uteretur." Translation is original.

27. Snorri Sturluson, *Gylfaginning* 31: "Ullr heitir einn, sonr Sifjar, stjúpsonr Þórs. Hann er bogmaðr svá góðr ok skíðfœrr svá at engi má við hann keppask. Hann er ok fagr álitum ok hefir hermanns atgervi. Á hann er ok gott at heita í einvígi." This and subsequent Sturluson *Edda* texts are taken from Anthony Faulkes, ed., *Snorri Sturluson, Edda; Prologue and Gylfaginning*, 4 vols. (Oxford: Clarendon Press, 1982–98).

28. Thor is described as "Ulls mágr" in a verse of Eystein Valdason that Snorri quotes at *Skáldskaparmál* 4 and as "Ullar mágr" in a verse from the *Haustlöng* of Þjoðolf of Hvinir, quoted at *Skáldskaparmál* 17. On the meaning of *mágr*, see Richard Cleasby,

Gudbrand Vigfusson, and Sir William Craigie, *An Icelandic-English Dictionary*, 2nd ed. (Oxford: Clarendon Press, 1957), p. 415.

29. Ullr is called "stjúpsonr Thórs" at *Gylfaginning* 31, "stjúp Thórs" at *Skáldskaparmál* 14.

30. Ullr is named "son(r) Sifjar" at *Gylfaginning* 31 and *Skáldskaparmál* 14. Sif is moður Ullar at *Skáldskaparmál* 21.

31. The phrase "Ullr . . . álmsíma" is found in the skaldic verse quoted in Njal's Saga 132.

32. The term is actually ambiguous, since Old Norse *skíð* most literally and immediately denotes a billet or stick of wood while also being used for skis and snowshoes. See further Cleasby, Vigfusson, and Craigie, *Icelandic-English Dictionary*, p. 550; de Vries, *Altnordisches etymologisches Wörterbuch*, p. 491; and Sigmund Feist, *Vergleichendes Wörterbuch der Gotischen Sprache* (Leiden: E. J. Brill, 1939), p. 427.

33. Thus de Vries, *Altgermanische Religionsgeschichte* 2:159–60, following S. Lindqvist, "Ynglingättens gravskick," *Fornvännen* (1921), p. 98.

34. At *Skáldskaparmál* 14, Snorri gives a list of kennings that might be used for Ullr. For the most part, this list mirrors his account of *Gylfaginning* 31, but includes a shield alongside skis and bow as prime attributes of the deity: "How shall one know Ullr? One calls him Sif's son, Thor's stepson, god of snowshoes, god of the bow, hunting god, god of the shield" (Hvernig skal kenna Ull? Sva at kalla hann son Sifjar, stjúp Þors, öndur ás, boga ás, veiði ás, skjaldar ás).

35. Cited from www.odins-gift.com/poth/L-Q/odetohuntinggod.htm (accessed June 6, 2011). The poem is accompanied by F. W. Heine's etching of Ullr (see plate 5 of the present text).

36. In comparing neopagans and ski enthusiasts, I do not mean to imply that religion plays the same kind of role in their lives. Indeed, this comparison—like all others—is instructive for both the differences and the similarity between the phenomena compared. Where the two groups differ most sharply, perhaps, is in the affective quality of their dealings with Ullr, i.e. the self-conscious earnestness of the neopagans and the levity of the skiers, whose operative ethic seems to demand that they take neither the gods nor themselves very seriously. Where they are most similar is in the extent to which they depend on Snorri's *Edda* for their information and imagine an Ullr consonant with the description they find there. This is to say that their relations to the text are equally faithful, even as their relations to the god are not.

37. For example, the devotional video *God Ullr (aka Ollerus)* posted at http://www.youtube.com/watch?v=Xfu105r43GQ (accessed June 6, 2011) is reasonably well informed.

38. Thus, for instance, one notes a certain measure of puerile novelty in the belief—now apparently widespread in certain ski clubs—that one can obtain snow from Ullr in exchange for an offering that wins his favor. Best suited to win such favor are photos of attractive, naked young women. Differences of opinion apparently exist about whether photos of such women playing in the snow or of those with whom the offerer has enjoyed sexual relations (and whom he thus shares with the deity and other viewers) are most effective of all. See several chains of discussion on this issue, complete with many photographic offerings, at http://www.tetongravity.com/forums/showthread.php/164302-Superbabes-of-snow (accessed June 6, 2011).

"The Cosmo-logic of Persian Demonology" was originally presented at "Competing Cosmologies: Intersections of Science and Religion," a conference organized by the Department of English at Duke University (January 2010).

1. European demonology has begun to receive more serious and more respectful attention in recent years, as in such works as Alain Boureau, *Satan the Heretic: The Birth of Demonology in the Medieval West* (Chicago: University of Chicago Press, 2006), Armando Maggi, *In the Company of Demons: Unnatural Beings, Love, and Identity in the Italian Renaissance* (Chicago: University of Chicago Press, 2006), Nathan Johnstone, *The Devil and Demonism in Early Modern England* (Cambridge: Cambridge University Press, 2006), Stuart Clark, *Thinking with Demons: The Idea of Witchcraft in Early Modern Europe* (Oxford: Clarendon Press, 1997), Sophie Houdard, *Les sciences du diable: Quatre discours sur la sorcellerie, XVe–XVIIe siècle* (Paris: Éditions du Cerf, 1992), and Isabel Grübel, *Die Hierarchie der Teufel: Studien zum christlichen Teufelsbild und zur Allegorisierung des Bösen in Theologie, Literatur und Kunst zwischen Frühmittelalter und Gegenreformation* (Munich: Tuduv, 1991).

2. The most thorough prior discussions of Zoroastrian demons and demonology are A. V. Williams Jackson, *Zoroastrian Studies* (New York: Columbia University Press, 1928), pp. 67–109; Arthur Christensen, *Essai sur la démonologie iranienne* (Copenhagen: Ejnar Munksgaard, 1941); Carsten Colpe, ed., *Altiranische und Zoroastrische Mythologie* (Stuttgart: Klett-Cotta, 1974–82); Carsten Colpe, *Iranier—Aramäer—Hebräer—Hellenen* (Tübingen: Mohr Siebeck, 2003), pp. 316–26, 470–72, and 567–602; and Éric Pirart, *Georges Dumézil face aux démons iraniens* (Paris: Éditions L'Harmattan, 2007). It goes beyond my ambitions to discuss the powerful influence Persian demonology exercised on Judaism, Christianity, Buddhism, Manichaeism, and other world religions, but it was of massive, enduring importance.

3. *Yašt* 18.1–2:

mraot Ahurō Mazdå Spitamāi Zaraθuštrāi. azəm daδąm airiianəm xᵛarənō gaomauuāitīm pouru.vaθwəm pouru.ištəm pouru.xᵛarənaŋhəm huš.hąm.bərətəm xraθβəm huš.hąm.bərətəm šaētəm Āzīm hamaēstārəm dušmainiiūm hamaēstārəm. tauruuaiieiti Aŋrəm Mainiiūm pouru.mahrkəm. tauruuaiieiti Aēšməm xruuīdrūm. tauruuaiieiti Būšiiąstəm zairinəm. tauruuaiieiti hąm.stərətəm Aēxəm. tauruuaiieiti daēum Apaošəm. tauruuaiieiti anairiiå daiŋhāiiō.

This and subsequent Avestan texts are taken from Karl F. Geldner, ed., *Avesta: The Sacred Books of the Parsis*, 3 vols. (Stuttgart: W. Kohlhammer, 1886–96). All translations are original. Other translations may be found in James Darmesteter, *Le Zend Avesta* (Paris: Annales du Musée Guimet, 1892–93) 2: 612, and Herman Lommel, *Die Yäšt's des Awesta* (Göttingen: Vandenhoeck & Ruprecht, 1927), p. 167.

4. *Yašt* 19 is a hymn devoted to *xvarənah*, and the Aryan monopoly on this power/entity/substance is treated in a mythic narrative recounted at verses 56–64. A related narrative at verses 45–50 describes the struggle between divine and demonic figures for its control. An extensive literature treats the ideology of *xvarənah*, including H. W. Bailey, *Zoroastrian Problems in the Ninth-Century Books* (Oxford: Clarendon Press, 1943; 2nd ed. 1971), pp. 1–77; Jacques Duchesne-Guillemin, "La Royauté iranienne et le *xvarənah*," in *Iranica*, ed. Gherardo Gnoli and Adriano V. Rossi (Naples: Istituto

Universitario Orientale, 1979), pp. 375–86; P. Oktor Skjærvø, "Farnah: Mot mède en vieux-perse," *Bulletin de la Société Linguistique* 78 (1983): 241–59; Bruno Jacobs, "Das Chvarnah—Zum Stand der Forschung," *Mitteilungen der Deutschen Orient Gesellschaft* 119 (1987): 215–48; Gherardo Gnoli, "Über das iranische *huarnah-*: Lautliche, morphologische und etymologische Probleme; Zum Stand der Forschung," *Altorientalische Forschungen* 23 (1996): 151–80; and Gherardo Gnoli, "*Xvarənah*," in *Encyclopaedia Iranica*, online at http://www.iranica.com/newsite/ (accessed June 6, 2011). Two excellent translations of *Yašt* 19 are available and include extensive commentary: Almut Hintze, ed. and trans. *Der Zamyād-Yašt: Edition, Übersetzung, Kommentar* (Wiesbaden: Ludwig Reichert, 1994), and Helmut Humbach and Pallan R. Ichaporia, trans., *Zamyād Yasht: Yasht 19 of the Younger Avesta; Text, Translation, Commentary* (Wiesbaden: Harrassowitz Verlag, 1998).

5. See, for instance, *Dēnkart* 3.157.18, which provides the basis for much medical practice.

> The reason healing of the body is necessary is the ceaseless evil assault of the cold-dry against the body's warm-moist blood, especially if the arrival of adversarial agents is simultaneous, such that the cold cools down the warmth of the body's blood and dryness dries out its moisture.

> ud bēšāz niyāzīh ī tan cim adrang sard hušk ud ēbgatīg petyārag ī ō garm-xwēd xōn tan mādag. kū hamēstārīg rahišnīg ⁺hambudast pad sardīh ī garmīh ī xōn afsārād pad huškīh xwēdīhā hōšēnād.

This and subsequent *Dēnkart* texts are taken from Dhanjishah Meherjibhai Madan, ed., *The Complete Text of the Pahlavi Dinkard* (Bombay: Society for the Promotion of Researches into the Zoroastrian Religion, 1911), and M. J. Dresden, *Dēnkart: A Pahlavi Text; Facsimile Edition of the Manuscript B of the K. R. Cama Oriental Institute, Bombay* (Wiesbaden: Otto Harrassowitz, 1966). All translations are original.

6. The Avestan phrases *daēuuanąm daēuuō* ("demon of demons") and *daēuuō daēuuanąm daēuuōtəmō* ("most demonic demon of demons") are used of Aŋra Mainiiu at *Vīdēvdāt* 19.43, where he appears with a long list of lesser demons. The Pahlavi equivalent (*dēwān dēw*, "demon of demons") occurs at *Dēnkart* 7.2.44 and elsewhere.

7. *Greater Bundahišn* 1.1–3: "pad wēh dēn owōn paydāg kū Ohrmazd bālistīg pad harwisp āgāhīh ud wehīh zamān ī akanārag andar rōšnīh hamē būd.... Ahreman andar tārigīh pad pas-dānišnīh ud zadār-kāmīh zofr-pāyag būd." This and subsequent texts from the *Greater Bundahišn* are taken from Fazlollah Pakzad, ed., *Bundahišn: Zoroastrische Kosmogonie und Kosmologie; Band I: Kritische Edition* (Tehran: Centre for the Great Islamic Encyclopaedia, 2005). All translations from the Pahlavi are original.
Note that Ahreman's ignorance is of a very particular sort. Most literally it is "after-knowledge" (*pas-dānišnīh*), which is to say that the Evil Spirit never properly anticipates the consequences of those actions it engenders. Impulsively destructive, it sets events in motion that always ironically backfire, producing not the destruction it intends but a mixed state in which creation and destruction temporarily coexist, but which ultimately resolves in favor of creation.

8. Cf. *Greater Bundahišn* 26.131 and 27.56: "The Ohrmazdian nature is made manifest as warm and moist and light and fragrant.... The nature of Ahreman is made manifest as cold and dry and demonic and dark and stinking" (gōhr ī Ohrmazdīg

garm ud xwēd ud rōšn ud hubōy ud sabuk ud andar frāz paydāg. . . . gōhrī Ahreman-
ig sard ud hušk ud gyāg tārīg ud gandag ud andar abrāz paydāg).

9. Priscilla Wald, *Contagious: Cultures, Carriers, and the Outbreak Narrative* (Durham,
NC: Duke University Press, 2008).

10. *Dādestān ī Dēnīg* 36.4–8:

> Thus, the Creator of the world made the spiritual creation pure and undefiled. He
> made the material creation immortal, unaging, without hunger, without bondage,
> without sorrow, and without pain. [That remained the state of things] until there
> erupted in the darkness the Lie of wickedness, who is not a right chooser of wisdom,
> goodness, and beneficence. He is a wrecker, murderous, ignorant, deceitful, mali-
> cious, misleading, destructive, wasteful, and envious. . . . In envy, full of vengeance,
> perfect in deceit, he rushed to seize, destroy, smash, and ruin this well-made creation
> of the gods.

> ōh-iz dādārī dahišn dād ān ī mēnōg dām abēzag anahōgēnēd ud ān-iz ī gētīgīg dām
> amarg a-zarmān ud suyišn ud abandišn abēš ud adard. tā ka candēd andar tom dušīh
> [ī] druz kē xrad rāst wizēngar nē wehīh ī spēnāgīg bē hast. škēnnāg margēnāg ud
> duš-āgāh ud frēbāg ud purr-kēn ud wiyābānēnāg ud wišōbāg ud wanīgar wanīgar
> ud purr-arešk. . . . u-š pad arešk ī purr-kēnwarīh ī spurr-druxtārīh nīxwarēd ō
> griftan wišuftan ud wanēnidan abēsīhēnidan ī im hukard dām ī yazdan.

This and subsequent *Dādestān ī Dēnīg* texts and translations are taken from Mahmoud
Jaafari-Dehaghi, ed., *Dādestān ī Dēnīg. Part I: Transcription, Translation, and Commentary*
(Paris: Association pour l'avancement des études iraniennes, 1998).

11. The verb that is used (Pahlavi *kirrenīdan*) is daēvic and connotes a violent,
messy process. Regarding its history and implications, see Bruce Lincoln, "Pahlavi
Kirrēnīdan and Traces of Iranian Creation Mythology," *Journal of the American Oriental
Society* 117 (1997): 681–85.

12. *Greater Bundahišn* 1.47: "from the material substance of self-indulgence, he
miscreated Lust, which is evil, which has the form of non-being" (u-š az stī ī xwad-
dōšagīh Waran ī wad ī nēst-kirb frāz kirrēnīd). The "material substance of self-
indulgence" (*stī ī xwad-dōšagīh*) would seem to be the ejaculate he produced through
masturbation.

13. *Mēnōg ī Xrad* 8.10: "The lying Evil Spirit spawned demons, lies, and other
sorcerors via self-sodomy" (ud Ahreman ī druwand ud dēwān ud druzān ud abārīg
⁺jādugān az kūnmarz ī xwēš wišūd).

14. *Greater Bundahišn* 1.16–17: "kirrenīd was dēw ān dām ī murnjēnidār... sahmgēn
ī pūdag ī wadag ud dušīh u-š nē burzīd hēnd."

15. Ibid., 4.19: "u-š Āz, Niyāz, Sēj, Dard, Yask, Waran, ud Būšāsp pad gāw ud
Gayōmard frāz hišt." Cf. *Dādestān ī Dēnīg* 36.31 and 36.38–45, which continues the
discussion, treating the members of the Evil Spirit's anticreation at considerable
length. Note also an Avestan passage, *Vīdēvdāt* 20.3, which speaks of "the evil eye,
putrefaction, and pollution, which the Evil Spirit created in opposition to this body
of mortal beings" (agašiiā pūitiiā āhitiiā yā Aŋrō Mainiiuš frākərəntat auui imąm
tanūm yąm mašiiānąm).

16. On these categories, see Shaul Shaked, "The Notions *Mēnōg* and *Gētīg* in the
Pahlavi Texts and Their Relation to Eschatology," *Acta Orientalia* 33 (1971): 59–107,

and Michael Stausberg, *Die Religion Zarathushtras: Geschichte—Gegenwart—Rituale* (Stuttgart: W. Kohlhammer, 2002) 1:333–38.

17. *Dādestān ī Dēnīg* 18.2: "It is said of the Evil Spirit that he does not exist as material being" (Ahreman rāy guft estēd kū gētīg nēst). Cf. *Ardā Wirāz Nāmag* 5.7, *Dēnkart* 5.7.1–2, and *Dādestān ī Dēnīg* 36.51. The material nonexistence of Ahreman has received much attention recently, including treatments by Shaul Shaked, "Some Notes on Ahreman, the Evil Spirit, and His Creation," in *Studies in Mysticism and Religion Presented to Gershom G. Scholem*, ed. E. E. Urbach et al. (Jerusalem: Magnes Press, 1967), pp. 227–34; Jes P. Asumssen, "Some Remarks on Sasanian Demonology," in *Commémoration Cyrus: Actes du Congrès de Shiraz* (Leiden: E. J. Brill, 1974), pp. 236–41; Hanns-Peter Schmidt, "The Non-Existence of Ahreman and the Mixture (*Gumēzišn*) of Good and Evil," in *K. R. Cama Oriental Institute: Second International Congress Proceedings* (Bombay: K. R. Cama Oriental Institute, 1996), pp. 79–95; and Antonio Panaino, "A Few Remarks on the Zoroastrian Conception of the Status of Angra Mainyu and of the Daēvas," *Res Orientales* 13 (2001): 99–107.

18. *Dādestān ī Dēnīg* 36.51: "The Wise Lord's creation is spiritual and also material. That of the Lie is not material. The Lie joins (its) bad spiritual being to the material being (of the Wise Lord's good creations)" (dām ī Ohrmazd mēnōg ud gētīg-iz. ōy <ī> druz nēst gētīg be wad mēnōgīh abyōzēd ō gētīg).

19. *Dēnkart* 3.105:

> hād mēnōg dahišn ast ahambūd ēwtag bawišn u-š ⁺waspuhrāgānīh ast hād mēnōg ud dahišn ast ī ahambūd awēnišnīg ud agīrišnīg ud az dādārīhišn dām fradom pad mēnōgīh bawišn ud būdan ahambūd awēnišnīg ud agīrišnīh. ud pad hambawēnidārīh ī bawišnīgān ō gētīgīh wašt ī wēnišnīg gīrišnīg ān paydagīh az-iz ēn ka gētīg tis wēnišnīg ud gīrišnīg ka az gētīg wēnišnīg gīrišnīg wišāyīhēd abāz ō bun bawišn awēnišnīg agīrišnīg mēnōg ast i-š bun šawēd. ud rōšn mēnōg pad garm-xwēd nērōg zīndag cihrīh az ahambūd mēnōg bawišn ō hambawišn ān gētīg waštan ud šāyēd. ān ī nūn-iz hamāg gētīg gētīg pad gētīhā winirdīh az ham nērōg. ud tār mēnōg marg gōhr sard hušk druwandīh rāy im ō hambawišnīg gētīg madan nē šāyēd. ān ī ō paydāg gētīhā mad nē xwēš gōhr be jud gōhr ⁺paymōxīg.

Cf. *Dādestān ī Dēnīg* 36.51 and *Dēnkart* 5.7.2.

20. *Greater Bundahišn* 27.53: "Ever-new demons come to people as a result of the ever-new crimes they commit against (good) creatures" (Nōg Nōg dēw ān ī nōg nōg az wināh ī dāmān kunēnd awiš jahēd). Cf. *Dēnkart* 5.23.21: "From babbling-while-eating, scurrying-about-with-one-shoe, urinating-while-standing, and other (unacceptable, demonic behaviors), from this kind of thing, it is as if new demons were born" (ud az drāyān-xwarišnīh ud ēw-mōg-dwārišnīh ud ⁺estān-mēzišnīh ud abārīg ī az ēn šōn dēw ciyōn <zāy az> zāyēnd). Note that the verbs used to describe the acts of speaking (Pahlavi *drāyīdan*) and locomotion (*dwāristan*) in the latter passage are daēvic, used only for irrational speech, erratically violent motion, and the morally defective beings of whom these are characteristic.

21. *Dādestān ī Dēnīg* 31.2–5:

> The fourth night after death, there is a reckoning for the soul of a liar at the Cinwad Bridge. It is turned upside down and falls. And the demon Wizarš leads him, tyrannically bound. He leads him to hell. And with him there are spiritual demons, which came into being from the evil he did in many forms and places, which resemble

spoilers, harmers, killers, destroyers, scoundrels, evil-bodies, wrongdoers, those who
are unseemly, most stingy, filthy, biting, and tearing vermin, stinking winds, dark,
stinking, burning, thirsting, hungry, inexpiably sinful, and other most sin-causing
and harm-causing demons, who become causes of pain for him in the material, as in
the spiritual creation. They have strength and power given them by his sin, as much
as it is great. And they ceaselessly cause him pain and suffering until the time of the
Renovation.

šāb ī tasum kard āmār az puhl ī Cinwad nigūn gardēd ud kafēnēd. u-š +Wizarš
dēw sezdēnīhā bastag nayēdu-š nayēd bē ō dušōx. u-š abāg bawēnd mēnōg dēw ī
hambust az ān ī ōy wināh pad was cihrag ud gāh mānāg ī wimuštārān-iz rešidārān
ōzanišngarān murnjēnidārān marān duškirbān bazag-ēwēnagān ud anabāyistān
an-iz-rātigān rēmān gazāgām darrāgān xrafstarān gandagān wādān tārigān
gandagān sōzāgān tišnigān +gušnāgān +anabuhlān ud abārīg frahist wināhēnāgān
ud dardēnāgān kē-š pad hangōšidag ī gētīg bēš-kardārān mēnōgīg abāg bawēnd.
u-š ham handāzag zōr nerōg i-šān az ān ī ōy wināh ud dād ān īta bē ō frašgird zamān
anāsānīhā dardēnēnd bēšišnēnēnd.

22. Avestan Āzi (= Pahlavi Āz) is derived from the verb āz-, "to strive for, long
after," on which see Christian Bartholomae, *Altiranisches Wörterbuch* (Berlin: Walter
de Gruyter, 1904; reprint ed. 1961), cols. 342–43. The word has been translated in
numerous different ways by scholars who unduly focus on just one of its various
aspects. Thus: "le démon du besoin" (Darmesteter), "Gier, Begierde" (Bartholomae, Colpe), "Habgier" (Lommel), "greed, selfish craving, and avidity" (Jackson),
"l'Avidité" (Christensen), "greed, lust" (D. N. MacKenzie, *A Concise Pahlavi Dictionary*
[London: Oxford University Press, 1971]), and "avidity, covetousness" (H. S. Nyberg,
A Manual of Pahlavi [Wiesbaden: Otto Harrassowitz, 1974] 2: 41). Most common is
"concupiscence," favored by R. C. Zaehner, *Zurvān: A Zoroastrian Dilemma* (Oxford:
Oxford University Press, 1955), Jacques Duchesne-Guillemin, *La religion de l'Iran ancien*
(Paris: Presses Universitaires de France, 1962), Geo. Widengren, *Die Religionen Irans*
(Stuttgart: W. Kohlhammer, 1965), and Pirart. While Pahlavi texts regularly identify
Āz as a demon (*dēw*), the Avesta does not give this title to his counterpart, preferring
to speak of Āzi as "demon-created" (*daēuuō.dāta*; cf. *Yasna* 16.8 and *Vīdēvdāt* 18.19).

23. *Greater Bundahišn* 27.34: "Āz dēw ān kē tis ōbārēd. ka Niyāz rāy tis nē mad estēd
az tan xwarēd. ān druz-ē(w) hast ī ka-š hamāg xwāstag ī gētīg be dād nē +ōbārēd ud
sagrnē bawēd." Two different terms are used to establish the demonic identity of Āz:
dēw, the unmarked term, and *druz*, which literally means "lie, falsehood," but is also
used for demonic beings of female gender. GBd 27.37 adds more information, citing
a lost Avestan passage: "This too one says: 'The power of the demon Āz comes from
that person who is not content in him/herself and who carries off others' things'"
(ēn-iz gōwēd kū Āz dēw zōr az ān tan kē pad zan ī xwēš nē hunsanēnd ud ān-iz ī
kasān be apparēd).

24. This point is taken up, inter alia, by *Dēnkart* 3.209:

> The definition of mankind in a state of purity is "life-force that is embodied and im-
> mortal." In the state of mixture produced by the Evil Spirit's Assault, the definition is
> "life-force that is embodied and mortal."

kē rāy wimand-īz mardōm andar abēzagīh axw ī astōmand amarg andar ēbgatīg
gumēzigīh axw ī astōmand margōmand.

Also, *Dēnkart* 3.317:

> Now, the mortality and immortality of mortal bodies come from the mixture of antithetical natures/substances produced by the Adversary's original Assault under the star station. The Creator does not preserve his creations as long as they are in the state of mixture produced by the Assault throughout the state of mixture. The reason (he lets) his progeny become mixed with mortality in the general course of things is so that the creations can participate in the Renovation, recovering that which they lost to the desire for death caused by the Adversary's Assault and putting an end to death itself and the Adversary.

> hād ōšōmandīh ud ahōšīh ōšōmandān tan az jud-gōhr ēbgat gumēzišn azēr star pāyag bawišn. andar ēbgatīg gumēzišn abāz nē ⁺dāštēd dādār az dahišnān tā andar gumēzišn. cim pad amaragānīg rawāg paywandīh ī andar gumēzišn abāg ⁺ōšōmandīh bawēd āyēd dahišnān pad be paywastan ī ō frašgird abāz wardēnīdan ān-iš zyān abar kām ōš wihān ēbgat pad frazām ošīh ī xwad ēbgat u-š.

25. *Dēnkart* 3.235: "hād tan andarōn xwadīg bōy az cihr u-š gand az Āz. . . . ud gand wiš ud hixr jōyišn." Note that the last word of this passage—Pahlavi *jōyišn*—is daēvic in its semantics, which is to say that it describes a demonic form of eating, immoderate, ugly, vicious, and destructive of the eater as well as the eaten.

26. *Greater Bundahišn* 1.48 explains that all stench originates with demons: "First, the Evil Spirit created the essence of the demons, the spirit of their evil motion. The stench of the Wise Lord's creatures comes into being from that" (u-š nazdist dēwān xwadīh dād dušrawišnīh ān mēnōg ī-š gannāgīh ī dāmān ī Ohrmazd azīš būd).

27. *Dēnkart* 5.24.19a:

> When the body is dead, the demon Astwihād, the death-maker, the author of powerlessness, the defeater of the soul, comes to it triumphantly. He seizes it and brings his brothers to the body, to inhabit its every place of life. These are the stench-makers, creators of foulness, and other demons who make the body useless and who drive off the opponents antithetical to themselves, like sweet fragrance, purity, good conduct, beauty, and others that are necessary. Residing in the body, they increase, so there are more of them all together in the body, so that they breathe corpse pollution and all illnesses. One can say, without dispute, that the residence of demons is in that pollution.

> ud tan ka murd abarwēzīhā madan ⁺margīhkardār ud agārēnidār Astwihād stōwēnidār ī gyān u-š abāz grift i-š gyāg gyāg ī zindagīh ud pad mehmānīh andar burdan i-š brādarān gandēnidārān ⁺pudagēnidārān abārīg anabēdān kardarān dēwān ō tan ⁺ānāftan i-šan jud jud xwēš hambadīg ciyōn hubōyīh pākīh huburdīh hucihrīh ud abārīg ī abāyišnīg az tan mehmānīhā wālīdan i-šan andar ham tan owōn frāyīhā kū ō-iz bē nasuš wisp wēmārīh ⁺damēnd ud ānōh kū dēwān mēhmānīh pad ān ewēnag rēmanīh guftan abē-pahikār spēd bawēd.

28. *Greater Bundahišn* 27.57: "As regards hell, one says: It is a darkness one can grasp in the hand and a stench one can cut with a knife" (dušōx rāy gōwēd kū tār ī pad dast šāyēd griftan ud gandagīh pad kārd šāyēd brīdan). Cf. *Ardā Wirāz Nāmag* 5.5, 18.2–4, and 54.1–6.

29. *Dēnkart* 5.8.8–11:

> The resurrection comes into being at the end with the destruction of the Adversary. The beneficent Creator brings all humanity back to life. . . . No creature remains in

the state produced by the Adversary's original assault. The Evil Spirit, also the other demons and lies, are conquered, killed, and destroyed. All stain and evil are carried away from good creatures. And all creatures like us, whose original substance is light, are established in a state of holiness, purity, freedom from blemish, absence of need, with one's desires accomplished, without misfortune, and all-happiness.

Ristāxēz pad abdomīg be abesīhēnišnīh ī petyārag bawēd. xwābar dādār ud hamāg ⁺mardōm zīndag abāz kunēd. . . . ud ēc dām andar petyārag ōmandīh be nē mānēd ud Ahreman ud abārīg-iz dēwān ud druzān wānīd ud zad ān ōzad bawēnd ud hamāg petyārag ud āhōg az weh dahišnān bē barīhēd ud hāmist dām ciyōn mān bun gōhr rōšnīh pad abēzagīh ud pākīh ud an-āhōgīh ud abē-niyāzīh ud hanjāft-kāmīh ud apetyāragīh ud hamāg-šādīh winnārīhēd.

The complex Zoroastrian doctrines concerning resurrection (*ristaxēz*) and perfection of "the final body" (*tan ī pasēn*) are treated most extensively at *Greater Bundahišn* 34; *Selections of Zādspram* 34; *Pahlavi Rivāyat Accompanying the Dādestān ī Dēnīg* 48. See, most recently, Mihaela Timuš, "The 'Eschatological Body' (*tan ī pasēn*) according to the Zoroastrian Theology," *Studia Asiatica* 4–5 (2003–4): 779–808.

30. *Selections of Zādspram* 34.32–33:

Then the Evil Spirit made Appetite his chief commander, and four subordinate commanders were created, who are Wrath [Xešm], Winter [Zamestān], Old Age [Zarmān], and Distress [Sēj], who are homologous with east, west, south, and north.

u-š pas wazēd spāhbed sālār ī xwad ast ⁺Āz. u-š čahār spāhbed pad hamkārīh frāz dād hēnd <ī> ast Xešm ud Zamestān ud ⁺Zarmān ud Sēj hōmānāgīh ī xwarāsān ud xwarōfrān ud nemrōz ud abāxtar spāhbed.

31. *Selections of Zādspram* 34.32–45 give the most extensive account of Appetite's fate at the end of time. At 34.36, it describes the decision of Appetite to divide itself into three separate forms, which may be described as gustatory, sexual, and aesthetic forms of desire. As humanity renounces each of these, the power of Appetite is correspondingly weakened.

Appetite, being one in nature, was not able to corrupt the creatures when they are scattered. So it divided its powers into three portions: that which is natural, that which is not natural, and that which is beyond nature. The natural is the state when one's life force is in bondage to eating. The unnatural is excessive desire for sexual intercourse, which itself is called Lust [*waran*] and is aroused by seeing that which is inside so that the nature of the body is excited. That beyond nature is the desire for whatever beauty one sees or hears.

ud Āz ēk cihrīhā nē tuwān būd ahōgēnīd tā dāmān pargandag bawēd. ān-iš zōrān pad jomā rawāg būdan ī andar dām rāy ō se baxt ī ast cihrīg ⁺cihrīg ud bērōn az cihr. cihrīg ān kā andar xwardārīh kē-š gyān awiš bastag. be-cihrīg kāmagōmandīh ī abar gumēzišn kē xwad waran xwandīhēd kē pad wēnišn ī ō be ān ī andarōn hangēzīhēd ud cihr ī tan awištābīhēd. berōn az cihr ārzōg ī ō kadār-iz-ē nēkīh ī wēnēd ayāb ašnawēd.

32. Ibid., 1.30:

Time said to the Evil Spirit: "Assisting them is a weapon: Appetite [Āz], who will devour you and die herself of hunger, if at the end of 9000 years, it is not completed as he promised you, as the pact was made and time fulfilled."

u-š pad frāz barišnīh guft kū: pad awēšān zay abāgīh Āz ēd ī tō bē jōyēd xwad pad suy frōd mīrēd agar pad sar ī 9000 sāl ciyōn-it ⁺padistēd ud pašt abar kard ud zamān abar grift nē frazāmēnēd.

33. Thus, *Selections of Zādspram* 34.32–45; *Mēnōg ī Xrad* 8.15–16; *Pahlavi Rivāyat Accompanying the Dādestān ī Dēnīg* 48.90–96; *Greater Bundahišn* 34.27–30.

34. The name is translated variously, but always with reference to excessive fatigue. Thus: "le démon du long et paresseux sommeil" (Darmesteter), "Schläfrigkeit" (Bartholomae, Colpe), "lethargy, long sleep, and sloth" (Jackson), "Schlafhexe" (Lommel), "sleepiness, somnolence" (Nyberg), "sleep, sloth" (MacKenzie), and "Statut de ce qui reste à l'état de projet, indolence, paresse" (Pirart).

35. *Vīdēvdāt* 18.16: "hā vīspəm ahūm . . . hakat raocaŋhaṃ fraɣrātō nixuuabdaiieiti."

36. *Greater Bundahišn* 27.32: "dēw ān kē ajgahānīh kunēd."

37. Ibid., 4.19 (cited above). *Dādestān ī Dēnīg* 36.31 gives a different list of eleven demons who participated in the original attack. Three demons are found in both lists: Torpor, Deprivation (Niyāz), and Lust (Waran). Those not found in the *Bundahišn* list are Evil Mind (Akōman), Wrath (Xēšm), Old Age (Zarmān), Distress (Tangīh), Buddha-Idol (Būd), Expiration (Wāy), and the two bringers of death (Astwihād and Wizarš).

38. Fragment Westergaard 42: "Now the scoundrel Torpor of the long paws stormed forth from the northern direction, babbling thus: 'Sleep, little people, sleep!'" (āat maire fraduuaraiti Būšiiąsta darəɣō.gauua apāxtarat haca naēmāt uiti daomna xvafsata mašiiākåŋhō).

39. *Vīdēvdāt* 18.16 warns against the demon's insidious urgings.

> Get up people, praise Best Truth, revile the demons. Torpor of the long paws storms at you, she who puts all embodied existence to sleep, even when it has awakened with the daylight, (saying): "Sleep long, little people. Your time hasn't arrived."

> usəhištata mašiiāka staota ašəm yat vahištəm nīsta daēuua aēša vō duuaraiti būšiiąsta darəɣō.gauua hā vīspəm ahūm astuuantəm hakat raocåŋhaṃ fraɣrātō nixvabdaiieiti. xvafsa darəɣō mašyāka noit tē sacaite.

40. *Mēnōg ī Xrad* 2.29–30: "Do not succumb to Torpor, so that your work and the virtuous deeds it is necessary to do do not remain undone" (Būšāsp ō warz kū-t kār ud kirbag ī abāyēd kardan akard nē mānēd). Cf. *Mēnōg ī Xrad* 16.57–59.

41. *Dādestān ī Dēnīg* 36.39–40:

> u-š Būšāsp dēw pad nizārēnidan wēn abespārd ud Tab dēw pad stardēnidan ud ōš āšōbēnēd ud Āz dēw zōr ogārdan ud pēš [?] sēnišnēnēd. u-š Zarmān dēw pad kirb wināhīdan ud [?] appurdan ud wattar Wāy wisānišn gyān az tan stōwēnidan Xēšm dēw pad kōxšišn sārēnidan ud ōzānišn abzāyēnidan ud tamīgān xrafstarān pad gazišn kardan wināhēnidan ud ⁺Zarīz dēw pad xwarišnān zahrēnidan margīh wihānēnidan abāg Niyāz ī nihān rawišn ud Sahm bīm-kun ud xīndagīh tabišn afsār ud was wināhišnīg ⁺zōrān wināhatārān dēwān hamē āyar kard ō Astwihād pad margēnidārīh.

Cf. *Dādestān ī Dēnīg* 22.3.

42. *Greater Bundahišn* 26.69–70:

ēn-iz gowēd kū: harw šab ⁺Būšāsp homānāg nasrust pad zamīg ud āb ud dām-iz ī
ahlawān be dwārēd ka xwaršēd ūl āyēd hamāg zamīg dēwān be zanēd yōjdahr be
kunēd. ēn-iz gowēd kū ka xwaršēd ēk zamān pas abar ayēd dēwān hamāg dām be
murnjēnd.

43. The only examples I have found either have been discussed above or will be
treated shortly. These include the association of non-Aryan countries with certain
demonic powers (*Yašt* 18.1–2), accounts of Ahreman's primordial assault (*Greater
Bundahišn* 4.19, *Dādestan ī Dēnīg* 36.31), discussions of death's onset (*Dādestan ī Dēnīg*
36.39), and the great list of demons found in *Greater Bundahišn* 27.

44. *Dēnkart* 3.374:

hat mardōm pad zāyišn fradom petyāragēnīdār druz Akōman pad anāg pēš frazāmīh
ī bēš ī ō zahag pad zāyišn nimūdārīh ī ast <tan ī pasēn> margīh. u-š nīšān zamānīg
⁺griyīg ī aburnāyīg pad zāyišn hamēstār ī ēn druz Wahman pad nēk abdom frazāmīh
rāmišn nimūdārīh ī ast tan ī pasēn hamē zīndagīh. u-š nīšān mehmānīg rāmišn ī
aburnāyīg. dudigar petyāragēnīdār druz Āz pad tan nizārēnāg ud suy ud ⁺tišn
abzārīh ud bōzag ī az dādār āfurišn abāyišn pad xwāstārīh ud mizagīh suy ī ud
⁺tišn spōz pēm ayār ī cihr ud zadār ī Āz srāyīdanag ī tan. sidigar petyāragēnitār druz
sustgar murnjenāg ī tan apaymān Būšāsp abāz ī dāštārīh ud wizend u-š āsānitār ī tan
paymān aram.

45. Consider, for example, the analysis of digestion found at *Greater Bundahišn*
28.10:

In material existence, people commit sins and good deeds. When someone dies, they
calculate his sins and good deeds. All those who are pure go to heaven. All those who
are liars are thrown into hell. Homologous to this is people's eating of food. All that
is good goes to the brain, where it becomes pure blood. All that is mixed with poison
goes from the stomach to the intestine and they throw it outside through the anus,
which is just like hell.

owōn ciyōn andar gētīg mardōm wināh ud kirbag kunēnd. ka mīrēd wināh ud
kirbag āmārēnēnd. harw cē abēzag ō garōdmān šawēd. harw cē druwand ō dušōx
abganēnd. hamgōnag mardōm-īz xwarišn ī xwarēnd. harw cē abēzag ō mazg ī
sar šawēd xōn ī pāk bawēd. ō dil rasēd hamāg tan nērōg aziš bawēd. harw cē wiš
gumēxtag az kumīg ō rōdīg šawēd pad ⁺kūn bērōn abganēnd ī handāzag ī dušōx.

Or that of respiration at 28.12:

Just as the Wise Lord is at the highest station, so the Evil Spirit is at the lowest depth,
and as their power is equal, their relations are conflictual in the material world.
People also have two struggling entities in their bodies. Thus, there is one breath of
knowledge, which is the soul, whose seat is in the brain, whose nature is warm-moist,
whose motion goes to the navel. And there is one breath of sin, whose nature is cold-
dry, whose seat is in the anus, whose motion goes to the sex organs.

owōn ciyōn Ohrmazd bālist ud Ahreman zofāyīg. u-š āgenēn nērōg andar gētīg ēk
ō did kōxšišnīg mardōm-iz dō andar tan ēk wād ī dānāgīh ast ī ruwān kē-š gāh pad
mazg ī sar ud gōhr garm xwēd ⁺rawišn ō nāfag, ēk wād ī bazag kē gōhr sard hušk ud
gāh pad kūn ⁺rawišn ō zahār.

46. See, for example, the analysis of hail at *Greater Bundahišn* 21.c.11:

When the demons arrive for the assault, they let cold loose on the cloud. They freeze its water and make it dry, so that it does not rain. They freeze the drops and hail falls.

dēwān ō petyaragīh rasēnd sardīh padiš hilēnd ān āb afsārēnēnd ud āb owōn hušk kunēnd kū tā nē wārēd. ast-iz ka sresk afsārēnēnd ud tagarg wārēd.

47. See, for instance, the analysis of swarming insects like ants at *Greater Bundahišn* 22.4:

Their material being, the light of their eyes, and the breath of their spirit are Ohrmazdian, from that which is similar in the world, and their poison, sinfulness, and malevolence are that which is Ahremanian.

u-šān stī ud rōšnīh ī cašm ud wād ī gyānīg ī Ohrmazdig az ān ciyōn andar gēhān u-š wīš bazagīh ud wadkāmagīh ān ī ahremanīg.

48. For a small sampling of an enormous, wide-ranging, and fast-growing literature, see David Frankfurter, *Evil Incarnate: Rumors of Demonic Conspiracy and Ritual Abuse in History* (Princeton, NJ: Princeton University Press, 2006), Nahi Alon and Haim Orner, *The Psychology of Demonization: Promoting Acceptance and Reducing Conflict* (Mahwah, NJ: Lawrrence Erlbaum, 2006), Tom De Luca and John Buell, *Liars! Cheaters! Evildoers! Demonization and the End of Civil Debate in American Politics* (New York: New York University Press, 2005), James Waller, *Becoming Evil: How Ordinary People Commit Genocide and Mass Killing* (Oxford: Oxford University Press, 2002), Norman Cohn, *Europe's Inner Demons: The Demonization of Christians in Medieval Christendom*, rev. ed. (Chicago: University of Chicago Press, 2000), and Robert Wistrich, ed., *Demonizing the Other: Antisemitism, Racism and Xenophobia* (Amsterdam: Harwood Academic Publishers, 1999).

49. The significance of Old Persian *daiva* in Xerxes's inscription at Persepolis has been much discussed, and opinion is divided as to whether it means "old gods," "foreign gods," or "demons." If the last is correct—as would be consistent with the cognate terms in other Iranian languages (Avestan *daēva*, Pahlavi *dēw*), one would translate the relevant passage (XPh §§4–6) as follows:

Proclaims Xerxes the King: When I became king, there was among the lands/peoples inscribed above one that was seething (in rebellion). Then the Wise Lord bore me aid. By the Wise Lord's will, I smote that land/people and set it in place. And among these lands/peoples there was one where formerly demons were worshipped. Then, by the Wise Lord's will, I demolished that demon temple. And I ordered that the demons not be worshipped there, where formerly demons were worshipped. There I worshipped the Wise Lord at the proper time and in the proper ritual style. And there were more that were ill-done; these I made good. That which I did, I did all of it by the Wise Lord's will. The Wise Lord bore me aid until I did what was done.

yaθā taya adam xšāyaθiya abavam, asti antar aitā dahyāva, tayai upari nīpištā, ayauda; pasāvamai Auramazdā upastām abara. vašnā Auramazdahā avām dahyāvam adam ajanam utašim gāθavā nīšādayam. utā antar aitā dahyāva āha, yadātaya paruvam daivā ayadiya; pasava vašnā Auramazdahā adam avam daivadānam viyakanam utā patiyazbayam: "daivā mā yadiyaiša"; yadāyadā paruvam daivā ayadiya. avadā adam Auramazdām ayadai ṛtācā brazmanīya; utā anīyašci āha, taya duškṛtam akariya, ava adam naibam akunavam; aita taya adam akunavam, visam vašnā Auramazdahā akunavam; Auramazdāmai upastām abara, yātā kṛtam akunavam.

This and subsequent Old Persian texts are taken from Rüdiger Schmitt, *Die altper-sischen Inschriften der Achaimeniden* (Wiesbaden: Reichert, 2009). Translations are original.

50. See, for example, a passage from one of Darius's inscriptions at Susa (DSe §4):

> Proclaims Darius the King: Much that was ill-done, I made good. The lands/peoples were seething (in rebellion), one smote the other. This I did by the Wise Lord's will, so that one does not smite the other any more. Each one is in place. My law—of that they feel fear, so that he who is stronger does not smite, does not destroy him who is weak.

> θāti Dārayavauš XŠ: vasai taya duškr̥tam āha, ava naibam akunavam; dahyāva ayauda; aniya aniyam aja; ava adam akunavam vašnā Auramazdāhā, yaθā aniya aniyam nai janti cinā, gāθavā kašci asti: dātam, taya manā, hacā avanā tr̥santi, yaθā haya tauvīyā tayam skauθim nai janti nai vimr̥dati.

I have treated the religious bases of Achaemenian imperialism more thoroughly in *Religion, Empire, and Torture: The Case of Achaemenian Persia; With an Appendix on Abu Ghraib* (Chicago: University of Chicago Press, 2007) and "*Happiness for Mankind*": *Achaemenian Religion and the Imperial Project* (Leuven: Peeters, Acta Iranica vol. 53, forthcoming).

51. Such lists are found at *Vīdēvdāt* 10.9–17, 19.40–47; *Yašt* 3.5–17; *Greater Bundahišn* 5.1–3; *Dādestān ī Dēnīg* 36.31, 36.37–46.

52. I am excluding from consideration the six "chief demons" (*kamālīgān dēwān*) discussed in *Greater Bundahišn* 27.6–12. This set has its own complex history and logic, which has received much discussion. Most recently, see Pirart, pp. 34–55.

53. As regards the whirlwind demon, see Bruce Lincoln, "Cēšmag, the Lie, and the Logic of Zoroastrian Demonology," *Journal of the American Oriental Society* 129 (2009): 45–55.

54. *Dēnkart* 3.271:

> The material existence of demonic evil is the power of nonbeing [*nērōg ī anast*] and invisibility, like darkness. And the material dissemination of evil will be permitted in the semblance of material existence, in the power of good, and in the creation itself.

> ud wattarīh druzīg u-š gētīg stī nērōg ī anast ud apaydāgīh ciyōn tārīgīh. ud wattarīh rawāgīh gētīgīhā pad hāwandīh gētīg stī nērōg ī ud wehīh ud dām xwēš ud hilēh.

CHAPTER FIVE

"Anomaly, Science, and Religion" was originally presented at a miniconference on Ira-nian religions organized by the University of Chicago Divinity School (May 2007), and first published in *History of Religions* 49 (2009): 270–83. Reprinted by permission.

1. This narrative has been recounted endlessly, always in heroic fashion and always as a hallmark of the rupture between science and religion, reason and faith, individual genius and church authority, the modern and the medieval. Among recent retellings, note, for instance, Elizabeth Spiller, *Science, Reading, and Renaissance Literature: The Art of Making Knowledge, 1580–1670* (Cambridge: Cambridge University Press, 2004), Kitty Ferguson, *The Nobleman and His Housedog: Tycho Brahe and Johannes Kepler; The Strange Partnership That Revolutionized Science* (London: Review, 2002), Juan Luis Garcia Hour-cade, *La rebellion de los astónomos: Copérnico y Kepler* (Madrid: Nivola Libros Ediciones, 2000), John Robert Christianson, *On Tycho's Island: Tycho Brahe and His Assistants,*

1570–1601 (Cambridge: Cambridge University Press, 2000), Job Kozhamthadam, *The Discovery of Kepler's Laws: The Interaction of Science, Philosophy, and Religion* (Notre Dame, IN: University of Notre Dame Press, 1994), Owen Gingrich, *The Eye of Heaven: Ptolemy, Copernicus, Kepler* (New York: American Institute of Physics, 1993), Henriette Chardak, *Kepler, le chien des étoiles* (Paris: Librairie Séguier, 1989), and Edward Rosen, *Three Imperial Mathematicians: Kepler Trapped between Tycho Brahe and Ursus* (New York: Abaris Books, 1986). For less conventional variants and attempts to spice up the familiar story, see Joshua Gilder and Anne-Lee Gilder, *Heavenly Intrigue: Johannes Kepler, Tycho Brahe, and the Murder behind One of History's Greatest Scientific Discoveries* (New York: Doubleday, 2004), and James A. Connor, *Kepler's Witch: An Astronomer's Discovery of Cosmic Order amid Religious War, Political Intrigue, and the Heresy Trial of his Mother* (San Francisco: Harper San Francisco, 2004).

2. Thomas S. Kuhn, *The Structure of Scientific Revolutions* (Chicago: University of Chicago Press, 1962; 2nd ed. 1970; 3rd ed. 1996).

3. For a general summary, see Ch. Brunner, "Astronomy and Astrology in the Sassanian Period," *Encyclopaedia Iranica* (London: Routledege & Kegan Paul, 1987), 2:862–68, esp. p. 867.

4. For Copernicus's use of Islamic astronomical sources, see George Saliba, *Islamic Science and the Making of the European Renaissance* (Cambridge, MA: MIT Press, 2007), which also contains a superb discussion of the way Islamic cosmologists struggled to account for planetary motion.

5. *Yasna* 2.11, 3.13, 4.16, 7.13; *Yašt* 10.145, 12.25; and *Vīdēvdāt* 2.40, 7.52 list these realms in ascending order (stars, moon, sun); *Yašt* 13.16 and *Vīdēvdāt* 9.41 move from the top down (sun, moon, stars), but the picture is the same in either case. The only relevant passage of the Older Avesta (*Yasna* 44.3) shows neither of these patterns, but first names "the path of sun and stars" (*xvə̄ṇg strə̄mca . . . aduuānəm*), then speaks of the moon and its phases (*kə yā må uxšiieiti nərəfsaiti*). The fullest discussion of this system and its historic origins is Antonio Panaino, "Uranographia Iranica I: The Three Heavens in the Zoroastrian Tradition and the Mesopotamian Background," in *Au Carrefour des religions: Mélanges offerts à Philippe Gignoux*, ed. Rike Gyselen (Paris: Groupe pour l'Étude de la Civilisation du Moyen-Orient, 1995), pp. 205–25.

6. Thus *Yasna* 1.11, 1.16, 71.9; *Vīdēvdāt* 11.1–2, 11.10.

7. *Yašt* 12.29–35, which lists in ascending order (1) stars that contain the seeds of water, (2) stars that contain the seeds of earth , (3) stars that contain the seeds of plants, (4) stars that contain the Good Mind, (5) the moon, which contains the seeds of cattle, (6) the sun, possessed of swift horses, (7) the Endless Lights, (8) the Best Existence, and (9) the House of Song.

8. Panaino, "The Three Heavens in the Zoroastrian Tradition," p. 210 et passim.

9. *Yašt* 13.57:

> ašāunąm . . . yazamaide
> yå strąm måŋhō hūrō
> anaγranąm raocaŋąm
> paθō daēsaiiən ašaonīš
> yōi para ahmāt hame gātuuō darəyəm
> hištənta afrašīmantō
> daēuuanąm parō tbaēšaŋhat
> daēuuanąm parō draomōhu.

āat tē nūra̦m frauuazənti
dūraēuruuaēsəm aδuuanō uruuaēsəm nāšəmna
yim frašō.kərətōit vaŋhuiiå.

This and subsequent Avestan texts are taken from Karl F. Geldner, ed., *Avesta: The Sacred Books of the Parsis*, 3 vols. (Stuttgart: W. Kohlhammer, 1886–96). All translations are original.

Cf. *Greater Bundahišn* 2.19:

> Until the coming of the Adversary's Assault, the moon, sun, and stars stood still and did not move. Time ever passed in pure fashion [*abēzagīhā*] and it was always noon. Then, from the coming of the Adversary's Assault, they were set in motion (which will continue) until the End.

tā madan ī ēbgat māh ud xwaršēd ud awešān stāragān estād nē raft hēnd abēzagīhā zamān hamē widard ud hamwār nēmrōz būd. pas az madan ī ēbgat ō rawišn estād hēnd ud tā frazām.

This and subsequent texts from the *Greater Bundahišn* are taken from Fazlollah Pakzad, ed., *Bundahišn: Zoroastrische Kosmogonie und Kosmologie; Band I: Kritische Edition* (Tehran: Centre for the Great Islamic Encyclopaedia, 2005). All translations from the Pahlavi are original.

10. In Avestan texts, "infinite time" appears at *Vīdēvdāt* 19.9, and "long time" at *Yašt* 13.53, 19.26; *Yasna* 62.3. The two are set in contrast at *Yasna* 72.10; *Vīdēvdāt* 19.13; and *Nyayiš* 1.8, although in these passages, finite historic time is designated "time of the long dominion" (*zruuān darəγō.xvaδāta*).

11. *Yašt* 8.44: "ratūm paiti.daēmca vīspaēša̦m stāra̦m."

12. *Yašt* 8.8:

> Tištrīm stārəm raēuuantəm
> xvarənaŋuhatəm yazamaide
> yō pairikå tauruuaiieiti
> yō pairikå titāraiieiti
> yå stārō kərəmå patanti
> antarə za̦m asmanəmca.

13. Antonio Panaino, *Tištrya* (Rome: Istituto Italiano per il Medio ed Estremo Oriente, 1990–95), 1:97, 2:1, and 19–23.

14. Thus David Pingree, *From Astral Omens to Astrology, from Babylon to Bīkāner* (Rome: Istituto Italiano per l'Africa e l'Oriente, 1997), esp. pp. 39–50; idem, "History of Astronomy in Iran," *Encyclopaedia Iranica* (London: Routledge & Kegan Paul, 1987), 2:858–62, esp. pp. 859–60; idem, "Astronomy and Astrology in India and Iran," *Isis* 54 (1963): 229–46, esp. pp. 241–42; and Otto Neugebauer, "The Transmission of Planetary Theories in Ancient and Medieval Astronomy," *Scripta Mathematica* 22 (1956): 165–92, esp. p. 172.

15. See, for example, Pingree, "Astronomy and Astrology in India and Iran," pp. 241–43; and idem, *From Astral Omens to Astrology*, pp. 39–40.

16. H. W. Bailey, *Zoroastrian Problems in the Ninth-Century Books* (Oxford: Clarendon Press, 1943; 2nd ed., 1971), pp. 147–48.

17. Wilhelm Eilers, "Stern—Planet—Regenbogen," in *Der Orient in der Forschung: Festschrift für Otto Spies*, ed. Wilhelm Hoenerbach (Wiesbaden: Otto Harrassowitz, 1967), pp. 112–16.

18. *Greater Bundahišn* 5A.9–10: "ēn abāxtarān . . . hamāg rāyēnišn ī āwām čiyōn band ō axtarān čiyōn čašm-dīd paydāg wišōbēnd ul frōdēnd ud kast abzōn kunēnd. u-šān rawišn-īz nē čiyōn axtarān čē hast ka tēz hast ī dagrand hast ka abāz rawišn hast ka estādag hēnd." This passage has been much discussed, as has the chapter in which it occurs. Inter alia, see the painstaking philological work of D. N. MacKenzie, "Zoroastrian Astrology in the *Bundahišn*," *Bulletin of the School of Oriental and African Studies* 27 (1964): 511–29.

19. *Greater Bundahišn* 6H.0: "the lying planets," *druzān abāxtarān*.

20. *Greater Bundahišn* 5.4: "the most destructive planets," *murnjēnīdarān abāxtarān*.

21. *Greater Bundahišn* 5A.10: "they are demons," *dēw hēnd*.

22. *Greater Bundahišn* 5A.10: "maker of old age and harm," *zarmānīh ud anāgīh kardār*.

23. *Greater Bundahišn* 5A.10:

This light of [the planets] is revealed to be the same light of Ohrmazdean creatures, in the same manner of evil men who are dressed in brocade garments or like the light in the eyes of vermin.

u-šān ēn rošnīh aziš paydāg ham-rošnīh ī Ohrmazdīg handāzag ī wattarān kē paymōzan ī ⁺dēbāg paymōxt hēnd ciyōn rošnīh andar cašm ī xrafstarān.

Cf. *Škend Gūmanīg Wizār* 4.21–27.

24. *Greater Bundahišn* 5A.3, 27.54; *Škend Gūmanīg Wizār* 4.30.

25. *Mēnōg ī Xrad* 8.17, 8.20.

26. *Škend Gūmanīg Wizār* 4.27: "nē ō xwēškārān arzānīgān bē ō wināhkārān axwēškārān jēhān rōspīgān anarzānīgān baxšēnd ud dahēnd." Cf. *Mēnōg ī Xrad* 12.8–10, conceivably also *Dādestān ī Dēnīg* 36.44.

27. *Greater Bundahišn* 5A.9: "The planets [*abāxtarān*] are thus named 'non-zodiacal constellations [*nē axtar*]'" (u-šān abāxtarān namīh ēd kū nē axtar hēnd).

28. *Škend Gūmanīg Wizār* 4.7: "bagān ī nēkīh baxtārān." Cf. *Mēnōg ī Xrad* 8.17, 12.8–10; *Škend Gūmanīg Wizār* 4.5–10. The opposition of planets and zodiacal constellations is thematized at *Mēnōg ī Xrad* 8.17–21, 12.7; *Greater Bundahišn* 4.27, 5.4, 5A.3, 5A.9, 6H.

29. As the name of a cardinal direction, Pahlavi *abāxtar* derives from Avestan *apāxtara-*, on which see Christian Bartholomae, *Altiranisches Wörterbuch*, reprint ed. (Berlin: Walter de Gruyter, 1961; original 1904), cols. 79–80, and texts like *Vīdēvdāt* 19.1: "From the northern side, from the northern regions, the Evil Spirit scurried forth, he of many deaths, the demon of all demons" (apāxtarat haca naēmāt apāxtaraēibiiō haca naēmaēibiiō fraduuarat aŋrō mainiiuš pouru.mahrkō daēuuanąm daēuuō). Cf. *Hadoxt Nask* 2.25; *Vīdēvdāt* 7.2, 8.16; and such Pahlavi texts as *Selections of Zād Spram* 30.48, 30.51; *Dādestān ī Dēnīg* 24.5, 32.6; *Pahlavi Rivāyat Accompanying the Dādestān ī Dēnīg* 31a2, 31c8, 45.1, 58.63; *Supplementary Texts to the Šāyest nē-Šāyest* 12.18, 14.2; *Ardā Wirāz Nāmag* 22.20–23.2.

30. *Mēnōg ī Xrad* 8.17–21:

harw nēkīh ud juttarīh ī ō mardōmān ud ⁺abārīg-īz dāmān rasēd pad 7-ān ud 12-ān rasēd. 12 axtar ciyōn pad dēn 12 spāhbēd ī az kustag ī Ohrmazd ān 7 abāxtar 7 spāhbēd ī az kustag ī Ahreman guft estēd. ud harwisp dām ud dahišn ōy 7 abāxtarān tarwēnēnd ud ō margīh ud harw anāgīh abespārēnēnd. ud ciyōn awēšān 12 axt[arān] ud 7 abāxtar[ān] brēhēnāg ud rāyēnāg ī <ud rāyēnāg ī> gēhān hēnd.

Cf. *Mēnōg ī Xrad* 12.4–10.

31. *Mēnōg ī Xrad* 12.7:

Then the Evil Spirit created the seven planets that are said to be like generals of the Evil Spirit, to take and destroy that goodness from the Wise Lord's creatures by assault on the sun, moon, and twelve zodiacal constellations.

ud pas Ahreman ān 7 abāxtar ciyōn 7 spāhbed ī Ahreman guft estēd pad wišuft bē stadan ān nēkīh az dāmān ī Ohrmazd pad petyāragīh ī mihr ud māh ud awēšān 12 axtarān dād.

Cf. *Greater Bundahišn* 4.27. The verb *dwāristan* is regularly used of Ahriman, as, for instance, in descriptions of his motion toward Ohrmazd's creation, when he launched his primordial assault. Thus *Greater Bundahišn* 4.10; *Dēnkart* 5.24.3; *Selections of Zād Spram* 3.7.

32. *Yašt* 8.8: "pairikå . . . yå stārō kərəmå patanti antarə zạm asmanəmca."

33. *Škend Gūmanīg Wizār* 4.9–10:

The seven stars and the witches-cum-shooting stars [*parīgān*] who slither [*dwarēnd*] beneath them are thieves who distribute in antagonistic fashion. The religion names them sorcerors [*yadūgān*].

haftān stār karbān parīgān ī azēr awēšān dwārēnd appurdārān ī jud-baxtārān kē-šān dēnīg nām yadūgān.

Cf. *Greater Bundahišn* 5.4, 5A.6–7, 27.54.

34. The basic cosmology is sketched out in *Greater Bundahišn* 1.1–5.

It is revealed thus in the good religion: Ohrmazd is highest in omniscience and goodness, for infinite time always exists in the light. That light is the seat and place of Ohrmazd, which one calls "Endless Light." Omniscience and goodness exist in infinite time, just as Ohrmazd, his place and religion exist in the time of Ohrmazd. Ahriman exists in darkness, with total ignorance and love of destruction, in the depths. His crude love of destruction and that place of darkness are what one calls "Endless Darkness." Between them a Void existed.

pad weh dēn owōn paydāg kū Ohrmazd bālistīg pad harwisp āgāhīh ud wehīh zamān ī akanārag andar rōšnīh hamē būd. ān rōšnīh gāh ud gyāg ī Ohrmazd hast kē asar rōšnīh gōwēd. ān harwisp āgāhīh ud wehīh ud zamān ī akanārag ciyōn Ohrmazd wehīh ud dēn ud zamān i Ohrmazd būd hēnd. Ahreman andar tārigīh pad pas-dānišnīh ud zadār-kāmagīh zofr-pāyag būd. u-š zadār-kāmagīh xām ud ān tārigīh gyāg hast kē asar tārigīh gōwēd. u-šān mayān tuhīgīh būd hast.

35. Three texts preserve different versions of this story. The relations among the variants are as follows:

Selections of Zād Spram 1.31–33	*Greater Bundahišn* 4.10	*Škend Gūmanīg Wizār* 4.16
At the same time the Evil Spirit, together with his associated powers, came to the star station. *pad ham zamān Ahreman az ham-zōrān hammis bē ō star pāyag āmad.*	Then the Evil Spirit, together with powerful demons, rose up against the lights. *pas āxist Gannag Mēnōg abāg hamist dēwān abzārān ō padīrag ī rōšnān.*	as the Lie leapt toward his lights *ciyōn-iš ōy druz ō rōšnān frazast*

(*continued*)

Selections of Zād Spram 1.31–33	Greater Bundahišn 4.10	Škēnd Gūmanīg Wizār 4.16
	He saw the sky, which was shown to him spiritually, even if it was still not created in bodily/material fashion. *u-š ān asmān dīd ī-šān mēnōgīhā nimūd ka nē astōmand dād estēd.*	
The base of the sky is kept in the star station. *bun ī asmān ī pad star pāyag +dāšt.*	Enviously and desirously, he attacked the sky, which stood in the star station. *arēšk kāmagīha tag abar kard. asmān pad star pāyag estād.*	
He pulled it out from there to the void, outside the foundation of the lights and darknesses, *az anōh frōd ō tuhīgīh āhixt ī +bērōn ī buništ ī rōšnān ud tārān*	He led it down to the void, which, as I wrote at the beginning, was between the foundation of the lights and the darknesses. *frōd ō tuhīgīh hāxt ī-m pad bun nipišt kū andarag ī buništag ī rōšnān ud tomīgān būd*	
to the place of battle, where there is the motion of both. *ud gyāg ī ardīg kē-š tazišn ī harw dōān pad-iš.*		
And that darkness he kept with himself; he brought that to the sky. *u-š tārīgīh ī abāg xwēš +dāšt andar ō asmān āwurd.*		and he was ensnared, so that all his powers and instruments, sins and lies of many species, are not left to pursue individually the accomplishment of their own desire, they are mixed with the material existence of the lights, *ud pēcīd adag-iš hamāg zōrān abzārān āšan bazagān druzān ī was-sardag jud-jud pad xwēš kāmišnkārīh nē hištan rāy hast ī ō gētīh ī rōšnān gumēxtag*
The sky was pulled so far into darkness that within the vault of the sky, just one third reached above the star station. *asmān ōwōn ō tom āhixt kū andarōn ī aškōb ī asmān cand se ēk-ē azabar star pāyag bē rasēd.*	He stood as if one third above the star station, from inside the sky. *owōn kū abar azabar ī star pāyag az andarōn ī asmān tā se ēk-ē(w) be estād.*	

36. Most fully on the theory of celestial cords and its historic diffusion, see Antonio Panaino, *Tessere il Cielo: Considerazioni sulle Tavole astronomiche, gli Oroscopi, e la Dottrina dei Legamenti tra Induismo, Zoroastrismo, Manicheismo e Mandeismo* (Rome: Istituto Italiano per l'Africa e l'Oriente, 1998).

37. *Škēnd Gūmanīg Wizār* 4.39-44:

ud ēn panj abāxtar dādār Ohrmazd xwēš-kāmagīhā nē hištan rāy harw ēk pad dō zīh ō Mihr ud Māh bast estēnd. u-šān frāz-rawišnīh ud abāz-rawišnīh az ham cim, hast kē-š drahnāy ī ān ī drāztar ciyōn Kēwān ud Ohrmazd, ud hast ē kāstar ciyōn Tīr ud Anāhīd, harw ka ō abdom ī zīh šawēnd pad pas abāz āhanjēnd. u-šān xwēš-kāmagīhā raftan nē hilēnd.

Cf. *Greater Bundahišn* 5A.6-8, which includes calculations taken directly from Indian sources.

38. On the way revised understandings of natural philosophy as a part of religious discourse paved the way for crucial developments in the history of science, see now Stephen Gaukroger, *The Emergence of a Scientific Culture: Science and the Shaping of Modernity, 1210-1685* (Oxford: Oxford University Press, 2006).

CHAPTER SIX

"Between History and Myth" was originally presented as the keynote for a workshop on the theme "Making Meaning through Myth, East and West," organized by the Department of Asian Studies at Cornell University (July 2010).

1. See above all Raffaele Pettazzoni, "Verità del Mito," *Studi e Materiali di Storia delle Religioni* 21 (1947-48): 104-16, trans. H. J. Rose under the title "The Truth of Myth," in Pettazzoni, *Essays on the History of Religions* (Leiden: E. J. Brill, 1967), pp. 11-23; Mircea Eliade, *Le mythe de l'éternel retour* (Paris: Gallimard, 1949), trans. Willard Trask under the title *The Myth of the Eternal Return* (Princeton, NJ: Bollingen Books, 1954); and idem, *Myth and Reality* (New York: Harper Torchbooks, 1963). The rather disappointing correspondence of the two foremost historians of religions of their era has been published by Natale Spineto, *L'histoire des religions a-t-elle un sens? Correspondance, Mircea Eliade et Raffaele Pettazzoni 1926-1959* (Paris: Éditions du Cerf, 1994).

2. See, for instance, Patrick Geary, *The Myth of Nations: The Medieval Origins of Europe* (Oxford: Oxford University Press, 2003); Anthony D. Smith, *Chosen Peoples: Sacred Sources of National Identity* (Oxford: Oxford University Press, 2003); idem, *Myths and Memories of the Nation* (Oxford: Oxford University Press, 1999); and Geoffrey Hosking and George Schöpflin, eds., *Myths and Nationhood* (New York: Routledge, 1997).

3. I treat these materials at greater length in *Between History and Myth: Stories of Harald "Fairhair" and the Founding of the State* (forthcoming).

4. On the Kings' Sagas in general, see Theodore M. Andersson, "Kings' Sagas," in *Old Norse-Icelandic Literature: A Critical Guide*, ed. Carol Clover and John Lindow (Ithaca, NY: Cornell University Press, 1985), pp. 197-238. The best general overview of *Heimskringla* and its importance is Diana Whaley, *Heimskringla: An Introduction* (London: Viking Society for Northern Research, 1991).

5. *Ágrip* 2:

Haraldr tók eftir Hálfdan ríki þat er faðir hans hafði haft, ok aflaði sér meira ríkis með þeim hætti—er maðrinn var snemma rǫskr ok risuligr vexti—at hann helt orrostu við næsta konunga ok sigraði alla, ok eignaðisk hann fyrstr konunga einn Nóreg á tvítøgs aldri.

This and susbsequent *Ágrip* texts are taken from M. J. Driscoll, *Ágrip af Nóregskonunga sǫgum* (London: Viking Society for Northern Research, 1995). All translations are original. As regards dating and provenance of the text, see pp. ix–xii.

6. *Historia Norwegiæ* 11: "De hoc memorantur multa et mirabilia, quæ nunc longum est narrare per singula." For dating and provenance of the text, see now Lars Boje Mortensen, in Inger Ekrem and Lars Boje Mortensen, eds., *Historia Norwegie*, trans. Peter Fisher (Copenhagen: Museum Tusculanum Press, 2003), pp. 11–24.

7. Theodricus Monachus, *Historia de Antiquitate Regum Norwagiensum* 1:

> Hunc numerum annorum Domini, investigatum prout diligentissime potuimus ab illis, quos nos vulgato nomine Islendinga vocamus, in hoc loco posuimus: quos constat sine ulla dubitatione præ omnibus aquilonaribus populis in hujusmodi semper et peritiores et curiosiores extitisse.

On dating the text and the identity of the author, see Peter Foote, introduction to David and Ian McDougall, trans., *Theodoricus Monachus: Historia de Antiquitate Regum Norwagiensium; An Account of the Ancient History of the Norwegian Kings* (London: Viking Society for Northern Research, 1998), pp. ix–xiii. The text is found in Gustav Storm, ed., *Monumenta Historica Norvegæ: Latinske Kildeskrifter til Norges Historie in Middelalderen* (Christiana [Oslo]: A.W. Brøgger, 1880).

8. The body of legend surrounding Harald has been discussed by Jan de Vries, "Harald Schönhaar in Sage und Geschichte," *Beiträge zur Geschichte der deutschen Sprache* 66 (1942): 55–116; and Gert Kreutzer, "Das Bild Harald Schönhaars in der altisländischen Literatur," in *Studien zum Altgermanischen: Festschrift für Heinrich Beck*, ed. Heiko Uecker (Berlin: Walter de Gruyter, 1994), pp. 443–61.

9. *Fagrskinna* 3 (from the B-Text) and appendix 3 (from the A-Text). The most recent discussion of the text is Alison Finlay, trans., *Fagrskinna: A Catalogue of the Kings of Norway* (Leiden: E. J. Brill, 2004), pp. 1–39. The standard edition of the text remains Bjarni Einarsson, ed., *Ágrip af Nóregskonunga Sögum [ok] Fagrskinna—Nóregs Konunga Tal* (Rejkhavík: Íslenzka Fornritafélag, 1984).

10. These are Harald Fairhair's Saga 4 (from Snorri's *Heimskringla*), Egil's Saga 3, Greater Saga of Olaf Tryggvason 2 (included in *Flateyjarbók* 1.40), and the "Tale of Harald Fairhair" ("þáttr Haralds hárfagra," included in *Flateyjarbók* 1.569).

11. Cf. Harald Fairhair's Saga 3 (from *Heimskringla*) and Greater Saga of Olaf Tryggvason 2 (in *Flateyjarbók* 1.39–40), which resemble each other so closely that it is generally assumed that the latter relies on the former. The variant in the "Tale of Harald Fairhair" 3 (in *Flateyjarbók* 1.569) is extremely short and identifies itself as an abbreviation of the variant from the Saga of Olaf Tryggvason.

12. Harald Fairhair's Saga 18 (cf. *Flateyjarbók* 1.573). Gyða's father is first identified at Harald Fairhair's Saga 3.

13. Harald Fairhair's Saga 20–21 (cf. *Flateyjarbók* 1.42 and 1.575–76).

14. *Fagrskinna*, appendix 3 (= chapters 15–17 in the A-Text, as first edited by Peter Andreas Munch and Carl Rikard Unger, *Fagrskinna: Kortfattet Norsk Konge-Saga* (Christiana [Oslo]: P. T. Malling, 1847), pp. 10–11.

15. A tabular comparison of the two variants is extremely revealing.

	A. Harald Fairhair's Saga	B. *Fagrskinna*, appendix 3 (from the A-Text)
1	King Harald sent his men after a maiden named Gyða . . . *Haraldr konungr sendi menn sína eptir meyju einni, er Gyða er nefnd . . .*	Harald fell greatly in love with Ragna. *En Haraldr lagði elsku mikla á Rǫgnu.*
2	Harald wanted to take her as his concubine . . . *er hann vildi taka til frillu sér . . .* (Cf. B6)	
3	But when the messengers came there and presented their message to the young woman, *en er sendimenn kómu þar, þá báru þeir upp erendi sín fyrir meyna,*	But when he let his words of love to Ragna be known, *En þá er Haraldr lét ástaryrði sín í ljós við Rǫgnu,*
4	she answered in this manner. *hon svaraði á þessa lund.*	she answered in this manner: *svaraði hón á þessa lund:*
5		"I say this surely in truth, that I could have no better sweetheart than you. This is because of both your kingly birth and all the kingly rank and beauty that are yours. But before I give my full love to you, I would like to know this: Who shall be the heir of your kinsman Nerið the Wise in Council—you, lord King, or Gandalf's sons?" *"Þat mæli ek víst með sannyndum, at eigi em ek betra unnusta verð en þér eruð. Veldr því hvárttveggja konunglig byrð yður ok svá ǫll konunglig tign ok fegrð, er á yðr er. En þó áðr en ek fella fulla ást til yðar, þá vil ek þess verða vǫr, hvárt heldr skulu verða arfar Neriðs ens ráðspaka, frænda yðvars, herra konungr, þér eða synir Gandálfs."*
6		Then Harald answered angrily and said, "I thought, Ragna, that you would be led to my bed with great honor for the sake of love, but because you have upbraided me with these reproaches, it is now the case that you should be led to my bed as a poor concubine." *Þá svaraði Haraldr reiðr ok mælti svá: "Þat ætlaða ek, Ragna, at þú skyldir fyrir ástar sakar með ágætri sæmð vera leidd til minnar sængr, en fyrir því at þú hefir brugðit mér þessum brigzlum, þá er nú þess vert, at þú sér svá leidd til minnar sængr sem ein fátæk frilla."* (Cf. A2)

(continued)

	A. Harald Fairhair's Saga	B. *Fagrskinna*, appendix 3 (from the A-Text
7		Ragna said this to the King: "Do not be angry, lord King, although we speak playfully and it does not exalt your kingship to contend with women, still less with a small girl like me. Better it is, lord King, to wage war against other kings, who now occupy all the land within. *Þat mælti Ragna við konunginn: "Eigi skulu þér, herra konungr, reiðask við, þó at vér mælim oss gaman ok hæfir þat ekki konungdómi yðrum at brjóta kapp við kvenmenn ok þó allra sízt við meybǫrn smá, sem ek em, heldr er yður sæmð þat, herra konungr, at deila kappi við konunga aðra, er nú skipaðir um allt land innan.*
8	She was not going to waste her maidenhood in order to take a man who, as king, has no more realms than a few districts to manage. *at eigi vill hon spilla meydómi sínum, til þess at taka til mannz þann konung, er eigi hefir meira ríki, en nǫkkur fylki, til forráða.*	And I want to tell you this, if I had my own way, I would neither be your concubine, nor that of any other man. *Þat vil ek ok segja yðr, ef ek ræð mér sjálf, þá verð ek hvártki yður frilla né einskis manns annars.*
9	"But it seems extraordinary to me," she said, "that there is no king who wants to take possession of Norway and to be sole ruler over it, like King Gorm in Denmark or Eirik in Uppsala." *"en þat þykki mér undarligt, segir hon, er engi er sá konungr, er svá vill eignask Nóreg ok vera einvaldi yfir, sem hefir Gormr konungr at Danmǫrku eða Eiríkr at Upsǫlum."*	I would have that man who will make all Norway's men his subjects or I shall have no one at all." *ok annat hvárt skal ek hafa þann at eignum manni, er alla Nóregs menn gørir sér at þegnum eða skal ek engan hafa."*
10	... The messengers now went to King Harald and told him the maiden's words ... *... Sendimenn fara nú aptr til Haraldz konungs ok segja honum þessi orð meyjarinnar ok telja ...*	
11	And then he said: "This vow I swear and I call on God to witness it, he who created me and rules over all. *ok enn mælti hann: "þess strengi ek heit, ok því skýt ek til guðs, þess er mik skóp ok ǫllu ræðr.*	When King Harald heard this speech, he straightaway swore an oath, swearing on his head, *Þá er Haraldr konungr heyrði þessi orð, þá strengði hann þegar heit ok sór við hǫfuð sitt,*

	A. Harald Fairhair's Saga	B. *Fagrskinna*, appendix 3 (from the A-Text
12		that he would have no wife in Norway, save Ragna, although with this stake *at hann skyldi enga eigna konu eiga í Nóregi nema Rǫgnu ok þó með þeim hætti*
13	Never shall I cut or comb my hair, until I have taken possession of all Norway, with its tributes and taxes and administration, or otherwise to die." *at aldri skal skera hár mitt né kemba, fyrr en ek hefi eignazk allan Nóreg með skǫttum ok skyldum ok forráði, en deyja at ǫðrum kosti."*	—that he would make all men in Norway his subjects. *at hann gǫrði alla menn at þegnum sér í Nóregi.*
14		He also let that follow, that a woman who has so manly a speech in her mouth as Ragna deserved to have a noble king rather than some district ruler. *Þat lét hann auk fylgja, at sú kona var verðari at eiga ágætan konung heldr en einhvern heraðs hǫlð, er svá skǫrulig orð hefir í munni sér sem Ragna.*

16. Chapter 1: "Harald Haarfagr."

17. Chapter 5: "The Story of the Norse-Kings."

18. Edward Everett Hale et al., eds., *The Young Folks Treasury*, vol. 2, *Myths and Legendary Heroes* (New York: University Society, 1909), pp. 396–98.

19. Jennie Hall, "Gyda's Saucy Message," from Jennie Hall, *Viking Tales* (Chicago: Rand McNally, 1902), at the website A Celebration of Women Writers,; online at http://digital.library.upenn.edu/women/hall/viking/viking-IX.html (accessed June 8, 2011).

20. *Alt for Gyda og Litt for Norge* (*All for Gyða and Little for Norway*, a production of the Brage Theater, Drammen, Norway); online at http://www.brageteatret.no/alt_for_gyda_og_litt_for_norge (accessed June 8, 2011).

21. *Hårfagre: Et musikkspill om Harald* (*Fairhair: A Musical Comedy about Harald*, book and lyrics by Jan Petersen); online at http://www.harfagre.com/content.aspx?page=10893 (accessed June 8, 2011).

22. Sandra Hill, *The Blue Viking*; online at http://www.sandrahill.net/blueviking excerpt.html (accessed June 8, 2011); Sandra Hill, *The Reluctant Viking*; online at http://www.wattpad.com/215360?p=42 (accessed June 8, 2011).

23. *Gyda på Kvie* (*Gyða at Kvie*, a summer production for schoolchildren); online at http://www.kvien.no/html/kvien/gyda/gyda.htm (accessed June 8, 2011).

24. A tableau of Harald and Gyða appears in the entry hall of the Nordvegen History Centre in Avaldsnes, which claims to be the original site of Harald's kingdom; see http://en.vikingkings.com/PortalDefault.aspx?portalID=116&activeTabID=825&parentActiveTabID=824 (accessed June 8, 2011). For further information on the excavations and museum at Avaldsnes, see "Culture Residence of the First King of Norway Found," online at http://www.bitsofnews.com/content/view/4436/42/ (accessed June 8, 2011).

25. "Age of Kings, Heaven: 'Gyda's Challenge'"; online at http://aok.heavengames

.com/features/blacksmith-features/gydas-challenge/ (accessed June 8, 2011); "Total War Center: 'Fallen Sword'"; online at http://www.twcenter.net/forums/showthread .php?t=205761 (accessed June 8, 2011).

26. *Lørdags Barnetimen: Harald Hårfagre* (*Friday's Children's Time: Harald Hairfair*, text of a radio drama broadcast in 2007 by Norwegian Public Radio [NRK]); online at http://fil.nrk.no/programmer/radio/lordags__barnetimen/1.3207858 (accessed June 8, 2011).

27. Rebellion, "Harald Harfager"; song lyrics online at http://www.kovideo.net/ harald-harfager-lyrics-rebellion-623918.html (accessed June 8, 2011).

28. "Harald Hårfagres saga" ("Harald Fairhair's Saga," instructional materials developed for the Avaldsnes Primary School; online at http://www.karmoyped.no/ sagaoya/bakgrunn/Harald.html [accessed June 8, 2011]).

29. "My Little Norway: Discover the Kingdom of the North," online at http:// mylittlenorway.com/2008/08/how-norway-become-a-country-in-love-and-folklore/ (accessed June 8, 2011).

30. "How Norway Became a Country—in Love and Folklore" (http://mylittle norway.com/2008/08/how-norway-become-a-country-in-love-and-folklore/ [accessed June 8, 2011]); "The Most Important Fact in My Country's History—Norway" (http://one-at-all.blogspot.com/2006/11/most-important-fact-in-my-countrys_11 .html [accessed July 5, 2010]).

CHAPTER SEVEN

"Poetic, Royal, and Female Discourse" was orginally published in *Métis* 5 (2007): 205–20. Reprinted by permission.

1. *Theogony* 81–84:

> Whenever the daughters of great Zeus observe
> And honor the birth of a king reared by Zeus,
> They pour sweet dew [γλυκερήν . . . ἐέρσην] on his tongue
> And soothing words [ἔπε᾽ . . . μείλιχα] flow from his mouth.

This and subsequent texts are taken from M. L. West, ed., *Hesiod, Theogony* (Oxford: Clarendon Press, 1966). All translations are original.

2. See, for instance, the rather loosely structured discussion of West, *Hesiod, Theogony*, p. 183, which starts by acknowledging that ἐέρση denotes "any liquid distilled from heaven," then devotes all its attention to traditions relating honey to speech, including Philostratos, *Heroicus* 19.19; the *Homeric Hymn to Hermes* 558ff.; Pindar, frag. 152 (Bowra); Pausanias 9.23.2; Virgil, *Georgic* 4.1; Ezekiel 3:3; and Old Norse traditions concerning the "mead of poetry." The scholion to this line reads: "ἐέρση: literally, 'dew'; metaphorically, 'honey'" ἐέρση · ἡ δρόσος κυρίως · νῦν δὲ μεταφορικῶς τὸ μέλι. Hans Flach, *Glossen und Scholien zur hesiodischen Theogonie* (Leipzig: B. G. Teubner, 1876; reprint ed. Osnabrück, 1970), p. 216. For their part, the ancient lexicographers gloss ἐέρση as δρόσος, "dew" (thus both Apollonius the Sophist and Hesychius).

3. Deborah Boedeker, *Descent from Heaven: Images of Dew in Greek Poetry and Religion* (Chico, CA: Scholars Press, 1984). For her discussion of the relations between dew and honey, see pp. 46–49 and 84–88.

4. Ibid., 80–99; Marilyn B. Arthur, "The Dream of a World without Women: Poetics and the Circles of Order in the *Theogony* Prooemium," *Arethusa* 16 (1983): 97–135.

5. On these myths and associations, see Bruce Lincoln, *Myth, Cosmos, and Society: Indo-European Themes of Creation and Destruction* (Cambridge, MA: Harvard University Press, 1986). I have since come to understand them as much more widely diffused, and not limited to any linguistic, ethnic, or social group, the category of "Indo-European" being particularly problematic. For my most recent reflections on these materials and their locus, see "Hegelian Meditations on 'Indo-European' Myths," *Papers from the Mediterranean Ethnographic Summer Seminar* 5 (2003): 59–76.

6. Consider, for example, the *Greater Bundahišn* 28.4, an Iranian text in which blood is homologized to water, veins to rivers, and the belly (together with its gastric juices) to the ocean.

7. See, for instance, two anthropogonic texts in Old English, the *Rituale Ecclesiae Dunelmensis* and the "Dialogue of Solomon and Saturn," discussed in Lincoln, *Myth, Cosmos, and Society*, pp. 17 and 178.

8. Thus *Iliad* 14.346–51:

> The son of Cronus seized his wife in his arms.
> And beneath them the earth grew fresh grass,
> Dewy lotus, crocus, and hyacinth,
> Thick and soft, which stays up high, off the earth.
> They lay down there and were clothed in nothing but a cloud—
> A beautiful, golden cloud. And it dripped glistening dew [στιλπναὶ ἔερσαι] down
> on them.

This and subsequent translated passages from the *Iliad* are quoted from A. T. Murray, ed., *Homer: The Iliad* (London: William Heinemann, 1971).

On the frequent erotic associations of dew, in association with semen and other sexual fluids, see Boedecker, *Descent from Heaven*, 2–4, 11–20, 54–60; and W. M. Clarke, "The God in the Dew," *L'antiquité classique* 43 (1974): 57–73.

9. Thus the Slavic anthropogony of 2 Enoch 8–9, and the Rumanian "Questions and Answers," on which see Lincoln, *Myth, Cosmos, and Society*, pp. 11, 15, 17. Note also *Iliad* 11.52–54: "Zeus, son of Cronus, stirred up an evil panic and down from the heavens, he let fall dewdrops dripping with blood [ἐέρσας αἵματι μυδαλέας] from the aither." See further Boedeker, *Descent from Heaven*, 73–77.

10. Thus *Iliad* 24.419 and 757, where the miraculously preserved body of Hektor is "dewy."

11. Thus the Old Norse tradition, as attested in *Vafthruðnismál* 14, *Helgakviða Hjörvarðsson* 29, *Gylfaginning* 10.

12. Notwithstanding the excellence of her analysis, Boedeker misses this association with saliva. This is a consequence of the excessive value she attaches to the derivation of Greek ἔέρση from Indo-European **wers-*, which leads her to view the symbolic associations of dew to rain, fructifying fluids, and processes of generation as primary, from which most other associations are extensions of one sort or another. Alternatively, I would suggest that dew—denoted by terms of whatever etymology—was consistently available for homologic association with a wide variety of bodily fluids. Semen, to be sure, is among the most important, but the others, saliva included, are in no way secondary or derivative.

13. *Theogony* 83–84. A direct etymological connection of μείλιχος, "soothing," to μέλι, "honey," is possible but unlikely, given the difference in the initial vowels. From an early date, however, the two were constantly associated via folk interpretations.

See further Pierre Chantraine, "Grec μελίχος," in *Mélanges Émile Boisacq* (Brussels: Institut de philologie et d'histoire orientales et slaves, 1937), 1:169ff.

14. *Theogony* 84–87 describes this process. Note also *Iliad* 1.249, where Nestor is credited with "speech that flows sweeter than honey from his tongue." In the passage that follows, however, this master of royal oratory is unable to calm the anger of Achilles and Agamemnon. The scene thus serves to establish that there are limits to the power of royal speech while also underscoring the enormity of this quarrel.

15. The strongly marked difference in the way kingship is treated in the two Hesiodic texts has frequently been noted. For a recent discussion, which recognizes the extended analogy

> *Theogony* 80–92: *Works and Days* 248–64
> :: Ideal: Actual
> :: Golden Age: Iron Age

see Sabrina Salis, "Le due facce del βασιλεύς in Esiodo: Alcune Osservazioni," *Annali della Facoltà di Lettere e Filosofia dell' Università di Cagliari* 20 (2002): 97–107.

16. *Works and Days* 709.

17. Ibid., 320–24.

18. The account of poets (*Theogony* 94–103) follows that of kings (80–93) and resonates with Hesiod's earlier description of his own *Dichterweihe* (23–34). The relevant literature includes, inter alia, Kathryn Stoddard, "The Programmatic Message of the 'Kings and Singers' Passage: Hesiod, *Theogony*, 80–103," *Transactions of the American Philological Association* 133 (2003): 1–16; Derek Collins, "Hesiod and the Divine Voice of the Muses," *Arethusa* 32 (1999): 241–62; André Laks, "Le double du roi: Remarques sur les antecedents Hésiodiques du philosophe-roi," in *Le métier du mythe: Lectures d'Hésiode*, ed. Fabienne Blaise et al. (Lille, France: Presses Universitaires de Septentrion, 1996), pp. 83–91; Jean Rudhardt, "Le préambule de la *Théogonie*: La vocation du poète; Le langage des Muses," in Blaise, et al., *Le métier du mythe*, pp. 25–40; Francesco Bertolini, "Muse, re e aeidi nel proemio della *Teogonia* di Esiodo," in *Studia Classica Iohanni Tardini oblata*, ed. Luigi Belloni et al. (Milan: Vita e Pensiero, 1995), pp. 127–38; Marie-Christine Leclerc, *La parole chez Hésiode: À la recherché de l'harmonie perdue* (Paris: Les Belles Lettres, 1993); Gregory Nagy, "Authorisation and Authorship in the Hesiodic *Theogony*," *Ramus* 21 (1992): 119–30; Graziano Arrighetti, "Esiodo e le Muse: Il dono della verità e la conquista della parola," *Athenaeum* 80 (1992): 45–63; Claude Calame, "L'ispirazione delle Muse Esiodee: Autenticità o convenzione letteraria?," in *Scrivere e recitare: Modelli di trasmissione del testo poetico nell' antichità e nel medioevo*, ed. Giovanni Cerri (Rome: Edizioni dell' Ateneo, 1986), pp. 85–101; Arthur, "Dream of a World without Women"; Jeffrey M. Duban, "Poets and Kings in the *Theogony* Invocation," *Quaderni Urbinati di Cultura Clasica*, n.s., 4 (1980): 7–21; Heinz Neitzel, "Hesiod und die Lügenden Musen," *Hermes* 108 (1980): 387–401; Pietro Pucci, *Hesiod and the Language of Poetry* (Baltimore: Johns Hopkins University Press, 1977); Jesper Svenbro, *La parole et le marbre: Aux origins de la poétique grecque* (Lund, Sweden: Studentlitteratur, 1976), pp. 46–73; Catharine P. Roth, "The Kings and the Muses in Hesiod's *Theogony*," *Transactions of the American Philological Association* 106 (1976): 331–38; Athanassios Kambylis, *Die Dichterweihe und ihre Symbolik* (Heidelberg: Carl Winter, 1965); and Kurt Latte, "Hesiods Dichterweihe," *Antike und Abendland* 2 (1946): 152–63. Many of these issues are treated more broadly in Gregory Nagy's

rich discussion, "Early Greek Views of Poets and Poetry," in *The Cambridge History of Literary Criticism*, vol. 1, *Classical Criticism*, ed. George A. Kennedy (Cambridge: Cambridge University Press, 1989), pp. 1–77.

19. The formulae read as follows:

Theogony 84: Soothing words [ἔπε' . . . μείλιχα] flow from (the king's) mouth
Theogony 98: Sweet [γλυκερή] is the speech [αὐδή] that flows from (the poet's) mouth
Theogony 39–40: Sweet speech [αὐδή . . . ἡδεῖα] flows inexhaustible (or: effortless, ἀκάματος) / from (the Muses') mouths.

20. *Theogony* 31–32: ἐνέπνευσαν δέ μοι αὐδὴ / θέσπιν.

21. The etymological relation of αὐδή to ἀείδω (to sing, to celebrate with a hymn), ἀοιδός (singer, poet), and ἀηδών (nightingale, literally, the songstress), is discussed in Hjalmar Frisk, *Griechisches etymologisches Wörterbuch* (Heidelberg: Carl Winter 1973), 1:184, and Pierre Chantraine, *Dictionnaire étymologique de la langue grecque* (Paris: Éditions Klincksieck, 1968–80), 1:137. Leclerc, *La parole chez Hésiode*, 45–46, argues persuasively that αὐδή implicitly contains what philosophers will later call λόγος. In contrast, Francesca Berlinzani, "La voce e il canto nel proemio della *Teogonia*," *Acme* 55 (2002): 193–96, is inclined to stress the sonoric beauty of αὐδή that gives it the quality of music and song. Berlinzani denies that αὐδή includes λόγος, while granting it is by its very nature persuasive, a view that strikes me as contradictory. I am thus inclined to view αὐδή as utterances that are strongly marked for both their logical-verbal *and* their aesthetic-musical qualities. Also relevant are Collins, "Hesiod and the Divine Voice of the Muses," and Antonín Bartoněk, "Die Wortparallelen αὐδή und φωνή in der archaischen epischen Sprache," *Sborník Prací Filosofické Fakulty Brněnské University, Rada Archeologicko-Klasická* E4 (1959): 67–74.

22. *Shield of Herakles* 393–97:

Sitting on the green branch, the dark-winged, chirping cicada
Begins to sing to people in summer.
The dew [ἐέρση] is his drink and nourishing food,
All day long and at dawn, he pours out his speech [αὐδή]
In the worst hot weather, when Sirius burns the skin.

The text is from R. Merkelbach and M. L. West, eds., *Hesiodi: Theogonia, Opera et Dies, Scutum* (Oxford: Oxford University Press, 1990). Translation is original.

The cicada's relation to dew, song, nutrition, and mortality is a well-developed theme in Greek myth. See Boedeker, *Descent from Heaven*, pp. 43–46 and 81–84.

23. *Odyssey* 21.411.

24. *Iliad* 15.270 (Apollo, speaking to Hektor), *Odyssey*, 2.297 (Athene to Telemakhos), 4.831 (Athene to Penelope), 14.89 (the suitors [wrongly] believe they have received news of Odysseus's death direct from the speech of a god, θεοῦ . . . αὐδήν). In the formulaic line *Odyssey*, 2.268 = 2.401 = 22.206 = 24.503 = 24.548, Athene impersonates Mentor, taking on the form of his body and the sound of his speech.

25. *Theogony* 31 (Hesiod, inspired by the Muses) and 97 (speech of him whom the Muses love), frag. 64.15 ([Merkelbach and West] the poet-diviner Philammōn, son of Apollo); *Iliad* 19.407 and 418 (Xanthos, inspired by Hera, prophesies Akhilles's death).

26. *Iliad* 19.250 (the herald Talthybios); *Odyssey* 4.160 (the great king Menelaus), 1.371 (the poet Phemios), 9.4 (the poet Demodokos).

27. *Shield of Herakles* 278 (a male chorus sings during a festival); *Odyssey* 10.311 = 10.481 (Odysseus addresses Circe).

28. On the adjective θέσπις, which appears at *Theogony* 32, see Hermann Koller, "ΘΕΣΠΙΣ ΑΟΙΔΟΣ," *Glotta* 43 (1965): 277–85.

29. *Works and Days* 507–8.

30. Those who do such breathing-in are Zeus (*Iliad* 17.456), Apollo (*Iliad* 15.60, 15.262, 20.110), Athene (*Iliad* 10.482; *Odyssey* 24.520), and an unnamed δαίμων (*Odyssey* 9.381, 19.138). Those who receive this in-spiration are Diomedes (*Iliad* 10.482), Hektor (*Iliad* 15.60, 15.262), Aeneas (*Iliad* 20.110), Odysseus (*Odyssey* 9.381), Penelope (*Odyssey* 19.138), Laertes (*Odyssey* 24.520), and the horses of Akhilles (*Iliad* 17.456 and 502).

31. The incident of Laertes's invigoration occurs at *Odyssey* 24.520. Other instances of μένος being blown into human recipients are found at *Iliad* 10.482, 15.60, 15.262, 17.456, 20.110.

32. *Odyssey* 9.381.

33. Ibid., 19.138, where she receives the ingenious idea of weaving and unweaving her tapestry.

34. *Theogony* 96–97.

35. Richard Broxton Onians, *The Origins of Greek Thought* (Cambridge: Cambridge University Press, 1951), pp. 23–40 and 66–67. For more recent discussions, see Bruno Snell, "φρένες—φρόνησις," *Glotta* 55 (1977): 34–64, and Shirley Darcus Sullivan, "Phrenes in Hesiod," *Revue Belge de Philologie et d'Histoire / Belgisch Tijdschrift voor Filologie en Geschiedenis* 67 (1989): 5–17.

36. In these instances, the lungs generally function as an organ for the reception—and not the production—of speech, it being understood that through them one can absorb what others have said at an extremely deep level. Thus, on two occasions Hesiod expresses the desire to "hurl" his speech into the φρένες of his brother (the verb used is βάλλω), so that the wayward Perses can be transformed by it (*Works and Days* 106–7 and 274). Similarly, at *Odyssey* 1.328, when the poet's account of Odysseus enters Penelope's φρένες, it moves her so deeply that she has to make him stop his song (*Odyssey* 1.341–42).

37. *Odyssey* 22.344–47. Translation is original.

38. The verb suggests a vegetative metaphor rather than the imagery (and ideology) of inspiration. The verb for the latter (ἐμ πνέω) occurs with φρένες as its indirect object at *Odyssey* 19.138, where a δαίμων breathes the idea of her tapestry into Penelope's φρένες. This scene, however, is consistent with the treatment of the φρένες as a seat of thought and emotion, but with no particular role in the production of speech.

39. Joshua T. Katz and Katharina Volk, "'Mere Bellies'?: A New Look at *Theogony* 26–8," *Journal of Hellenic Studies* 120 (2000): 122–31.

40. *Theogony* 26.

41. The scholia gloss γαστέρες οἶον as "being occupied with the belly only and thinking only of the belly" (περὶ τὴν γαστέρα μόνην ἀσχολούμενοι καὶ μόνα τὰ τῆς γαστρὸς φρονοῦντες). Hesychius makes the same point: "caring only about food" (τροφῆς μόνης ἐπιμελούμενοι).

For the fullest discussion of the image of the γαστήρ, see Svenbro, *La parole et le marbre*, pp. 50–59.

42. Katz and Volk, "'Mere bellies'?," pp. 124–29. On the ἐγγαστρίμυθοι, see further E. R. Dodds, *The Greeks and the Irrational* (Berkeley: University of California Press, 1951), pp. 70–72.

43. *Iliad* 18.417–20.

44. As ibid., 18.418 makes clear, the *automata* are not living maidens but "like" living maidens (ζωῆσι νεήνισιν εἰοκυῖαι). Being made of gold, they are presumably immortal, incapable of aging, and untiring, i.e., the ideal laborers.

45. *Works and Days* 60–68:

> Ἥφαιστον δ᾿ ἐκέλευσε περικλυτὸν ὅττι τάχιστα
> γαῖαν ὕδει φύρειν, ἐν δ᾿ ἀνθρώπου θέμεν αὐδήν
> καὶ σθένος, ἀθανάτης δέ θεῆς εἰς ὦπα ἐίσκειν,
> παρθενικῆς καλὸν εἶδος ἐπήρατον· αὐτάρ Ἀθήνην
> ἔργα διδασκῆσαι, πολυδαίδαλον ἱστὸν ὑφαίνειν·
> καὶ χάριν ἀμφιχέαι κεφαλῇ χρυσῆν Ἀφροδίτην,
> καὶ πόθον ἀργαλέον καὶ γυιοβόρους μελεδώνας·
> ἐν δέ θέμεν κύνεόν τε νόον καὶ ἐπίκλοπον ἦθος
> Ἑρμείην ἤνωγε διάκτορον ἀργειφόντην.

Text is taken from M. L. West, *Hesiod, Works and Days* (Oxford: Clarendon Press, 1978).

Use of the same verbal form (θέμεν, Aorist Infinitive from τίθημι) in lines 61 and 67 serves to bring the subjects of those verbs (Hephaistos and Hermes) and their objects (αὐδήν, σθένος, νόος, and ἦθος) into close association.

46. West's discussion of these differences is most unsatisfactory. See his editions of the *Theogony*, pp. 326–29, and the *Works and Days*, pp. 158–67, esp. 160–61, where he lamely suggests that when *Works and Days* 70–82 contradicts lines 60–68 of the same text, it "slip[s] back into" the version of *Theogony* 571–84, and "nothing is more natural" than its doing so. The latter text, like *Works and Days* 70–82, describes Pandora as she was actually made, but this does not explain—nor does it obviate the need for explaining—the striking fact that this final product differed markedly from what Zeus had intended, as reported in *Works and Days* 60–68. Including the *Theogony* passage in the discussion complicates the problem, but hardly resolves it.

47. *Works and Days* 67–68. Hermes's identity as god of thieves makes him the appropriate donor of these gifts (cf. *Homeric Hymn to Hermes* 292 passim).

48. On the gender politics of the Hesiodic texts, with particular reference to the Pandora myth, see Vigdis Songe-Møller, *Philosophy without Women: The Birth of Sexism in Western Thought* (London: Continuum, 2002); Pierre Lévèque, "Pandora ou la terrifiante féminité," *Kernos* 1 (1988): 49–62; Jean Rudhardt, "Pandora: Hésiode et les femmes," *Museum Helveticum* 43 (1986): 231–46; Arthur, "Dream of a World Without Women"; idem, "Cultural Strategies in Hesiod's *Theogony*: Law, Family, Society," *Arethusa* 15 (1982): 63–82; Patricia A. Marquardt, "Hesiod's Ambiguous View of Woman," *Classical Philology* 77 (1982): 283–91; Angelo Casanova, *La famiglia di Pandora: Analisi filologica dei miti di Pandora e Prometeo nella tradizione esiodea* (Florence: Cooperativa Libraria Universitatis Studii Fiorentini, 1979); Linda Sussman, "Workers and Drones: Labor, Idleness and Gender Definition in Hesiod's Beehive," *Arethusa* 11 (1978): 27–37; and several articles conveniently collected in Blaise et al., eds., *Le métier du mythe*: Pierre Judet de la Combe, "La dernière ruse: 'Pandora' dans la *Théogonie*,"

pp. 263–299; Pierre Judet de la Combe and Alain Lernould, "Sur la Pandore des *Travaux*: Esquisses," pp. 301–13; Daniel Saintillan, "Du festin à l'échange: Les graces de Pandore," pp. 315–48; Froma Zeitlin, "L'origine de la femme et la femme origine: La Pandore d'Hésiode," pp. 349–80; and Jean-Pierre Vernant, "Les semblances de Pandora," pp. 381–92.

49. Warriors: *Shield of Herakles* 420; mythic heroes: *Works and Days* 598, 615, 619; frag. 204.56 (Merkelbach and West); laboring animals: *Works and Days* 437; *Shield of Herakles* 97; frag. 75.22 Merkelbach and West.

50. Wild animals: *Iliad* 5.139, 5.783, 12.42, 17.22; rivers: *Iliad* 17.751, 18.607, 21.195; Hephaistos's automata: *Iliad* 18.420.

51. *Odyssey* 24.530; *Theogony* 685.

52. Battle cries: *Iliad* 14.400, 15.686, 18.221; *Shield of Herakles* 382. Men and dogs use their φωναί together: *Iliad* 17.111.

53. Imitation: *Odyssey* 4.279; cf. Patroclus's shade, *Iliad* 23.67, and Eurycleia's recognition of Odysseus, *Odyssey* 19.381.

54. *Theogony* 39. Cf. *Iliad* 18.571.

55. Thus *Works and Days* 448 (a crane); *Theogony* 584 (the golden beasts on Perse-phone's crown); *Odyssey* 10.239 (pigs), 12.396 (cattle), 17.111 (dogs), 19.521 (the nightingale, singing in lament), 19.545 (an eagle).

56. *Theogony* 685 has the gods and Titans engaging in battle cries together. *Works and Days* 104 attributes φωναί to diseases. Most dramatic, however, is the description of Typhōn given at *Theogony* 824–35.

> From his shoulders,
> There were one hundred heads of a monstrous, serpentine dragon,
> Licking with dark tongues. . . .
> And in all those monstrous heads there were voices [φωναὶ],
> Spouting unspeakable horrors in every direction, for sometimes
> They spoke as if addressing the gods, and sometimes
> Their force was that of a loud-bellowing, irresistible bull, proud of voice [ὄσσαν],
> Sometimes they seemed like a lion of merciless spirit,
> Sometimes like puppies, a wonder to be heard,
> And sometimes like hissing that resounds beneath great mountains.

57. *Iliad* 18.219.

58. *Works and Days* 77–78.

59. *Theogony* 86. The full passage also notes the king's discriminating judgment (διακρίνοντα θέμιστας, 1.85), his self-assurance in assembly (ἀσφαλέως ἀγορεύων, 1.86), and his intelligence and knowledge (ἐπισταμένως, 1.87; βασιλῆες ἐχέφρονες, 1.88).

60. *Works and Days* 7–9.

61. Ibid., 35–39.

62. Ibid., 194. Also relevant are the crooked accusations of line 258.

63. Ibid., 219, 221, 250, 262, and 264.

64. Ibid., 225–37.

65. Ibid., 248–55.

66. Ibid., 256–64:

ἡ δέ τε παρθένος ἐστὶ Δίκη, Διὸς ἐκγεγαυῖα,
κυδρή τ' αἰδοίη τε θεοῖς οἳ Ὄλυμπον ἔχουσιν·
καί ῥ' ὁπότ' ἄν τίς μιν βλάπτῃ σκολιῶς ὀνοτάζων,
αὐτίκα πάρ Διὶ πατρὶ καθεζομένη Κρονίωνι
γηρύετ' ἀνθρώπων ἀ ἄδικον νόον, ὄφρ' ἀποτείσῃ
δῆμος ἀτασθαλίας βασιλέων οἳ λυγρά νοέοντες
ἄλλῃ παρκλίνωσι δίκας σκολιῶς ἐνέποντες.
ταῦτα φυλασσόμενοι, βασιλῆς, ἰθύνετε μύθους,
δωροφάγοι, σκολιῶν δέ δικέων ἐπὶ πάγχυ λάθεσθε.

Text is taken from West, *Hesiod, Works and Days.*

CHAPTER EIGHT

"Ancient and Post-Ancient Religions" was originally published as the epilogue to
Religions of the Ancient World: A Guide, ed. Sarah Iles Johnston (Cambridge, MA: Harvard University Press, Belknap Press, 2004), pp. 657–67. Copyright © 2004 by the President and Fellows of Harvard College.

1. Cf. the discussions of Wilfred Cantwell Smith, *The Meaning and End of Religion: A New Approach to the Religious Traditions of Mankind* (New York: Macmillan, 1963), and Talal Asad, *Genealogies of Religion: Discipline and Reasons of Power in Christianity and Islam* (Baltimore: Johns Hopkins University Press. 1993).

2. "A Cosmological Incantation: The Worm and the Toothache" (E. A. Speiser, trans.), in James Pritchard, ed., *Ancient Near Eastern Texts relating to the Old Testament*, 3rd ed. (Princeton, NJ: Princeton University Press, 1969), pp. 100–101.

3. Cicero, *De Divinatione* 1.95.

4. Hesiod, *Theogony* 782–806.

5. Herodotus 7.150, e.g.

6. See, inter alia, Cornelius Loew, *Myth, Sacred History, and Philosophy: The Pre-Christian Religious Heritage of the West* (New York: Harcourt, Brace and World 1967); Mircea Eliade, *Le mythe de l'éternel retour* (Paris: Gallimard, 1949), trans. Willard Trask under the title *The Myth of the Eternal Return* (Princeton, NJ: Princeton University Press, 1954); and Henri Frankfort, *Kingship and the Gods: A Study of Ancient Near Eastern Religion as the Integration of Society and Nature* (Chicago: University of Chicago Press. 1948).

7. Wilhelm Nestle, *Vom Mythos zum Logos: Die Selbstentfaltung des griechischen Denkens von Homer bis auf die Sophistik und Sokrates* (Stuttgart: A. Kröner. 1940); Francis Macdonald Cornford, *From Religion to Philosophy: A Study in the Origins of Western Speculation* (London: E. Arnold, 1912); and Jean-Pierre Vernant, *The Origins of Greek Thought* (Ithaca, NY: Cornell University Press, 1982). Cf. Richard Buxton, ed., *From Myth to Reason? Studies in the Development of Greek Thought* (Oxford: Oxford University Press, 1999).

8. Xenophanes, frag. 21B11 and 21B112 (Diels-Kranz).

9. Ibid., frag. 21B15. Cf. 21B16.

10. Ibid., frag. 21B1, lines 13–16.

11. Ibid., lines 21–23.

12. Plato, *Apology* 20e-23c.

13. Ibid., 40ac.

14. Plato, *Republic* 614b-621d; cf. *Phaedrus* 246d-249d.

15. Hippocratic corpus, *On the Sacred Disease* (*Peri Hierês Nousou*).

16. Cicero, *De Divinatione* 2.52.

17. Thucydides 5.89.

18. Bruce Lincoln, *Holy Terrors: Thinking about Religion after September 11* (Chicago: University of Chicago Press, 2003), 5–7.

19. Knowledge and use of nonalphabetic scripts (cuneiform, hieroglyphics, e.g.) were much more restricted than those of alphabetic, since the scripts were so much more demanding and cumbersome. As a result, these normally were the province of scribal—and priestly—elites, who employed them for a small set of tasks, including sacred texts (myths, ritual programs, records of omens and divination, etc.) and palace records.

20. Hesiod, *Theogony* 31–32: "enepneusan de moi audên thespin." M. L. West, ed., *Hesiod, Theogony* (Oxford: Clarendon Press, 1966).

21. More likely rapt than wild; Christopher Forbes, *Prophecy and Inspired Speech in Early Christianity and Its Hellenistic Environment* (Tübingen, Germany: J. C. B. Mohr, 1995), and Lisa Maurizio, "Anthropology and Spirit Possession: A Reconsideration of the Pythia's Role at Delphi," *Journal of Hellenic Studies* 115 (1995): 69–86.

22. Plutarch, *De Defectu Oraculorum*.

23. Marcel Detienne, *The Masters of Truth in Archaic Greece* (New York: Zone Books, 1996; French original 1967).

24. James Kugel, ed., *Poetry and Prophecy: The Beginnings of a Literary Tradition* (Ithaca, NY: Cornell University Press, 1990).

25. Eric Alfred Havelock, *Preface to Plato* (Cambridge, MA: Harvard University Press, 1963); Jack Goody, *The Interface between the Written and the Oral* (Cambridge: Cambridge University Press, 1987); and Walter Ong, *Orality and Literacy: The Technologizing of the Word* (London: Methuen, 1982).

26. Suetonius, *Divus Augustus* 31.1; Fenestella, frag. 18 (Peter).

27. A. Leo Oppenheim, *Ancient Mesopotamia: Portrait of a Dead Civilization* (Chicago: University of Chicago Press, 1964).

28. "Temple Program for the New Year's Festival at Babylon," lines 396–400 (A. Sachs, trans.), in Pritchard, *Ancient Near Eastern Texts*, p. 334:

> [Marduk], exalted among the gods,
> [Who dwells in the temple Esag]il, who creates the laws,
> [Who . . .] to the great gods,
> [. . .] I praise your heroism.
> [May] your heart [be sympathetic] to whoever seizes your hands.

29. W. Robertson Smith, *Lectures on the Religion of the Semites: First Series; The Fundamental Institutions* (New York: Appleton, 1889); Henri Hubert and Marcel Mauss, *Sacrifice: Its Nature and Function* (Chicago: University of Chicago Press, 1964; French original 1899); Paul Thieme, "Vorzarathustrisches bei den Zarathustriern und bei Zarathustra," *Zeitschrift der deutschen morgenlandischen Gesellschaft* 107 (1957): 67–104; Walter Burkert, *Homo Necans: The Anthropology of Ancient Greek Sacrificial Ritual and Myth* (Berkeley: University of California Press, 1983; German original 1972); Réné Girard, *Violence and the Sacred* (Baltimore: Johns Hopkins University Press, 1977; French original 1972); Marcel Detienne and Jean-Pierre Vernant, *The Cuisine of Sacrifice among the Greeks* (Chicago: University of Chicago Press, 1991); Bruce Lincoln, *Death, War, and*

Sacrifice: Studies in Ideology and Practice (Chicago: University of Chicago Press, 1991), 198–208; and Cristiano Grottanelli, *Il Sacrificio* (Rome: Laterza, 1999).

30. Jean-Pierre Vernant, "At Man's Table: Hesiod's Foundation Myth of Sacrifice," in *The Cuisine of Sacrifice among the Greeks,* edited by Marcel Detienne and Jean-Pierre Vernant (Chicago: University of Chicago Press, 1989 ;French original 1979), pp. 21–86; and Cristiano Grottanelli and Nicola Parise, *Sacrificio e società nel mondo antico* (Rome: Laterza, 1988).

31. Bruce Lincoln, *Myth, Cosmos, and Society: Indo-European Themes of Creation and Destruction* (Cambridge, MA: Harvard University Press, 1986).

32. Cristiano Grottanelli, "Healers and Saviors of the Eastern Mediterranean," in *La soteriologia dei culti orientali nell' Impero Romano,* ed. Ugo Bianchi and Martin Vermaseren, pp. 649–70 (Leiden: E. J. Brill, 1982).

33. Martin Riesebrodt, *The Promise of Salvation: A Theory of Religion* (Chicago: University of Chicago Press, 2010), treats soteriological concerns as the centerpiece of religion in general. I would be more inclined to see this as characteristic of certain types of religion, especially those of the post-ancient era.

34. Matthew 10:37, Luke 14:26.

35. Jonathan Z. Smith, *Map Is Not Territory: Studies in the History of Religions* (Leiden: E. J. Brill, 1978).

36. Raymond Bowman, *Aramaic Ritual Texts from Persepolis* (Chicago: University of Chicago Press, 1970).

CHAPTER NINE

"Sanctified Violence" was originally presented at a conference on the theme "Sanctified Violence in Ancient Mediterranean Religions: Discourse, Ritual, Community," organized by the Department of Classical and Near Eastern Studies at the University of Minnesota (October 2007), and first published as "Sanctified Violence in the Ancient Mediterranean" in *The Cambridge Companion to Ancient Mediterranean Religions,* ed. Barbette Stanley Spaeth (New York: Cambridge University Press, 2011). Copyright © 20011 by Bruce Lincoln. Reprinted with the permission of Cambridge University Press.

1. The text was originally written in 1940, shortly after the Nazi occupation of France. A convenient English translation has regularly been reprinted by Pendle Hill and the Society of Friends since 1956, but see now James P. Holoka, ed., *Simone Weil's The Iliad; or, The Poem of Force: A Critical Edition* (New York: Peter Lang, 2003).

2. Alexandre Kojève, *Introduction to the Reading of Hegel: Lectures on the Phenomenology of Spirit,* trans. James H. Nichols (New York: Basic Books, 1969; French original, 1947, based on lectures given at the École des hautes-études in 1933–39, as the Third Republic descended into terminal crisis).

3. Orlando Patterson, *Slavery and Social Death: A Comparative Study* (Cambridge, MA: Harvard University Press, 1982).

4. Comparison between murder and surgery may also be instructive, insofar as it shows that violence is not simply a type of action—e.g. the rending of another person's flesh—but more important, a type of effect and a type of intention. Thus, where the killer transforms what was once a fully human subject into a dead object, the surgeon's actions (ideally) restore a patient (i.e., one whose physical personhood is

compromised in some fashion) to health. Notwithstanding bloody, greedy, and arrogant aspects of their practice, surgeons (are supposed to) respect their patients' essential humanity, which they endeavor to preserve and repair. That killers and surgeons both achieve their results (and reap their profits) in similar bloody fashion is a coincidence that obscures their much more important difference: one practices violence, destroying the subjectivity of others; the other attempts to repair it.

5. Although this formulation is heuristically useful, it ignores some crucial points. Most important of these is the need to distinguish between the immediate victims of lethal violence—those whom it converts into corpses—and others for whose eyes this spectacle may be intended, with the expectation that they will be intimidated by it and thereafter submit more readily to those who showed themselves willing and able to kill. The immediate victims are fully objectified by lethal violence; the others—who may be designated mediated victims, victims at a second remove, or spectator-victims—only partially so. One can also theorize this distinction in other ways, contrasting the physical and discursive effects of lethal violence, for example, or its use-value and its sign-value.

6. In its incipient moments, insurrectionary violence reverses the subject-object relations in the existing system of domination, with liberatory intention and effects. If successful, however, those who have waged such campaigns regularly establish structures of domination that are formally identical to those they overthrew, changing only the identity of who holds the whip hand and who lives in fear. This is not to say that such victories are sterile, ironic, or inconsequential, but violence that actually ends domination, instead of just inverting it, is regrettably rare.

7. The literature on this topic grows whenever a state that defines itself as Christian finds itself making war. Most recently, see John Mark Mattox, *Saint Augustine and the Theory of Just War* (London: Continuum, 2006).

8. Søren Kierkegaard, *Fear and Trembling*, ed. and trans. Howard V. Hong and Edna H. Hong (Princeton, NJ: Princeton University Press, 1983; Danish original, 1843).

9. Along these lines, I am fond of a moment in the 1956 film *Friendly Persuasion*, when Elder Purdey (played by Richard Hale) explains fine points of the Quakers' peace testimony to a more reluctant Jess Birdwell (Gary Cooper), as Confederate raiders bear down on their Indiana farms.

> "If thee wants to help, pick up a gun and fight, the same as I'm doing."
> "I'm not ready to do that."
> "What does thee aim to do, sit here and turn the other cheek?"
> "That's what I aim to do, if I can."
> "Thee has got to face the fact, Jess, that *wartime calls for another kind of thinking*."

The film, directed by William Wyler, came out at the height of the cold war and was based on Jessamyn West's novel, which appeared toward the end of World War II (New York: Harcourt, Brace, 1945). The incident seems to me typical in many ways and helps us understand that many of the assumptions that normally organize human experience leave little trace in the historic record, since the taken-for-granted need not speak itself until it faces some difficulty or challenge. The situation most likely to force the kind of articulation that remains available for subsequent scrutiny is one in which those who wish to practice violence (for whatever reason), while still wishing to regard themselves as moral and religious persons, struggle to reconcile these contradictory impulses. The situation is always instructive, not least for the ingenuity exhibited.

10. David Frankfurter thus suggests to me:

> The kind of violence you don't address is that conceived to obliterate, purify, or somehow neutralize bodies/objects that are perceived as polluting, which I don't think are best described under the rubric of "conquest." While I agree that one of the governing pretexts of violence is depersonalization/dehumanization, one of the fascinating/horrifying aspects of purification—in lynching, in mutilation of witches, or even of mass rape—is the designation of the body of the other as the site of purification/cosmic transformation/conversion/what-have-you. Dehumanization occurs, yet the human body—marked as demonic—is still necessary to contextualize the meaningful gesture.

Private communication, September 11, 2007. On this theme, see further Frankfurter's *Evil Incarnate: Rumors of Demonic Conspiracy and Ritual Abuse in History* (Princeton, NJ: Princeton University Press, 2006), and Natalie Zemon Davis, "The Rites of Violence," in *Society and Culture in Early Modern France* (Stanford, CA: Stanford University Press, 1975), pp. 152–87. I have little to add on this topic, save the observation that the phenomenon and dynamic at issue might aptly be called "purgation," a term that combines the senses of purification and annihilation.

11. Bruce Lincoln, *Religion, Empire, and Torture: The Case of Achaemenian Persia* (Chicago: University of Chicago Press, 2007).

12. Eve Adler, *Vergil's Empire: Political Thought in the Aeneid* (Lanham, MD: Rowman & Littlefield, 2003); Francesco Lucrezi, *Messianismo, Regalità, Impero: Idee religiose e idea imperiale nel mondo romano* (Florence: Editoriale La Giuntina, 1996), pp. 1–14; and Paul Zanker, *The Power of Images in the Age of Augustus* (Ann Arbor: University of Michigan Press, 1988). Here, as in other notes of this sort, I have pointed to only a few items in an enormous bibliography.

13. Klaus Martin Girardet, *Die konstantinische Wende: Voraussetzungen und geistige Grundlägen der Religionspolitik Konstantins des Grossen* (Darmstadt: Wissenschaftliche Buchgesellschaft, 2006); Charles Matson Odahl, *Constantine and the Christian Empire* (New York: Routledge, 2004); and H. A. Drake, *Constantine and the Bishops: The Politics of Intolerance* (Baltimore: Johns Hopkins University Press, 2000).

14. A. Tafazzoli, *Sassanian Society* (New York: Bibliotheca Persica, 2000); Shaul Shaked, *Dualism in Transformation: Varieties of Religion in Sasanian Iran* (London: School of Oriental and African Studies, University of London, 1994); and Karin Mosiq-Walburg, *Die frühen sasanidischen Könige als Vertreter und Förderer der zarathustrischen Religion: Eine Untersuchuing der zeitgenössischen Quellen* (Frankfurt am Main: Peter Lang, 1982).

15. Karl-Heinz Öhlig and Gerd-Rainer Puin, eds., *Die dunklen Anfänge: Neue Forschungen zur Entstehung und frühen Geschichte des Islam* (Berlin: Hans Schiller, 2006); Wilferd Madelung, *The Succession to Muhammad: A Study of the Early Caliphate* (Cambridge: Cambridge University Press, 1997); John Walter Jandora, *The March from Medina: A Revisionist Study of the Arab Conquests* (Clifton, NJ: Kingston Press, 1990); Patricia Cone and Martin Hinds, *God's Caliph: Religious Authority in the First Centuries of Islam* (Cambridge: Cambridge University Press, 1986); and Fred Donner, *The Early Islamic Conquests* (Princeton, NJ: Princeton University Press, 1981).

16. I have treated this pattern in a very different historical context. See Bruce

Lincoln, "Jihads, Jeremiads, and the Enemy Within," in *Holy Terrors: Thinking about Religion after September 11* (Chicago: University of Chicago Press, 2005), pp. 33–50.

17. Oded Lipschitz, *The Fall and Rise of Jerusalem: Judah under Babylonian Rule* (Winona Lake, IN: Eisenbrauns, 2005); Jom Kiefer, *Exil und Diaspora: Begrifflichkeit und Deutungen im antiken Judentum und in der Hebräischen Bibel* (Leipzig: Evangelische Verlagsanstalt, 2005); Rainer Albertz, *Israel in Exile: The History and Literature of the Sixth Century B.C.E.* (Leiden: E. J. Brill, 2004); Christopher Seitz, *Theology in Conflict: Reactions to the Exile in the Book of Jeremiah* (Berlin: De Gruyter, 1989); and Daniel Smith, *The Religion of the Landless: The Social Context of the Babylonian Exile* (Bloomington, IN: Meyer-Stone Books, 1989).

18. This is evident in texts that depict Babylon's last king, Nabonidus, as having so offended the god Marduk that he shifted his favor to the Persians; these texts are available in James B. Pritchard, *Ancient Near Eastern Texts relating to the Old Testament,* 3rd ed. (Princeton, NJ: Princeton University Press, 1969), pp. 305–16. For discussion, see Amélie Kuhrt, "Nabonidus and the Babylonian Priesthood," in *Pagan Priests: Religion and Power in the Ancient World,* ed. Mary Beard and John North (Ithaca, NY: Cornell University Press, 1990), pp. 119–55; Paul-Alain Beaulieu, *The Reign of Nabonidus, King of Babylon 556–539 B.C.* (New Haven, CT: Yale University Press, 1989); and Wolfram von Soden, "Kyros und Nabonid: Propaganda und Gegenpropaganda," in *Kunst, Kultur und Geschichte der Achamenidenzeit und ihr Fortleben,* ed. Heidemarie Koch and D. N. MacKenzie (Berlin: Dietrich Reimer, 1983), pp. 61–68.

19. The classic work is Samuel K. Eddy, *The King Is Dead: Studies in the Near Eastern Resistance to Hellenism, 334–31 B.C.* (Lincoln: University of Nebraska Press, 1961). More recently, see Mary Boyce and Frantz Grenet, *A History of Zoroastrianism,* vol. 3, *Zoroastrianism under Macedonian and Roman Rule* (Leiden: E. J. Brill, 1991).

20. Note, for instance, the description of omens, divine displeasure, and human guilt in the context of Civil War that is found in Dio Cassius 47.40; Paul Jal, *La guerre civile à Rome: Étude littéraire et morale* (Paris: Presses Universitaires de France, 1963); idem, "Les dieux et les guerres civiles dans la Rome de la fin de la république," *Revue des etudes latines* 40 (1962): 170–200; and idem, "La propagande réligieuse à Rome au cours des guerres civiles de la fin de la république," *L'antiquité classique* 30 (1962): 395–414.

21. John J. Collins, ed., *The Encyclopedia of Apocalypticism,* vol. 1, *The Origins of Apocalypticism* (New York: Continuum, 1998); Richard A. Horsley, *Bandits, Prophets, and Messiahs: Popular Movements in the Time of Jesus* (San Francisco: Harper & Row, 1988); Peter Schäfer, *Der Bar Kokhba-Aufstand: Studien zum zweiten jüdischen Krieg gegen Rom* (Tübingen, Germany: J. C. B. Mohr, 1981); and S. G. F. Brandon, *Jesus and the Zealots: A Study of the Political Factor in Primitive Christianity* (Manchester: Manchester University Press, 1967).

22. Anders Hultgård, "Persian Apocalypticism," in Collins, *Encyclopedia of Apocalypticism,* 1:39–83; Mary Boyce, "On the Antiquity of Zoroastrian Apocalyptic," *Bulletin of the School of Oriental and African Studies* 47 (1984): 57–75; John Hinnells, "The Zoroastrian Doctrine of Salvation in the Roman World: A Study of the Oracles of Hystaspes," in *Man and His Salvation: Studies in Honor of S. G. F. Brandon,* ed. E. J. Sharpe and J. R. Hinnells (Manchester: Manchester University Press, 1973), pp. 125–48.

23. Spartacus was said to bear signs of divine election according to Plutarch, *Life*

NOTES TO PAGES 88–91   179

of Crassus 8–11, the importance of which was noted by Cristiano Grottanelli, "Archaic Forms of Rebellion and Their Religious Background," in *Religion, Rebellion, Revolution*, ed. Bruce Lincoln (New York: St. Martin's Press, 1985), pp. 18–19; Tacitus's description of Civilis as one-eyed (*Histories* 4.13) suggests that his countrymen associated him with the god Woðanaz, and several authors report that he was the beneficiary of prophecies made by a Sibylline figure (Tacitus, *Histories* 4.61, 65; *Germania* 8; Statius, *Silvae* 1.4.90). Caesar scrupulously avoids reporting anything that would indicate the charismatic basis of Vercingetorix's claims, but the last element in the rebel's name (Gallic *-rix* = Latin *rex*) makes clear that he was regarded as rightful heir to royal status among the Arverni, and more broadly among the Gauls. See further Paul M. Martin, *Vercingétorix: Le politique, le stratège* (Paris: Perrin, 2000); Christian Goudineau, *Le dossier Vercingétorix* (Paris: Errance, 2001); Jean Markale, *Vercingétorix* (Monaco: Éditions du Rocher, 1995); or Camille Jullian, *Vercingétorix* (Paris: Hachette, 1903).

24. Maria Massi Dakake, *The Charismatic Community: Shi'ite Identity in Early Islam* (Albany: State University of New York Press, 2007); Mostafa Vaziri, *The Emergence of Islam: Prophecy, Imamate, and Messianism in Perspective* (New York: Paragon House, 1992); and Seyyed Hossein Nasr et al., eds., *Expectation of the Millennium: Shi'ism in History* (Albany: State University of New York Press, 1989).

25. Elizabeth Clark, *Reading Renunciation: Asceticism and Scripture in Early Christianity* (Princeton, NJ: Princeton University Press, 1999): Griet Petersen-Szemeredy, *Zwischen Wentstadt und Wüste: Römische Asketinnen in der Spätantike* (Göttingen: Vandenhoeck & Ruprecht, 1993): Peter Brown, *The Body and Society: Men, Women, and Sexual Renunciation in Early Christianity* (New York: Columbia University Press, 1988); and John Gager, "Body-Symbols and Social Reality: Resurrection, Incarnation, and Asceticism in Early Christianity," *Religion* 12 (1982): 345–64.

26. Jason BeDuhn, *The Manichaean Body in Discipline and Ritual* (Baltimore: Johns Hopkins University Press, 2000).

27. Einar Thomassen, *The Spiritual Seed: The Church of the "Valentinians"* (Leiden: E. J. Brill, 2006); John Douglas Turner, *Sethian Gnosticism and the Platonic Tradition* (Louvain: Éditions Peeters, 2001); and Maria Grazia Lancellotti, *The Naassenes: A Gnostic Identity among Judaism, Christianity, Classical and Ancient Near Eastern Traditions* (Münster: Ugarit Verlag, 2000).

28. Grottanelli, "Archaic Forms of Rebellion," pp. 22–24; M. J. Vermaseren, *Cybele and Attis: The Myth and the Cult* (London: Thames & Hudson, 1977); Britt-Mari Näsström, *The Abhorrence of Love: Studies in Rituals and Mystic Aspects in Catullus' Poem of Attis* (Stockholm: Almqvist & Wiksell, 1989); and J. Peter Södergård, "The Ritualized Bodies of Cybele's Galli and the Methodological Problem of the Plurality of Explanations," in *The Problem of Ritual*, ed. Tore Ahlbäck (Stockholm: Almqvist & Wiksell, 1993), pp. 169–93.

29. Richard Bramlich, *Weltverzicht: Grundlägen und Weisen islamischer Askese* (Wiesbaden: Otto Harrassowitz, 1997).

30. Eliezer Diamond, *Holy Men and Hunger Artists: Fasting and Asceticism in Rabbinic Culture* (Oxford: Oxford University Press, 2004).

31. Thomas Bénatouli, *Faire usage: La pratique du stoïcisme* (Paris: Vrin, 2006); John Sellars, *Stoicism* (Berkeley: University of California Press, 2006); Gretchen Reydams-Schils, *The Roman Stoics: Self, Responsibility, and Affection* (Chicago: University of Chicago

Press, 2005); Nancy Sherman, *Stoic Warriors: The Ancient Philosophy behind the Military Mind* (New York: Oxford University Press, 2005); and Ted Brennan, *The Stoic Life: Emotions, Duties, and Fate* (Oxford: Clarendon Press, 2005).

32. The topic has received a great deal of attention in recent years. Inter alia, see G. E. M. de Ste. Croix, *Christian Persecution, Martyrdom, and Orthodoxy* (New York: Oxford University Press, 2006); Paul Middleton, *Radical Martyrdom and Cosmic Conflict in Early Christianity* (London: T. & T. Clark, 2006); Elizabeth Castelli, *Martyrdom and Memory: Early Christian Culture Making* (New York: Columbia University Press, 2004); Margaret Cormack, ed., *Sacrificing the Self: Perspectives on Martyrdom and Religion* (New York: Oxford University Press, 2001); Daniel Boyarin, *Dying for God: Martyrdom and the Making of Christianity and Judaism* (Stanford, CA: Stanford University Press, 1999); Brent Shaw, "Body/Power/Identity: Passions of the Martyrs," *Journal of Early Christian Studies* 4 (1996): 269–312; G. W. Bowersock, *Martyrdom and Rome* (Cambridge: Cambridge University Press, 1995); Carlin Barton, "Savage Miracles: The Redemption of Lost Honor in Roman Society and the Sacrament of the Gladiator and the Martyr," *Representations* 45 (1994): 41–71; David S. Potter, "Martyrdom as Spectacle," in *Theater and Society in the Classical World*, ed. Ruth Scodel (Ann Arbor: University of Michigan Press, 1993), pp. 53–88; Arthur Droge and James Tabor, *A Noble Death: Suicide and Martyrdom among Christians and Jews in Antiquity* (San Francisco: Harper, 1992); Jan Bremmer, "'Christianus sum': The Early Christian Martyrs and Christ," in *Eulogia: Mélanges offerts à Antoon A. R. Bastiansen*, ed. G. J. M. Bartelink et al. (The Hague: Martinus Nijhoff, 1991), pp. 11–20; and Paul-Albert Février, "Les chrétiens dans l'arène," in *Spectacula I: Gladiateurs et amphitheatres*, ed. Claude Domerge et al. (Lattes, France: Éditions Imago, 1990), pp. 265–73. Although my discussion focuses on the early Christian martyrs, one ought to attend also to the ideology of martyrs in other traditions. See, inter alia, David Cook, *Martyrdom in Islam* (Cambridge: Cambridge University Press, 2007); J. W. van Henten, *Martyrdom and Noble Death: Selected Texts from Graeco-Roman, Jewish, and Christian Antiquity* (New York: Routledge, 2002); J. W. van Henten, ed., *Die Entstehung der jüdischen Martyrologie* (Leiden: E. J. Brill, 1989); Marta Sordi, ed., *Dulce et decorum est pro patria mori: La morte in combattimento nell' antichità* (Milan: Vita e pensiero, 1990); and Clemens Scholten, *Martyrium und Sophiamythos im Gnostizismus nach den Texten von Nag Hammadi* (Münster: Aschendorff, 1987).

33. An instructive example is the way local elites were eager to implement emperor worship and turn it to their advantage. See now Ittai Gradel, *Emperor Worship and Roman Religion* (Oxford: Clarendon Press, 2002); Steven J. Friesen, *Imperial Cults and the Apocalypse of John* (Oxford: Oxford University Press, 2001); and Morten Lund Warmind, "The Cult of the Roman Emperor before and after Christianity," in Ahlbäck, *The Problem of Ritual*, pp. 211–20.

34. Alison Futrell, *Blood in the Arena: The Spectacle of Roman Power* (Austin: University of Texas Press, 1997); Mark Gundarson, "The Ideology of the Arena," *Classical Antiquity* 15 (1996): 113–51; Cinzia Visnara, *Il supplizio come spettacolo* (Rome: Quasar, 1990); Ernst Baltrusch, "Die Verstaatlichung der Gladiatorenspiele," *Hermes* 116 (1988): 324–37; and Ramsay MacMullen, "Judicial Savagery in the Roman Empire," *Chiron* 16 (1986): 81–96.

35. Given the public nature, familiarity, and high drama of Christian martyrdom, I have chosen to highlight this case. In its broad outlines, this sketch is still applicable to the cases of the Maccabean martyrs and the suicides of noble Roman Stoics and

others who opposed imperial power on philosophical grounds (see further the classic discussion of Ramsay Macmullen, *Enemies of the Roman Order: Treason, Unrest, and Alienation in the Empire* [New York: Routledge, 1966; reprint ed. 1992], pp. 46–94), although some modifications would be necessary. The case of Socrates also holds interest, although it falls outside our temporal framework and stands in a context of a recently defeated imperial power.

36. Castelli, *Martyrdom and Memory*, is quite useful on this point. See also Ekkehard Mühlenberg, "The Martyr's Death and Its Literary Presentation," *Studia Patristica* 29 (1997): 85–93; and François Heim, "Les panegyriques des martyrs ou l'impossible conversion d'un genre littéraire," *Revue des Sciences des Religion* 61 (1987): 105–28.

37. The struggle of Donatists and Catholics in Roman North Africa is particularly instructive, but much too complex to pursue here. The classic account is W. H. C. Frend, *Martyrdom and Persecution in the Early Church: A Study of a Conflict from the Maccabees to Donatus* (Oxford: Blackwell, 1965), but more recently, see Michael Gaddis, *There Is No Crime for Those Who Have Christ: Religious Violence in the Christian Roman Empire* (Berkeley: University of California Press, 2005); Maureen Tilley, *The Bible in Christian North Africa: The Donatist World* (Minneapolis: Fortress Press, 1997); idem, *Donatist Martyr Stories: The Church in Conflict in Roman North Africa* (Liverpool: Liverpool University Press, 1996); and J. E. Atkinson, "Out of Order: The Circumcellions and Codex Theodosianus 16.5.52," *Historia* 61 (1992): 488–99.

38. For examples of the discursive campaign waged to discredit such actors, see Israel W. Chary, *Fighting Suicide Bombing: A Worldwide Campaign for Life* (Westport, CT: Praeger Security International, 2007); Mohammed M. Hafez, *Suicide Bombers in Iraq: The Strategy and Ideology of Martyrdom* (Washington, DC: United States Institute of Peace Press, 2007); Mia Bloom, *Dying to Kill: The Allure of Suicide Terror* (New York: Columbia University Press, 2005); Kenneth Cragg, *Faith at Suicide, Lives Forfeit: Violent Religion—Human Despair* (Brighton: Sussex Academic Press, 2005); Ami Pedahzur, *Suicide Terrorism* (Cambridge, MA: Polity, 2005); and countless others.

CHAPTER TEN

"Religious and Other Conflicts in Twentieth-Century Guatemala" was originally presented at a conference on the theme "Beyond 'Primitivism,'" organized by the Department of Religious Studies at the University of California, Davis (March 1996), and first published as "'He, Not They, Best Protected the Village': Religious and Other Conflicts in 20th Century Guatemala" in *Beyond "Primitivism": Indigenous Religious Traditions and Modernity*, ed. Jacob Olupona (New York: Routledge, 2004), pp. 149–63. Reprinted by permission.

1. A spate of good works on the colonial period has appeared in recent years, including Grant Jones, *Maya Resistance to Spanish Rule: Time and History on a Colonial Frontier* (Albuquerque: University of New Mexico Press, 1989); Inga Clendinnen, *Ambivalent Conquests: Maya and Spaniard in Yucatán, 1517–1570* (Cambridge: Cambridge University Press, 1987); and Nancy Farriss, *Maya Society under Colonial Rule: The Collective Enterprise of Survival* (Princeton, NJ: Princeton University Press, 1984). For more recent periods in Guatemalan history, see Carol Smith, ed., *Guatemalan Indians and the State, 1540–1988* (Austin: University of Texas Press, 1990); Jim Handy, *Gift of the Devil: A History of Guatemala* (Boston: South End Press, 1984); and Robert Carmack,

"Spanish-Indian Relations in Highland Guatemala, 1800–1944," in *Spaniards and Indians in Southeastern Mesoamerica*, ed. Murdo MacLeod and Robert Wasserstrom (Lincoln: University of Nebraska Press, 1983), pp. 215–53.

2. Charles Wagley, *The Social and Religious Life of a Guatemalan Village* (New York: American Anthropological Association, 1949), p. 51. All parenthetical phrases appear in the original.

3. Ibid., p. 50.

4. Wagley, *Social and Religious Life of a Guatemalan Village*, p. 52.

5. For a fuller discussion of this mythological theme, see Bruce Lincoln, *Discourse and the Construction of Society* (New York: Oxford University Press, 1989), pp. 38–50.

6. See the discussion of Fernando Cervantes, *The Devil in the New World: The Impact of Diabolism in New Spain* (New Haven, CT: Yale University Press, 1994), esp. pp. 38–39.

7. For different attempts to theorize ladino-Indian relations, see Carol A. Smith, "Race-Class-Gender Ideology in Guatemala: Modern and Anti-Modern Forms," *Comparative Studies in Society and History* 37 (1995): 723–49; *Guatemala: Seminario sobre la Realidad Etnica* ([Mexico City]: Centro de Estudios Integrados de Desarrollo Communal, 1990); Marta Elena Casaus Arzu, *Guatemala: Linaje y racismo* (San José: FLACSO, 1992); Hector Roberto Rosada Granados, *Indios y Ladinos (Un estudio Antropológico-Sociológico)* (San Carlos, Guatemala: Editorial Universitaria, 1987); John Hawkins, *Inverse Images: The Meaning of Culture, Ethnicity and Family in Postcolonial Guatemala* (Albuquerque: University of New Mexico Press, 1984); Douglas E. Brintnall, "Race Relations in the Southeastern Highlands of Mesoamerica," *American Ethnologist* 6 (1979): 638–52; Kay Warren, *The Symbolism of Subordination: Indian Identity in a Guatemalan Town* (Austin: University of Texas Press, 1978); Judith Friedlander, *Being Indian in Hueyapan* (New York: St. Martin's, 1975); Henning Siverts, "Ethnic Stability and Boundary Dynamics in Southern Mexico," in *Ethnic Groups and Boundaries: The Social Organization of Cultural Difference*, ed. Fredrik Barth (Boston: Little, Brown, 1969), pp. 101–16; Benjamin Colby and Pierre van den Berghe, *Ixil Country: A Plural Society in Highland Guatemala* (Berkeley: University of California Press, 1969); and Rudolfo Stavenhagen, "Classes, Colonialism, and Acculturation," in *Comparative Perspectives on Stratification: Mexico, Great Britain, Japan*, ed. Joseph Kahl (Boston: Little, Brown, 1969), pp. 31–63.

8. Ambiguity offers subordinate groups many strategic advantages, and the Indians of Mesoamerica have mastered the art of constructing texts that maximize this potential. Cf., for example, their Passion Plays, where "Roman centurions" torment Christ, clad in helmets that invite anyone so inclined to read them as conquistadores.

9. Wagley, *Social and Religious Life of a Guatemalan Village*, p. 52.

10. Ibid., pp. 56–57.

11. On the practices employed by these recruiters, see Charles Wagley, *Economics of a Guatemalan Village* (Menasha, WI: American Anthropological Association, 1941), p. 73.

12. Regarding the contrast between *santos* and Guardians of the mountains, see the insightful analysis of John Watanabe, "From Saints to Shibboleths: Image, Structure, and Identity in Maya Religious Syncretism," *American Ethnologist* 17 (1990): 131–50; and idem, *Maya Saints and Souls in a Changing World* (Austin: University of Texas Press, 1992), pp. 61–80.

13. On the Ubico regime, see Handy, *Gift of the Devil*, pp. 77–101, and Kenneth Grieb, *Guatemalan Caudillo: The Regime of Jorge Ubico, Guatemala, 1931–1944* (Athens: Ohio University Press, 1979).

14. Wagley, *Social and Religious Life of a Guatemalan Village*, pp. 8–9. More information is given about Diego Martín at pp. 51, 86–87, 97, and in Wagley, *Economics of a Guatemalan Village*, pp. 78–80, where we learn he was one of the largest landholders in Chimaltenango, something of a womanizer, and an iconoclast, as well as a man who consciously learned from ladinos how best to exploit hired labor.

15. On the almost mystic importance accorded the village's *titulo*, see Wagley, *Economics of a Guatemalan Village*, p. 62.

16. Wagley, *Social and Religious Life of a Guatemalan Village*, pp. 8–9 and n6.

17. Gillin's article first appeared in *Psychiatry* 11 (1948): 387–400, has been reprinted several times, and is most readily available in his collected essays, *Human Ways* (Pittsburgh: University of Pittsburgh Press, 1969), pp. 197–219. The healing ceremony was also observed by Gillin's field assistant, William Davidson, who made it the subject of his master's thesis, "A Method for Studying Religious Cult and Healing Ceremonies and Its application to a Guatemalan Indian Curing Ceremony" (unpublished M.A. thesis, Duke University Graduate School of Arts and Sciences, 1948). On San Luis in this period, see further Gillin, *Human Ways*, pp. 35–59; idem, *The Culture of Security in San Carlos: A Study of a Guatemalan Community of Indians and Ladinos* (New Orleans: Middle American Research Institute, Tulane University, 1951); idem, "San Luis Jilotepeque: 1942–55," in *Political Changes in Guatemalan Indian Communities*, ed. Richard Adams (New Orleans: Middle American Research Institute, Tulane University, 1957), pp. 23–27; and Melvin Tumin, *Caste in a Peasant Society* (Princeton, NJ: Princeton University Press, 1952). For an attempt to place this research in historical context, see Bruce Lincoln, "Revisiting 'Magical Fright,'" *American Ethnologist* 28 (2001): 778–802.

18. The chain of recriminations leads back to the beginning of the couple's relation, which Alicia described to Davidson ("A Method for Studying Religious Cult and Healing Ceremonies," pp. 79–80).

> "Fernando, my husband, is two years younger than I. He is the only man that I have ever had. I was never promised to another, nor did I have an affair previously. As a young man, Fernando had nothing and was much given to drink. He and my brothers were in the army together in Guatemala City. After returning from the service, Fernando came to our house one night. He was drunk and he got my family awake. He got my father out of bed and shared a half-bottle of aguardiente with him. They sat down to drink and to talk. Fernando had previously spoken with me when I was walking along the street. He had also spoken to my brother about me, but my brother did not like him since he was poor and a drunkard.

> "After a while my papa asked Fernando what his intentions were. Fernando said that he wanted to marry one of his daughters, me. By this time the bottle had been emptied, and my father said, 'What are we going to do about this without having some more aguardiente?' Fernando went out and got two more bottles, one for himself and one for papa. They sat down to drink some more and to talk some more. Before much time had passed, both bottles were empty, and my papa was very drunk. He became very friendly with Fernando, and soon told me that I had to marry this Fernando."

At first, Alicia refused to accept this arrangement. Then

"One day my father brought a big stone into the house and tied me to it. Then he started to whip me. He gave me three lashes, and then I cried out, 'If you wish, I shall marry him. But I must be married in the church.' My mother objected to my father, but he struck her and yelled to her, 'You are getting very brave, aren't you?' So it was that I was married to Fernando against my will."

More immediately, the spouse's quarrel was occasioned by a long series of misfortunes. Treatment of previous illnesses having been expensive (Alicia had been *espontada* on seven earlier occasions!), they had been forced to sell their land. After years of saving, they were ready to buy land again, but Fernando became drunk, dallied with a "loose woman," fell asleep, and when he awoke, the money was gone. Davidson, p. 82, gives a fuller account of these events than Gillin, who summarizes them briefly: *Human Ways*, p. 201.

19. In contrast, see the sensitive and moving treatment of Kaja Finkler, *Women in Pain: Gender and Morbidity in Mexico* (Philadelphia: University of Pennsylvania Press, 1994).

20. Gillin was among the first to write about this condition, which figures prominently in Mesoamerican theories of illness and healing. For later discussions, see Italo Signorini, *Los tres ejes de la vida: Almas, corpo, enfermedad entre los Nahuas de la Sierra de Puebla* (Xalapa, Mexico: Editorial UV, 1989), and Arthur Rubel, Carl O'Nell, and Rolando Collado-Ardón, *Susto: A Folk Illness* (Berkeley: University of California Press, 1984), along with the literature cited therein.

21. Gillin, *Human Ways*, p. 206. Davidson, "A Method for Studying Religious Cult and Healing Ceremonies," p. 116, quotes the phrases with which Manuel began his address to the chief of the spirits. These contain some striking details.

"Good evening, compadre Lucifer. Here [Alicia] lost her soul. She is a good woman. She has harmed no one. Now she suffers much. Santo Lucifer, I bring you gifts, a good cigar, good cigarettes, good bread, and a good drink. Please allow her soul to go free."

22. A significant difference is that the Chimalteco spirits are not held responsible for soul loss. The closest resemblance is to the Zinacanteco Earth Lord, "a fat and greedy ladino who wants meat with his tortillas," and who, if not placated with gifts, will "capture the souls of the inhabitants of the house and put them to work as slaves for many years, until the 'iron huraches he gives them all wear out.'" Evon Z. Vogt, *Tortillas for the Gods: A Symbolic Analysis of Zinacanteco Rituals* (Norman: University of Oklahoma Press, 1993), pp. 15–18 and 56–58.

23. The leader of the spirits, Don Avelín Caballero Sombrerón, is known only to Manuel, and according to his rivals is simply the healer's invention. His name, however, resembles that of Pedro Amalín, one of the conquistadores who captured San Luis in 1530. Don Manuel Urrutia was an *intendente* of the village in the 1890s, while Señor Don Justo Juez and Doña María Diego seem to have similar connections. Rounding out the set is Saint Gabriel, Manuel's patron *santo*. Gillin, *Culture of Security*, pp. 11, 106, 108.

24. Gillin, *Human Ways*, p. 207. Davidson, "A Method for Studying Religious Cult and Healing Ceremonies," p. 115, adds white bread to the list.

25. Gillin, *Culture of Security*, pp. 60–62. The fullest discussion of *compadrazgo* in Mesoamerica is Hugo Nutini and Betty Bell, *Ritual Kinship: The Structure and Histori-*

cal Development of the Compadrazgo System in Rural Tlaxcala (Princeton, NJ: Princeton University Press, 1980), with full citation of earlier literature.

26. Gillin, *Culture of Security*, p. 61.

27. Davidson notes that he and Gillin stayed in the home of a wealthy ladino, in which all their Indian visitors seemed ill at ease, save only Manuel ("A Method for Studying Religious Cult and Healing Ceremonies," pp. 53–54). He also quotes the response Manuel gave when he asked him what things he feared, a response which indicates his awareness of the current political situation: "Here we are not afraid of much. We are afraid of revolutions, but they do not come often. Our greatest fear is of the pesta which kills our children" (p. 49).

28. Gillin, "San Luis Jilotepeque: 1942–55," pp. 23–27, esp. p. 25. Further information may be obtained in Jim Handy, *Revolution in the Countryside: Rural Conflict and Agrarian Reform in Guatemala, 1944–1954* (Chapel Hill: University of North Carolina Press, 1994), esp. pp. 131–32.

29. On the revolutionary period, see Handy, *Revolution in the Countryside*; Marco Antonio Villamar, *Significado de la decada 1944–1954 conocido como la revolucion guatamalteca de octubre* (Guatemala City: n.p., 1993); Piero Gleijesis, *Shattered Hope: The Guatemalan Revolution and the United States, 1944–1954* (Princeton, NJ: Princeton University Press, 1991); and Robert Wasserstrom, "Revolution in Guatemala: Peasants and Politics under the Arbenz Government," *Comparative Studies in Society and History* 17 (1975): 443–78. Regarding the coup—which was largely orchestrated by E. Howard Hunt, of Watergate fame—see Stephen Schlesinger and Stephen Kinzer, *Bitter Fruit: The Untold Story of the American Coup in Guatemala* (Garden City, NY: Doubleday, 1982); Richard Immerman, *The CIA in Guatemala: The Foreign Policy of Intervention* (Austin: University of Texas Press, 1982); and José Aybar de Soto, *Dependency and Intervention: The Case of Guatemala in 1954* (Boulder, CO: Westview Press, 1978).

30. See Susanne Jonas, *The Battle for Guatemala: Rebels, Death Squads, and U.S. Power* (Boulder, CO: Westview Press, 1991); Jim Handy, "Insurgency and Counter-Insurgency in Guatemala," in *Sociology of "Developing Societies": Central America*, ed. Jan Flora and Edelberto Torres Rivas (New York: Monthly Review Press, 1989), pp. 112–39; Robert M. Carmack, ed., *Harvest of Violence: The Maya Indians and the Guatemalan Crisis* (Norman: University of Oklahoma Press, 1988); Jean-Marie Simon, *Guatemala: Eternal Spring—Eternal Tyranny* (New York: W. W. Norton, 1987); and Michael McClintock, *The American Connection: State Terror and Popular Resistance in El Salvador and Guatemala*, 2 vols. (London: Zed Books, 1985). The many reports filed by human rights organizations also make for grim reading: *Guatemala: Getting away with Murder* (New York: Americas Watch; Somerville, MA: Physicians for Human Rights, 1991); *Guatemala: Human Rights Violations under the Civilian Government* (New York: Amnesty International, 1989); *Closing the Space: Human Rights in Guatemala* (New York: Americas Watch, 1988); *Guatemala* (London: Catholic Institute for International Relations, 1988); *Guatemala: A Nation of Prisoners* (New York: Americas Watch, 1984); *Guatemala—Tyranny on Trial: Testimony of the Permanent People's Tribunal* (San Francisco: Synthesis Publications, 1984); *Report on the Situation of Human Rights in the Republic of Guatemala* (Washington, DC: General Secretariat of the Organization of American States, 1983); and *Guatemala: A Government Program of Political Murder* (London: Amnesty International, 1981).

31. See G. Asturias Montenegro, *Los 504 dias de Rios Montt* (Guatemala City: Gamma, 1995), as well as the literature cited in the preceding note.

32. Regarding patterns of religious change over the past twenty years, see Richard Wilson, *Maya Resurgence in Guatemala: Q'eqchi' Experiences* (Norman: University of Oklahoma Press, 1995); Luis Samandú, ed., *Protestantismos y procesos sociales en Centroamérica* (San José, Costa Rica: EDUCA, 1991), pp. 67–114; idem, *Guatemala. Retos de la iglesia católica en una sociedad en crisis* (San José, Costa Rica: DEI/CSUCA, 1990); David Stoll, *Is Latin America Turning Protestant? The Politics of Evangelical Growth* (Berkeley: University of California Press, 1990); Sheldon Annis, *God and Production in a Guatemalan Town* (Austin: University of Texas Press, 1987); Douglas Brintnall, *Revolt against the Dead: The Modernization of a Mayan Community in the Highlands of Guatemala* (New York: Gordon & Breach, 1979); and James Sexton, "Protestantism and Modernization in Two Guatemalan Towns," *American Ethnologist* 5 (1978): 280–302.

33. Watanabe, *Maya Saints and Souls*, pp. 194–216.

34. Regarding the use of civilian patrols to carry out terror at the local level, see Alice Jay et al., *Persecution by Proxy: The Civil Patrols in Guatemala* (New York: Robert F. Kennedy Memorial Center for Human Rights, 1993).

35. Watanabe, *Maya Saints and Souls*, pp. 214–15.

36. For theoretical reflections on syncretism, see Charles Stewart and Rosalind Shaw, eds., *Syncretism/Anti-Syncretism: The Politics of Religious Synthesis* (New York: Routledge, 1994). Recent attempts to make use of it for Mesoamerican data include Manuel Marzal, *El sincretismo iberoamericano: Un estudio comparativo sobre los quechuas (Cusco), los mayas (Chiapas), y los africanos (Bahia)* (Lima: Pontificia Universidad Catolica del Peru, 1985); Hugo Nutini, *Todos Santos in Rural Tlaxcala: A Syncretic, Expressive, and Symbolic Analysis of the Cult of the Dead* (Princeton, NJ: Princeton University Press, 1988); and Doren Slade, *Making the World Safe for Existence: Celebration of the Saints among the Sierra Nahuatl* (Ann Arbor: University of Michigan Press, 1992).

CHAPTER ELEVEN

"In Praise of the Chaotic" was originally presented at a conference on the theme of "Chaos" organized by the University of Copenhagen's Institute of History of Religions (April 2007), and first published in Danish translation in *Chaos* 49 (2008): 9–27.

1. Thus, to cite an obvious example, N. J. Girardot, "Chaos," in *The Encyclopedia of Religion*, ed. Mircea Eliade (New York: Macmillan, 1987), 3:213–18.

2. Hesiod, *Theogony* 104–15 (emphasis added). All translations are original, and texts are taken from the edition of M. L. West, *Hesiod, Theogony* (Oxford: Clarendon Press, 1966).

χαίρετε τέκνα Διός, δότε δ᾿ ἱμερόεσσαν ἀοιδήν
κλείετε δ᾿ ἀθανάτων ἱερὸν γένος αἰέν ἐόντων,
οἳ Γῆς ἐξεγένοντο καὶ Οὐρανοῦ ἀστερόεντος,
Νυκτός τε δνοφερῆς, οὕς θ᾿ ἁλμυρὸς ἔτρεφε Πόντος.
εἴπατε δ᾿ ὡς τά πρῶτα θεοὶ καὶ γαῖα γένοντο ...
ταῦτά μοι ἔσπετε Μοῦσαι Ὀλύμπια δώματ᾿ ἔχουσαι
ἐξ ἀρχῆς, καὶ εἴπαθ᾿, ὅτι πρῶτον γένετ᾿ αὐτῶν.

3. Even here, a slight variation occurs, for when Earth enters the story as part of the first-named tetrad (line 106), she bears the name Γῆ. When she next appears, as part of the second-named (but firstborn) tetrad, it is under the name Γαῖα (line 117). Elsewhere in the poem, γῆ is used only as a common noun denoting the physical

earth, not the goddess who is its embodiment (cf. lines 679, 720, 721, 723a, 728, 736, 762, 790, 807, 972). For the latter, the form Γαῖα is always employed elsewhere (23×, including lines 20, 45, 126, 147, 154, etc.). This point has been noted by West, p. 189, who takes the occurrence of Γῆ as a proper name at line 106 to be a Homeric usage. This may be so, but the contrast of nomenclature at lines 106 and 117 also advances a subtle theological point: existence of the earth as a deity (Γαῖα) is temporally prior to its realization in material form (Γῆ), insofar as spirit takes ontological precedence over matter.

4. For some recent attempts to interpret this concept, see John Bussanich, "A Theoretical Interpretation of Hesiod's Chaos," *Classical Philology* 78 (1983): 212–19; H. Podbielski, "Le Chaos et les confins de l'univers dans la *Théogonie* d'Hésiode," *Les Études Classiques* 54 (1986): 253–63; and Robert Mondi, "Chaos and the Hesiodic Cosmogony," *Harvard Studies in Classical Philology* 92 (1989): 1–41, with citation of earlier literature.

5. *Theogony* 114–22 (emphasis added):

ταῦτά μοι ἔσπετε Μοῦσαι Ὀλύμπια δώματ᾽ ἔχουσαι
ἐξ ἀρχῆς, καὶ εἴπαθ᾽, ὅτι πρῶτον γένετ᾽ αὐτῶν.

   ἤτοι μὲν πρώτιστα Χάος γένετ᾽· αὐτὰρ ἔπειτα
Γαῖ᾽ εὐρύστερνος, πάντων ἕδος ἀσφαλὲς αἰεὶ
ἀθανάτων οἳ ἔχουσι κάρη νιφόεντος Ὀλύμπου,
Τάρταρά τ᾽ ἠερόεντα μυχῷ χθονὸς εὐρυοδείης,
ἠδ᾽ ἔρος, ὃς κάλλιστος ἐν ἀθανάτοισι θεοῖσι . . .

6. *Theogony* 123–32:

From Chaos, Nether-Darkness [Erebos] and black Night were born,
And from Night, Celestial-Light [Aithêr] and Day came to birth,
Whom Night conceived and bore after mingling in love with Nether-Darkness.
Earth first gave birth to starry Sky [Ouranos],
Equal to herself, so that he might fully cover her,
And she was ever the unmovable seat for the blessed gods.
And she gave birth to great mountains, lovely divine haunts
Of the Nymphs, who dwell in the glen-filled mountains.
And she bore Pontos, the barren sea, with its swelling surface,
Without any act of desirous love.

ἐκ Χάεος δ᾽ Ερεβός τε μέλαινά τε Νὺξ ἐγένοντο,
Νυκτὸς δ᾽ αὖτ᾽ Αἰθήρ τε καὶ Ἡμέρη ἐξεγένοντο,
οὓς τέκε κυσαμένη Ἐρέβει φιλότητι μιγεῖσα.
Γαῖα δέ τοι πρῶτον μέν ἐγείνατο ἶσον ἑωυτῇ
Οὐρανὸν ἀστερόενθ᾽, ἵνα μιν περὶ πάντα καλύπτοι,
ὄφρ᾽ εἴη μακάρεσσι θεοῖς ἕδος ἀσφαλὲς αἰεί,
γείνατο δ᾽ οὔρεα μακρά, θεᾶν χαρίεντας ἐναύλους
Νυμφέων, αἳ ναίουσιν ἀν᾽ οὔρεα βησσήεντα,
ἠδέ καὶ ἀτρύγετον πέλαγος τέκεν οἴδματι θυῖον,
Πόντον, ἄτερ φιλότητος ἐφιμέρου

7. Being nonmaterial, nebulous, and somewhat indistinct, members of this lineage are thus hard to know, and their character often prompts a certain disquiet or anxiety, as in the case of Fate (Moros), Destiny (Kêr), Death (Thanatos), Grief (Oizys), Nemesis, and Strife (Eris). Others, however, remain ambiguous and ultimately unknowable,

but not necessarily threatening, as in the case of Sleep (Hypnos), Dreams (Oneiroi), and Love (Philotês). Regarding this lineage, as treated by Hesiod and others, see Clémence Ramnoux, *La nuit et les enfants de la nuit dans la tradition grecque* (Paris: Flammarion, 1986), and Giuliana Scalera McClintock, *Il Pensiero dell' invisibile nella Grecia arcaica* (Naples: Tempi Moderni Edizioni, 1989).

8. The exception is Typhôn, whom Earth bears to Tartaros, but who dies without issue (*Theogony* 820ff.). On the significance of this monster and the victory over him that confirms Zeus's power, see Alain Ballabriga, "Le dernier adversaire de Zeus: Le myth de Typhon dans l'épopée grecque archaïque," *Revue de l'histoire des religions* 207 (1990): 3–30; and Fabrienne Blaise, "L'épisode de Typhée dans la *Théogonie* d'Hésiode (v. 820–885): La stabilization du monde," *Révue des etudes grecques* 105 (1992): 349–70.

9. M. Hofinger, *Lexicon Hesiodeum* (Leiden: E. J. Brill, 1975), p. 700, translates τό χάος as "abîme, gouffre," when used as a common noun, τό χάος (i.e. the proper noun) as "Chaos, l'abîme personifié; dieu primordial." Later authors tend to associate Chaos either with the empty space between Earth and Sky above (thus Bacchylides 5.27; Aristophanes, *Clouds* 424, 627, *Birds* 1218) or that between Earth and Tartaros below (thus [Pseudo-]Plato, *Axiochus* 371e; Quintus Smyrnaeus 2.614). Etymologically, the attested form is derived from an earlier .χάος, closely related to the adjective χαῦνος, "insubstantial" (on which, see the splendid discussion of Mondi, "Chaos and the Hesiodic Cosmogony," pp. 22–26) and a bit more distantly to such terms as χάσκω, "to yawn, gape, open wide," and χάσμα, "chasm, gulf, wide opening." For fuller discussions, see West, *Hesiod, Theogony*, pp. 192–93; Hjalmar Frisk, *Griechisches etymologisches Wörterbuch* (Heidelberg: Carl Winter, 1973), 2:1072–73; and Pierre Chantraine, *Dictionnaire étymologique de la langue grecque* (Paris: Éditions Klincksieck, 1968–80), 4:1246.

10. Hermann Fränkel, "Drei Interpretationen aus Hesiod," in his *Wegen und Formen frühgriechischen Denkens* (Munich: Beck, 1955), p. 318.

11. The name Ginnungagap is unattested in any text prior to the *Edda* of Snorri Sturluson (1179–1241). In all likelihood, Snorri himself coined the term, drawing on *Völuspá* 3, a poem that probably dates to the late tenth century. This and subsequent translations are original. Texts are taken from Gustav Neckel, ed., *Edda: Die Lieder des Codex Regius* (Heidelberg: Carl Winter, 1962).

> It was early in time
> There where Ymir dwelt.
> Neither sand, nor sea was,
> Nor chill waves.
> The earth, not found,
> Nor heaven above.
> The void was vast [*gap var ginnunga*]
> And grass nowhere.
>
> Ár var alda
> Þar er Ymir byggði;
> Vara sandr né sær
> né svalar unnir.
> Iörð fannz æva
> né upphiminn:

gap var ginnunga,
en gras hvergi.

12. Jan de Vries, *Altnordisches etymologisches Wörterbuch* (Leiden: E. J. Brill, 1977), p. 156. Compare also Anglo-Saxon *geáp*, (noun) "expanse, room," (adjective) "open, spread out, extended, broad, roomy, spacious, wide"; *geápan* (verb), "to gape, open."

13. Thus ibid., p. 167–68; idem, "Ginnungagap," *Acta Philologica Scandinavica* 5 (1930): 41–66, who favors an association of *Ginnunga-* with Runic Danish *ginu-*, as attested in inscriptions that read *ginoronoR* (Stentoften, ca. 620 CE) and *ginArunAR* (Björketorp, ca. 650). Interpreting these forms to mean "zauberkräftige runen," he goes on to suggest that *Ginnungagap* most literally denotes "der mit magischen kräften erfüllte Weltraum."

14. Ursula Dronke, *The Poetic Edda* (Oxford: Clarendon Press, 1969-), 2:112–14, frankly acknowledged that *ginnunga* "presents a tortuous problem; it has no straight-forward linguistic interpretation in terms of Old Norse." She goes on to suggest that Old High German *ginunga* (with single *n*), which usually serves to gloss Latin *hiatus* and *rictus*, "may have been a term for the heathen Germanic *Chaos*." Going further still, she imagines it was borrowed into Old Norse, with doubling of the consonant as a result of associations with ON *ginn-*. While possible, the argument seems unlikely: more ingenious than persuasive.

15. Richard Cleasby, Gudbrand Vigfusson, and Sir William Craigie, *Icelandic-English Dictionary*, 2nd ed. (Oxford: Clarendon Press, 1957), p. 200, who derive *ginnunga* from Old Norse *ginn-* and connect the latter to Anglo-Saxon *gin* or *ginn*, "vast, wide," then go on to state, "It seems however better to derive it from the verb *beginnan*, English *begin*, a word used in all Teutonic languages, except the old Scandinavian tongue, where it is unknown, unless in this mythological prefix." The absence of corresponding terms in Scandinavian remains a significant difficulty.

16. *Gylfaginning* 5; this and subsequent translations from Old Norse are original. Text here and in subsequent references are taken from Anthony Faulkes, ed., *Snorri Sturluson: Edda; Prologue and Gylfaginning* (Oxford: Clarendon Press, 1982):

> Svá sem kallt stóð af Niflheimi ok allir hlutir grimmir, svá var þat er vissi námunda Muspelli heitt ok ljóst, en Ginnungagap var svá hlætt sem lopt vindlaust. ok þá er mœttisk hrímin ok blær hitans, svá at bráðnaði ok draup, ok af þeim kvikudropum kviknaði með krapti þess er til sendi hitann, ok varð mannz líkandi, ok var sá nefndr Ymir.

17. Comparison of the primordial gap to "windless air" (*lopt vindlaust*) suggests the presence of a minimal something that, like air, is of indispensable importance, however much it may be imperceptible.

18. On this passage, see Klaus von See, *Mythos und Theologie im skandinavischen Hochmittelalter* (Heidelberg: Carl Winter, 1988), pp. 52–55; Anthony Faulkes, "Pagan Sympathy: Attitudes to Heathendom in the Prologue to Snorra Edda," in *Edda: A Collection of Essays*, ed. R. J. Glendinning and H. Bessason (Winnipeg: University of Manitoba Press, 1983), pp. 282–314; Margaret Clunies Ross, *Prolonged Echoes: Old Norse Myths in Medieval Icelandic Society* (Odense: Odense University Press, 1994) 1:152–58; and Bruce Lincoln, "The Center of the World and the Origins of Life," *History of Religions* 40 (2001): 311–26.

19. Emphases added. All translations are original. This and subsequent

texts are taken from Fazlollah Pakzad, ed., *Bundahišn: Zoroastrische Kosmo-gonie und Kosmologie. Band I: Kritische Edition* (Tehran: Centre for the Great Islamic Encyclopaedia, 2005). Greater Bundahišn 1.1–8:

> pad wēh-dēn owōn paydāg kū Ohrmazd bālistīg pad harwisp-āgāhīh ud wehīh zamān ī a-kanārag andar rōšnīh hamē būd. ān rōšnīh gāh ud gyāg ī Ohrmazd ast kē asar-rōšnīh gōwēd. ud ān harwisp-āgāhīh ud wēhīh ud zamān ī a-kanārag čiyōn Ohrmazd ud gāh dēn ud zamān i Ohrmazd būd hēnd. Ahreman andar tārigīh pad pas-dānišnīh ud zadār-kāmīh zofr-pāyag būd. u-š zadār-kāmagīh xēm ud ān tārigīh gyāg ast kē asar-tārigīh gōwēd. u-šān mayān tuhīgīh būd ast kē Way kē gumēzišn padiš. har(w) dō(w)ān ⁺mēnōg kanāragōmand ud a-kānaragōmand. čē ān ī asar-rōšnīh gōwēd kū nē sarōmand ud zofr pāyag ān ī asar-tārigīh ud ān ast a-kanāragīh. pad wimand har(w) dō kanāragōmand kū-šān mayān tuhīgīh ud ēk ō did nē paywast hēnd. did har(w) dō(w)ān mēnōg pad xwēš-tan kanāragōmand.

20. The term is an abstract noun meaning "emptiness, void," built on the adjective *tuhīg*, "empty." As H. W. Bailey, *Zoroastrian Problems in the Ninth Century Books* (Oxford: Clarendon Press, 1943; 2nd ed. 1971), p. 135, first recognized, the same cosmic void is sometimes also denoted as *wišādagīh* ("openness, empty space"). Thus, for instance, *Selections of Zādspram* 1.1: "Now, in the Religion, it is revealed thus: 'Light was above and darkness below, and in between the two was empty space'" (hād pad dēn ōwōn paydāg kū: rōšnīh azabar ud tārīgīh azēr u-šān mayānag ī harw 2 wišādagīh būd). Translation is original. Text is taken from Ph. Gignoux and A. Tafazzoli, eds., *Anthologie de Zādspram* (Paris: Association pour l'avancement des études iraniennes, 1993).

21. *Dēnkart* 5.24.2–3, emphases added; translation is original. Text is taken from M. J. Dresden, *Dēnkart: A Pahlavi Text; Facsimile Edition of the Manuscript B of the K. R. Cama Oriental Institute, Bombay* (Wiesbaden: Otto Harrassowitz, 1966), p. 357, lines 6–11; and Dhanjishah Meherjibhai Madan, ed., *The Complete Text of the Pahlavi Dinkard* (Bombay: Society for the Promotion of Researches into the Zoroastrian Religion, 1911), p. 457, lines 4–8:

> hambadīg pad wihēz ī az gyāg [ō gyāg] andar tuhīgīh āyad. hambadīg az bun abēcim agārīhā dwārist pad tuwān jumbāgīh ud nē nāmcištīg-xwāhišnīhā mad ō sāmān ī ēn rōšn gōhr. ōh-īz ōy hambadīg abēcim ud halag-wadagār ud ka anāgāhīhā pahikafišnīg mad {ud} az jud-gōhrīh ōšmurīhist būd.

Subsequent texts are taken from these sources. All translations are original.

22. See *Greater Bundahišn* 6A.2–4; *Selections of Zādspram* 3.2–4; *Dēnkart* 3.107 (B Ms. 74.20–75.1).

23. *Selections of Zādspram* 1.31–32:

> Ahriman, together with his allies, came to the star station. The base of the sky is in the star station. He pulled it down from there to the Void, which is outside the foundation of the lights and the darkness, to the place of battle, where there is the motion of both.

> pad ham zamān Ahriman az ham-zōhrān hammis bē ō star pāyag āmad. bun ī asmān ī pad star pāyag ⁺dāšt. az anōh frōd ō tuhīgīh āhixt ī ⁺bērōn ī buništ ī rōšnān ud tārān ud gyāg ī ardīg kē-š tazišn ī harw dōān pad-iš.

Cf. *Greater Bundahišn* 4.10:

Then the Evil Spirit, together with powerful demons, rose up against the lights. He saw the sky, which was shown to him spiritually, even if it was still not created in bodily/material fashion. Enviously and desirously, he attacked the sky, which stood in the star station and led it down to the Void, which, as I wrote at the beginning, was between the foundation of the lights and the darknesses.

pas āxist Gannāg Mēnōg abāg hamist dēwān abzārān ō padīrag ī rōšnān. u-š ān asmān dīd ī-šān mēnōgīhā nimūd ka nē astōmand dād estēd. arēšk kāmagīha tag abar kard asmān pad star pāyag estād frōd ō tuhīgīh haxt ī-m ī pad bun nipišt kū andarag ī buništag ī rōšnān ud tomīgān būd.

It is not clear to me which stars Ahriman dragged into the Void, but it may have been the planets, which are marked by an awkward retrograde motion much like his own, and to which a malevolent nature is often attributed. See further such texts as *Greater Bundahišn* 2, 4.23, 4.27, 5.4–7, 5A.1–9, 6H, 6J, 27.52. Also relevant are *Selections of Zādspram* 1.26–33, 34.49; *Mēnōg ī Xrad* 8.17–21, 12.3–10, 49; and the *Pahlavi Rivāyat Accompanying the Dādestān ī Dēnīg* 35c.1–2 and 65.

24. Thus, for instance, *Greater Bundahišn* 34.30.

25. *Dēnkart* 5.24.9 (B MS. 358.14–18 [emphases added]):

abgandan <ud> ōbastan ī-š abāz ō tuhīgīh spurr-uzmāyišnīhā ud bowandag-stōwīhā ud agārīhā ud purr-waxrīhā ud zad-abzārīhā ud wašt-rōyīhā ud widārd ud garāntom ud awištābtom bim-paymōgīhā ud ān drubuštīh ī pērōzīh apērōzīh xwanihēd andaragīhā ud brīd-kōxšišnīhā ud an-ēmēdīhā pad ān ham nērōg ī yazd.

26. *Dēnkart* 5.24.10 (B MS. 358.19–359.2):

One reason he is not able to return to the struggle is that once he retreated [into the Void], there is no way for him to be able to come back. Here, no fear, lamentation, or thought of him remains. He is in that fortress "Victory that is Non-Victory": in terror, dread, self-made containment and total bondage. Thus, in no way is he able (to return to the struggle).

u-š abāz ō kōšišn mad<an> ⁺ayāristan nē sazistan cim ēk ān ī pēš abāz dwārīd u-š ēc ēwēnag abāz ayāristan. nē sazēd ud ēc homānāg-bahrīh nēst. ēc bim ud cēhišn <ud> handēšišn u-š ēdar nē mānēd ud pad-iz ān pērōzīh a-pērōzīh drubuštīh ud āhr ud sam ud xwadīk-kard pašn ud bandīh bowandag bast ēstēd ēc ēwēnag nē ayāristan cimīg.

27. *Gylfaginning* 5:

In no way may we acknowledge him a god. He was evil, as were all his kinsmen. We call them frost giants. It is also said that when he slept, he sweated. Then a man and woman grew under his left arm, and one foot begat a son with the other. From that came the lineages that were frost giants. The old frost giant we call Ymir.

Fyr øngan mun játum vér hann guð. Hann var illr ok allir hans ættmenn, þá kǫllum vér hrímþursa. Ok svá er sagt at þá er hann svaf, fekk hann sveita. þá óx undir vinstri hǫnd honum maðr ok kona, ok annarr fótr hans gat son við ǫðrum. En þaðan af kómu ættir, þat eru hrímþursar. Hinn gamli hrímþurs, hann kǫllum vér Ymi.

28. *Gylfaginning* 8 (emphasis added):

þeir tóku Ymi, ok fluttu í mitt Ginnungagap, ok gerðu af honum jǫrðina; af blóði hans sæinn og vǫtnin. Jǫrðin var gǫr af holdinu, en bjǫrgin af beinunum; grjót ok urðir gerðu þeir af tǫnnum ok jǫxlum, ok af þeim beinum, er brotin váru. . . . ok með þeiri sjávar strǫndu gáfu þeir lǫnd til bygðar jǫtna ættum. En fyrir innan á jǫrðunni gerðu þeir borg umhverfis heim fyrir ófriði jǫtna, en til þeirar borgar hǫfðu þeir brár Ymis jǫtuns, ok kǫlluðu þá borg Miðgarð.

This passage draws on older poetic traditions, including *Grímnismál* 40–41 and *Vafþrúðnismál* 21.

29. On this aspect of the Ymir myth, see John Lindow, "Bloodfeud and Scandinavian Mythology," *Alvíssmál* 4 (1994): 51–68.

30. *Theogony* 687–700 (emphasis added):

οὐδ᾽ ἄρ᾽ ἔτι Ζεὺς ἴσχεν ἑὸν μένος, ἀλλά νυ τοῦ γε
εἶθαρ μέν μένεος πλῆντο φρένες, ἐκ δέ τε πᾶσαν
φαῖνε βίην· ἄμυδις δ᾽ ἄρ᾽ ἀπ᾽ οὐρανοῦ ἠδ᾽ ἀπ᾽ Ὀλύμπου
ἀστράπτων ἔστειχε συνωχαδόν, οἱ δέ κεραυνοὶ
ἴκταρ ἅμα βροντῇ τε καὶ ἀστεροπῇ ποτέοντο
χειρὸς ἄπο στιβαρῆς, ἱερὴν φλόγα εἰλυφρόωντες,
ταρφέες· ἀμφὶ δέ γαῖα φερέσβιος ἐσμαράγιζε
καιομένη, λάκε δ᾽ ἀμφὶ περὶ μεγάλ᾽ ἄσπετος ὕλη·
ἔζεε δέ χθὼν πᾶσα καὶ Ὠκεανοῖο ῥέεθρα
πόντος τ᾽ ἀτρύγετος· τοὺς δ᾽ ἄμφεπε θερμὸς ἀυτμὴ
Τιτῆνας χθονίους, φλὸξ δ᾽ αἰθέρα δῖαν ἵκανεν
ἄσπετος, ὄσσε δ᾽ ἄμερδε καὶ ἰφθίμων περ ἐόντων
αὐγὴ μαρμαίρουσα κεραυνοῦ τε στεροπῆς τε.
καῦμα δέ θεσπέσιον κάτεχεν χάος

Typically, editors do not capitalize χάος here or in verse 814, treating it as a common rather than a proper noun. This reflects their sense that the usage in these passages differs from that of lines 116 and 123, where Chaos is fully personified; but it is an editorial decision and not part of the manuscript tradition. In the latter two passages, Chaos has become less nebulous and more objectified, also less independent an entity as it becomes an object on which Zeus's power makes itself felt. It is thus more proper (and more analytically revealing) to observe that the nature of Chaos changes in the course of the mythic narrative as the result of the action, than to posit two different entities: τό Χάος and τό χάος.

31. Thus, for instance, West, *Hesiod, Theogony*, p. 349.

32. It is hard to capture the full sense of the verb *katekhein*, which Hesiod employs here and at line 844 to describe acts of penetration and domination. Hofinger, *Lexicon Hesiodeum*, p. 339, offers the following definition: "envahir, occuper, régner sur, prendre possession de." The term appears more frequently in the Homeric epic, where its semantics include "to hold down, keep in a lowered position," and "to seize, detain, withhold from the rightful owner" (Richard Cunliffe, *A Lexicon of the Homeric Dialect* [Norman: University of Oklahoma Press, 1963], pp. 219–20).

33. For detailed discussion of this passage, see David M. Johnson, "Hesiod's descriptions of Tartarus (Theogony 721–819)," *Phoenix* 53 (1999): 8–28.

34. Theogony 813–14: "πρόσθεν δέ θεῶν ἔκτοσθεν ἁπάντων / Τιτῆνες ναίουσι, πέρην χάεος ζοφεροῖο." Modification of Chaos by the adjective *zopheros* in this line indicates the way it has been made just a bit more tangible and assimilated to Tartaros. Nowhere else is that term applied to Chaos, and this is the only time it appears in the Hesiodic corpus. *Zophos*, however, from which it is derived, is elsewhere associated with the subterranean murk of Tartaros (*Theogony* 653, 658, 729).

35. Smith has recently written about this period and his dealings with Eliade in *Relat-*

ing Religion: Essays in the Study of Religion (Chicago: University of Chicago Press, 2004), pp. 1–60, esp. 11–19. The course I took from Smith in Fall 1971 is described at pp. 10 and 39–41. Eliade has virtually nothing of interest to say about this period or his brilliant junior colleague, neither in his *Journal*, trans. Mac Linscott Ricketts, 4 vols. (Chicago: University of Chicago Press, 1990), nor in any of his autobiographical writings.

36. On some of the patterns one finds in such myths, see Jarich Oosten, *The War of the Gods: The Social Code in Indo-European Mythology* (London: Routledge & Kegan Paul, 1985).

CHAPTER TWELVE

"Theses on Comparison" (with Cristiano Grottanelli) was orginally presented at a conference on the theme "Les approches comparatives en histoire des religions antiques: Controverses et propositions," organized by the Atelier Chicago-Paris sur les religions anciennes (Paris, December 2010).

1. Grottanelli and I disagreed somewhat on this point. I quote from his letter dated July 7, 1983, responding to my earlier assertion that those things called "universals" are either nothing of the sort—i.e. misrepresentations of some privileged part for the whole—or "commonplaces," i.e. widespread banalities.

> I am glad to see that you accept the existence of "generally human" data; but I do not think that such data are banal or uninteresting. Is the incest prohibition uninteresting? Is the right vs. left classification, and are the other "simple" dual symbolic classifications uninteresting? Is the problem of purity and pollution uninteresting? This list could continue; but of course it is not boundless, for indeed the generally human problems and data are few. And, of course, they are always solved in different ways by the different societies: to see that there are "generally human" problems and data does not mean that all societies and cultures are "fundamentally alike." It only means that in order to study the specific, one has, first of all, to deal with the "general": only when one has understood what is not specific can one go on to specify. This is the very (implicit) basis of comparatism itself, for if there were not a general "human" similarity, comparison (i.e. comparison between utterly different human problems and data) would be impossible.

2. On the general nature and importance of the *Bundahišn*, see Carlo Cereti, *La Letteratura Pahlavi: Introduzione ai testi con riferimenti alla storia degli studi e alla tradizione manoscritta* (Milan: Mimesis, 2001), pp. 87–105. The standard edition is now Fazlollah Pakzad, *Bundahišn: Zoroastrische Kosmogonie und Kosmologie; Band I: Kritische Edition* (Tehran: Centre for the Great Islamic Encyclopaedia, 2005). All translations of the *Bundahišn* and other scriptural quotations/extracts that follow are original.

3. This is spelled out in *Greater Bundahišn* 1.1–11.

4. *Greater Bundahišn* 1.12:

> In his omniscience, the Wise Lord knows that the Foul Spirit exists, because he [i.e. Ahriman] draws up plans in envious desire, as he mixes things up from beginning to end in countless ways. Spiritually, [the Wise Lord] created the creation that is necessary for his power.

> Ohrmazd pad harwisp-āgāhīh dānist kū Gannāg-Mēnōg ast čē ⁺handāzēd{ud kunēd} pad arešk-kāmagīh ciyōn /andar\ gūmēzēd <az> fragān /ta\ frazām abāg cand abzārān. u-š mēnōgīhā ān dām ī pad ān abzār andar abāyēd frāz brēhēnīd.

Pahlavi *arešk* is derived from Avestan *araska-*, which also denotes "envy." The latter term occurs only three times in the Avestan corpus, in formulaic passages that describe the primordial Golden Age as a time when "there was neither cold nor heat, neither old age nor death, nor demon-created envy" (nōit aotəm åŋha nōit garəməm nōit zairuua åŋha nōit mərθiiuš nōit araskō daēuua.dātō: *Yasna* 9.5, *Yašt* 15.16, *Yašt* 19.33).

5. *Greater Bundahišn* 1.14–15:

Gannāg-Mēnōg pas-dānišnīh rāy az (h)astīh ī Ohrmazd an-āgāh būd. pas az ān zōfāyīg ⁺axēzīd ō wimand ī didār ī rōšnān mad. ka-š dīd Ohrmazd ud ān rōšnīh ī a-griftār frāz ⁺payrūd zadār-kāmagīh ud arešk-gōhrīh rāy pad murnjēnīdan tag abar kard.

Greater Bundahišn 4.10 describes Ahriman's primordial assault, once again tracing the violent acts he committed to his preexisting sense of envy: "Then the Foul Spirit rose up against the lights, together with his demons and powers. He saw the sky. In envious desire, he launched an attack" (pas āxist Gannāg-Mēnōg abāg hāmist dēwān abzārān ō padīrag ī rōšnān. u-š ān asmān dīd ī-šān mēnōgīhā nimūd ka nē astōmand dād estēd arešk-kāmagīhā tag abar kard).

6. Much recent scholarship has been concerned to show the association of Ahriman with nonbeing. See especially Shaul Shaked, "Some Notes on Ahreman, the Evil Spirit, and His Creation," in *Studies in Mysticism and Religion Presented to Gershom G. Scholem*, ed. E. E. Urbach et al. (Jerusalem: Magnes Press, 1967), pp. 227–34; Jes P. Asumssen, "Some Remarks on Sasanian Demonology," in *Commémoration Cyrus: Actes du Congrès de Shiraz* (Leiden: E. J. Brill, 1974), pp. 236–41; Hanns-Peter Schmidt, "The Non-Existence of Ahreman and the Mixture (*Gumēzišn*) of Good and Evil," in *K. R. Cama Oriental Institute: Second International Congress Proceedings* (Bombay: K. R. Cama Oriental Institute, 1996), pp. 79–95; Antonio Panaino, "A Few Remarks on the Zoroastrian Conception of the Status of Angra Mainyu and of the Daēvas," *Res Orientales* 13 (2001): 99–107; and chapter 4 of the present text.

7. *Dādēstān ī Dēnīg* 36.4–8:

ōh-iz dādār ī dahišn dād ān ī mēnōg dām abēzag anahōgēnēd ud ān-iz ī gētīgīg dām amarg a-zarmān ud suyišn ud abandišn abēš ud adard.... u-š pad arešk ī purr-kēnwarīh ī spurr-druxtārīh nīxwarēd ō griftan wišuftan ud wanēnidan abēsīhēnidan ī im hukard dām ī yazdan.

Text is taken from Mahmoud Jaafari-Dehaghi, ed., *Dādestān ī Dēnīg. Part I: Transcription, Translation, and Commentary* (Paris: Association pour l'avancement des études iraniennes, 1998).

8. *Dēnkart* 5.24.4 makes complex emotions of this sort responsible for Ahriman's assault, listing envy alongside others, but not granting it primacy. On this last point, it differs from the analysis of the *Bundahišn*.

The reason for his waging combat to mix up existence is his improper vindictiveness, greed, lust, enviousness [*areškanīh*], shame, thievishness, quarrelsomeness, arrogance, perversity, ignorance, his lie about being able to destroy the basis of the light-substance, his malevolence, injustice, foolhardy combativeness, and all his functions correlated with these.

ud kōxšišn ī pad andar gumēxtan wihān ān-ēwēn kēnwarīh ud āzwarīh ud waranīgīh ud areškanīh ud nangwarīh ud apparag-xēmīh ud stēzgārīh ud abar-menišnīh ud tar-menišnīh ud a-frazānagīh ud mituxtīh ī pad abesīhēnidan šāyistan ī buništ <ī>

rōšn gōhr ud anāk-kāmīh ud a-dādig-cihragīh ud halak-kōšāgīh ud hāmist imīn ham rāyēnišn.

Text is taken from from Jaleh Amouzgar and Ahmad Tafazzoli, eds., *Le cinquième livre du Dēnkard* (Paris: Association pour l'avancement des etudes iraniennes, 2000).

9. Any of the standard secondary sources contain summary discussions of these issues. See, for example, Herman Lommel, *Die Religion Zarathustras nach dem Awesta dargestellt* (Tübingen: J. C. B. Mohr, 1930), pp. 93–129, 205–46; Jacques Duchesne-Guillemin, *La religion de l'Iran Ancien* (Paris: Presses Universitaires de France, 1962), 308–54; Marijan Molé, *Culte, mythe et cosmologie dans l'Iran ancien* (Paris: Presses Universitaires de France, 1963), pp. 389–422; and Mary Boyce, *A History of Zoroastrianism*, vol. 1, *The Early Period* (Leiden: E. J. Brill, 1975), pp. 192–246.

10. For a variety of positions regarding the date of the text, see Colin Chase, ed., *The Dating of Beowulf* (Toronto: University of Toronto Press, 1997). Citations are taken from Fr. Klaeber, ed., *Beowulf and The Fight at Finnsburg*, 3rd ed. (Lexington, MA: D. C. Heath, 1950). All translations are original.

11. *Beowulf* 104–14:

	fifelcynnes eard
wonsǣli wer	weardode hwile,
siþðan him Scyppend	forscrifen hæfde
in Cāines cynne—	þone cwealm gewræc
ēce Drihten,	þæs þe hē Ābel slōg;
ne gefeah hē þǣre fǣhðe,	ac hē hine feor forwræc,
Metod for þȳ māne	manacynne fram.
Þanon untȳdras	ealle onwōcon,
eotenas ond ylfe	ond orcnēas,
swylce gigantas,	þā wið Gode wunnon
lange þrāge.	

12. The story of Cain appears at Genesis 4.1–16, and verses 3–5 establish his envy of Abel's privileged relation to God as motive for the murder. The theme of Cain's monstrous descendants entered Old English traditions via the pseudoepigraphical Book of Enoch. See further David Williams, *Cain and Beowulf: A Study in Secular Allegory* (Toronto: University of Toronto Press, 1982); Ruth Mellinkoff, "Cain's Monstrous Progeny in *Beowulf*: Part I, Noachic Tradition," *Anglo-Saxon England* 8 (1979): 143–97; idem, "Cain's Monstrous Progeny in *Beowulf*: Part II, Post-Diluvian Survival," *Anglo-Saxon England* 9 (1981): 183–97; Stephen C. Bandy, "Cain, Grendel and the Giants of *Beowulf*," *Papers on Language and Literature* 9 (1973): 235–49; and R. E. Kaske, "Beowulf and the Book of Enoch," *Speculum* 46 (1971): 421–31.

13. The classic discussion of envy, including envy at the creation, as prompting Grendel's assault remains Oliver Farrar Emerson, "Grendel's Motive in Attacking Heorot," *Modern Language Review* 16 (1921): 113–19.

14. *Beowulf* 86–103:

Ðā se ellengǣst	earfoðlīce
Þrāge geþolode,	sē þe in þȳstrum bād,
Þæt hē dōgora gehwām	drēam gehȳrde
hlūdne in healle;	þær wæs hearpan swēg,

swutol sang scopes.   Sægde sē þe cūþe
frumsceaft fīra   feorran reccan,
cwæð þæt se Ælmihtiga   eorðan worh(te),
wlitebeorhtne wang,   swā wæter bebūgeð
gesette sigehrēþig   sunnan ond mōnan
lēoman tō lēohte   landbūendum,
ond gefrætwade   foldan scēatas
leomum ond lēafum,   līf ēac gesceōp
cynna gehwylcum   þāra ðe cwice hwyrfaþ.—
Swā ðā drihtguman   drēamum lifdon,
ēadiglīce,   oð ðæt ān ongan
fyrene fre(m)man   fēond on helle;
wæs se grimma gæst   Grendel hāten,
mære mearcstapa,   sē þe mōras hēold,
fen ond fæsten;

15. On Heorot as mirroring the creation and the text's polysemic blurring of microcosm and macrocosm, see Alvin A. Lee, *Gold-Hall and Earth-Dragon: Beowulf as Metaphor* (Toronto: University of Toronto Press, 1998), pp. 152–76; Willem Helder, "The Song of Creation in *Beowulf* and the Interpretation of Heorot," *English Studies in Canada* 13 (1987): 243–55; and Paul Beekman Taylor, "Heorot, Earth, and Asgard: Christian Poetry and Pagan Myth," *Tennessee Studies in Literature* 11 (1966): 119–30.

     16. *Beowulf* 64–81:

Þā wæs Hrōðgāere   here-spēd gyfen,
wīges weorð-mynd,   þæt him his wine-māgas
georne hȳrdon,   oðð þæt sēo geogoð gewēox
magodriht micel.   Him on mōd bearn,
þæt healreced   hātan wolde,
medoærn micel   men gewyrcean
þon[n]e yldo bearn   æfre gefrūnon
ond þær on innan   eall gedælan
geongum ond ealdum,   swylc him God sealde
būton folcscare   ond feorum gumena.
Ðā ic wīde gefrægn   weorc gebannan
manigre mægþe   geond þisne middangeard,
folcstede frætwan.   Him on fyrste gelomp,
ædre mid yldum,   þæt hit wearð ealgearo,
healærna mæst ...
Hē bēot ne ālēh,   bēagas dælde,
sinc æt symle.

17. On the hall and its significance, see Hugh Magennis, *Images of Community in Old English Poetry* (Cambridge: Cambridge University Press, 1996).

     18. See further Bruce Lincoln, "Cristiano Grottanelli, in Memoriam et Gratitudinem," *Asdiwal* 5 (2010): 7–16.

CHAPTER THIRTEEN

"The (Un)discipline of Religious Studies" was originally presented at a symposium hosted by the Department of Religion at Columbia University (November 2007).

1. Karl Marx, first sentence of A *Contribution to the Critique of Hegel's Philosophy of Right: Introduction*, in *Marx, Early Political Writings*, ed. and trans. Joseph O'Malley (Cambridge: Cambridge University Press, 1994), p. 57.

2. Associate Justice Tom Clark, majority opinion statement, Abington School District v. Schempp, 374 U.S. 203 (1963); emphasis added.

3. Quoted by Jonathan Z. Smith, *Relating Religion: Essays in the Study of Religion* (Chicago: University of Chicago Press, 2004), p. 199. See further, pp. 198–201

4. "In a world where religion plays so central a role in social, political, and economic events, as well as in the lives of communities and individuals, there is a critical need for ongoing reflection upon and understanding of religious traditions, issues, questions, and values. The American Academy of Religion's mission is to promote such reflection through excellence in scholarship and teaching in the field of religion.

"As a learned society and professional association of teachers and research scholars, the American Academy of Religion has over 10,000 members who teach in some 1,000 colleges, universities, seminaries, and schools in North America and abroad. The Academy is dedicated to furthering knowledge of religion and religious institutions in all their forms and manifestations. This is accomplished through Academy-wide and regional conferences and meetings, publications, programs, and membership services.

"Within a context of free inquiry and critical examination, the Academy welcomes all disciplined reflection on religion—both from within and outside of communities of belief and practice—and seeks to enhance its broad public understanding." AAR mission statement; online at http://www.aarweb.org/About_AAR/Mission_Statement/default.asp (accessed June 10, 2011).

BIBLIOGRAPHY

Adler, Eve. 2003. *Vergil's Empire: Political Thought in the Aeneid*. Lanham, MD: Rowman & Littlefield.

Ahlbäck, Tore, ed. 1993. *The Problem of Ritual*. Stockholm: Almqvist & Wiksell.

Albertz, Rainer. 2004. *Israel in Exile: The History and Literature of the Sixth Century B.C.E.* Leiden: E. J. Brill.

Alon, Nahi, and Haim Orner. 2006. *The Psychology of Demonization: Promoting Acceptance and Reducing Conflict*. Mahwah, NJ: Lawrence Erlbaum.

Amouzgar, Jaleh, and Ahmad Tafazzoli, eds. 2000. *Le cinquième livre du Dēnkard*. Paris: Association pour l'avancement des etudes iraniennes.

Andersson, Theodore M. 1985. "Kings' Sagas." In *Old Norse-Icelandic Literature: A Critical Guide*, edited by Carol Clover and John Lindow, pp. 197–238. Ithaca, NY: Cornell University Press.

Anklesaria, Ervad Tahmuras Dinshaji. 1908. *The Būndahishn: Being a Facsimile of the TD 2 Manuscript Brought from Persia by Dastur Tîrandâz and Now Preserved in the Late Ervad Tahmuras' Library*. Bombay: British India Press.

Annis, Sheldon. 1987. *God and Production in a Guatemalan Town*. Austin: University of Texas Press.

Arrighetti, Graziano. 1992. "Esiodo e le Muse: Il dono della verità e la conquista della parola." *Athenaeum* 80: 45–63.

Arthur, Marilyn B. 1982. "Cultural Strategies in Hesiod's *Theogony*: Law, Family, Society." *Arethusa* 15: 63–82.

———. 1983. "The Dream of a World without Women: Poetics and the Circles of Order in the *Theogony* Prooemium." *Arethusa* 16: 97–135.

Arzu, Marta Elena Casaus. 1992. *Guatemala: Linaje y racismo*. San José, Costa Rica: FLACSO.

Asad, Talal. 1993. *Genealogies of Religion: Discipline and Reasons of Power in Christianity and Islam*. Baltimore: Johns Hopkins University Press.

Asmussen, Jes P. 1974. "Some Remarks on Sasanian Demonology." In *Commémoration Cyrus: Actes du Congrès de Shiraz*, pp. 236–41. Leiden: E. J. Brill.

Assmann, Jan, ed. 1993. *Die Erfindung des inneren Menschen: Studien zur religiösen Anthropologie*. Gütersloh: G. Mohn.

Asturias Montenegro, G. 1995. *Los 504 dias de Rios Montt*. Guatemala City: Gamma.

Atkinson, J. E. 1992. "Out of Order: The Circumcellions and Codex Theodosianus 16.5.52." *Historia* 61: 488–99.

Aybar de Soto, José. 1978. *Dependency and Intervention: The Case of Guatemala in 1954*. Boulder, CO: Westview Press.

Baetke, Walter. 1964. *Yngvi und die Ynglinger: Eine quellenkritische Untersuchung über das nordische "Sakralkönigtum."* Berlin: Akademie Verlag.

Bailey, H. W. 1943 (2nd ed. 1971). *Zoroastrian Problems in the Ninth-Century Books.* Oxford: Clarendon Press.

Ballabriga, Alain. 1990. "Le dernier adversaire de Zeus: Le myth de Typhon dans l'épopée grecque arrchaïque." *Revue de l'histoire des religions* 207: 3–30.

Baltrusch, Ernst. 1988. "Die Verstaatlichung der Gladiatorenspiele." *Hermes* 116: 324–37.

Bandy, Stephen C. 1973. "Cain, Grendel and the Giants of *Beowulf.*" *Papers on Language and Literature* 9: 235–49.

Bartholomae, Christian. 1904 (reprint ed. 1961). *Altiranisches Wörterbuch.* Berlin: Walter de Gruyter.

Barton, Carlin. 1994. "Savage Miracles: The Redemption of Lost Honor in Roman Society and the Sacrament of the Gladiator and the Martyr." *Representations* 45: 41–71.

Bartoněk, Antonín. 1959. "Die Wortparallelen αὐδή und φωνή in der archaischen epischen Sprache." *Sborník Prací Filosofické Fakulty Brněnské University, Rada Archeologicko-Klasická* E4: 67–74.

Beaulieu, Paul-Alain. 1989. *The Reign of Nabonidus, King of Babylon 556–539 B.C.* New Haven, CT: Yale University Press.

BeDuhn, Jason. 2000. *The Manichaean Body in Discipline and Ritual.* Baltimore: Johns Hopkins University Press.

Bénatouli, Thomas. 2006. *Faire usage: La pratique du stoïcisme.* Paris: Vrin.

Berlinzani, Francesca. 2002. "La voce e il canto nel proemio della *Teogonia.*" *Acme* 55: 189–204.

Bertolini, Francesco. 1995. "Muse, re e aeidi nel proemio della *Teogonia* di Esiodo." In *Studia Classica Iohanni Tardini oblata,* edited by Luigi Belloni et al., pp. 127–38. Milan: Vita e Pensiero.

Bianchi, Ugo, and Martin Vermaseren, eds. 1982. *La soteriologia dei culti orientali nell'Impero romano.* Leiden: E. J. Brill.

Blaise, Fabrienne. 1992. "L'épisode de Typhée dans la *Théogonie* d'Hésiode (v. 820–885): La stabilization du monde." *Révue des etudes grecques* 105: 349–70.

Blaise, Fabrienne et al., eds. 1996. *Le métier du mythe: Lectures d'Hésiode.* Lille, France: Presses Universitaires de Septentrion.

Bloom, Mia. 2005. *Dying to Kill: The Allure of Suicide Terror.* New York: Columbia University Press.

Boedeker, Deborah. 1984. *Descent from Heaven: Images of Dew in Greek Poetry and Religion.* Chico, CA: Scholars Press.

Boureau, Alain. 2006. *Satan the Heretic: The Birth of Demonology in the Medieval West.* Chicago: University of Chicago Press.

Bowersock, G. W. 1995. *Martyrdom and Rome.* Cambridge: Cambridge University Press.

Bowman, Raymond. 1970. *Aramaic Ritual Texts from Persepolis.* Chicago: University of Chicago Press.

Bowra, C. M., ed. 1947. *Pindari Carmina cum Fragmentis.* Oxford: Clarendon Press, 1947.

Boyarin, Daniel. 1999. *Dying for God: Martyrdom and the Making of Christianity and Judaism.* Stanford, CA: Stanford University Press.

Boyce, Mary. 1975. *A History of Zoroastrianism.* Vol. 1, *The Ancient Period.* Leiden: E. J. Brill.

———. 1984. "On the Antiquity of Zoroastrian Apocalyptic." *Bulletin of the School of Oriental and African Studies* 47: 57–75.

Boyce, Mary, and Frantz Grenet. 1991. *A History of Zoroastrianism.* Vol. 3, *Zoroastrianism under Macedonian and Roman Rule.* Leiden: E. J. Brill.

Bramlich, Richard. 1997. *Weltverzicht: Grundlägen und Weisen islamischer Askese.* Wiesbaden: Otto Harrassowitz.

Brandon, S. G. F. 1967. *Jesus and the Zealots: A Study of the Political Factor in Primitive Christianity.* Manchester: Manchester University Press.

Bremmer, Jan. 1991. "'Christianus sum': The Early Christian Martyrs and Christ." In *Eulogia: Mélanges offerts à Antoon A. R. Bastiansen,* edited by G. J. M. Bartelink et al., pp. 11–20. The Hague: Martinus Nijhoff.

Brennan, Ted. 2005. *The Stoic Life: Emotions, Duties, and Fate.* Oxford: Clarendon Press.

Briant, Pierre. 1996. *Histoire de l'empire perse de Cyrus à Alexandre.* Leiden: Nederlands Instituut voor het Nabije Oosten.

Brintnall, Douglas E. 1979a. "Race Relations in the Southeastern Highlands of Mesoamerica." *American Ethnologist* 6: 638–52.

———. 1979b. *Revolt against the Dead: The Modernization of a Mayan Community in the Highlands of Guatemala.* New York: Gordon & Breach.

Brown, Peter. 1982. *Society and the Holy in Late Antiquity.* Berkeley: University of California Press.

———. 1988. *The Body and Society: Men, Women, and Sexual Renunciation in Early Christianity.* New York: Columbia University Press.

Brunner, Ch. 1987. "Astronomy and Astrology in the Sassanian Period." *Encyclopaedia Iranica,* 2:862–68. London: Routledge & Kegan Paul.

Burkert, Walter. 1983 (German original 1972). *Homo Necans: The Anthropology of Ancient Greek Sacrificial Ritual and Myth.* Berkeley: University of California Press.

Bussanich, John. 1983. "A Theoretical Interpretation of Hesiod's Chaos." *Classical Philology* 78: 212–19.

Buxton, Richard, ed. 1999. *From Myth to Reason? Studies in the Development of Greek Thought.* Oxford: Oxford University Press.

Calame, Claude. 1986. "L'ispirazione delle Muse Esiodee: Autenticità o convenzione letteraria?" In *Scrivere e recitare: Modelli di trasmissione del testo poetico nell' antichità e nel medioevo,* edited by Giovanni Cerri, pp. 85–101. Rome: Edizioni dell' Ateneo.

Carmack, Robert. 1983. "Spanish-Indian Relations in Highland Guatemala, 1800–1944." In *Spaniards and Indians in Southeastern Mesoamerica,* edited by Murdo MacLeod and Robert Wasserstrom, pp. 215–53. Lincoln: University of Nebraska Press.

———, ed. 1988. *Harvest of Violence: The Maya Indians and the Guatemalan Crisis.* Norman: University of Oklahoma Press.

Casanova, Angelo. 1979. *La famiglia di Pandora: Analisi filologica dei miti di Pandora e Prometeo nella tradizione esiodea.* Florence: Cooperativa Libraria Universitatis Studii Fiorentini.

Casaus Arzu, Marta Elena. 1992. *Guatemala: Linaje y racismo*. San José, Costa Rica: FLACSO.

Castelli, Elizabeth. 2004. *Martyrdom and Memory: Early Christian Culture Making*. New York: Columbia University Press.

Cereti, Carlo. 2001. *La Letteratura Pahlavi: Introduzione ai testi con riferimenti alla storia degli studi e alla tradizione manoscritta*. Milan: Mimesis.

Cervantes, Fernando. 1994. *The Devil in the New World: The Impact of Diabolism in New Spain*. New Haven, CT: Yale University Press.

Chantraine, Pierre. "Grec μελίχος." In *Mélanges Émile Boisacq*, 1:169ff. Brussels: Institut de philologie et d'histoire orientales et slaves, 1937.

———. 1968–80. *Dictionnaire étymologique de la langue grecque*. 4 vols. Paris: Éditions Klincksieck.

Chardak, Henriette. 1989. *Kepler, le chien des étoiles*. Paris: Librairie Séguier.

Chary, Israel W. 2007. *Fighting Suicide Bombing: A Worldwide Campaign for Life*. Westport, CT: Praeger Security International.

Chase, Colin, ed. 1997. *The Dating of Beowulf*. Toronto: University of Toronto Press.

Christensen, Arthur. 1941. *Essai sur la démonologie iranienne*. Copenhagen: Ejnar Munksgaard.

Christianson, John Robert. 2000. *On Tycho's Island: Tycho Brahe and His Assistants, 1570–1601*. Cambridge: Cambridge University Press.

Clark, Stuart. 1997. *Thinking with Demons: The Idea of Witchcraft in Early Modern Europe*. Oxford: Clarendon Press.

Clark, Elizabeth. 1999. *Reading Renunciation: Asceticism and Scripture in Early Christianity*. Princeton, NJ: Princeton University Press.

Clarke, W. M. 1974. "The God in the Dew." *L'antiquité classique* 43: 57–73.

Cleasby, Richard, Gudbrand Vigfusson, and Sir William Craigie. 1957. *Icelandic-English Dictionary*. 2nd ed. Oxford: Clarendon Press.

Clendinnen, Inga. 1987. *Ambivalent Conquests: Maya and Spaniard in Yucatán, 1517–1570*. Cambridge: Cambridge University Press.

Closing the Space: Human Rights in Guatemala. New York: Americas Watch, 1988.

Cohn, Norman. 2000. *Europe's Inner Demons: The Demonization of Christians in Medieval Christendom*. Rev. ed. Chicago: University of Chicago Press.

Colby, Benjamin, and Pierre van den Berghe. 1969. *Ixil Country: A Plural Society in Highland Guatemala*. Berkeley: University of California Press.

Collins, Derek. 1999. "Hesiod and the Divine Voice of the Muses." *Arethusa* 32: 241–62.

Collins, John J., ed. 1998. *The Encyclopedia of Apocalypticism*. Vol. 1, *The Origins of Apocalypticism*. New York: Continuum.

Colpe, Carsten, ed. 1974–82. *Altiranische und Zoroastrische Mythologie*. Stuttgart: Klett-Cotta.

———. 2003. *Iranier—Aramäer—Hebräer—Hellenen*. Tübingen: Mohr Siebeck.

Cone, Patricia, and Martin Hinds. 1986. *God's Caliph: Religious Authority in the First Centuries of Islam*. Cambridge: Cambridge University Press.

Connor, James A. 2004. *Kepler's Witch: An Astronomer's Discovery of Cosmic Order amid Religious War, Political Intrigue, and the Heresy Trial of His Mother*. San Francisco: Harper San Francisco.

Cook, David 2007. *Martyrdom in Islam* Cambridge: Cambridge University Press.

Cormack, Margaret, ed. 2001. *Sacrificing the Self: Perspectives on Martyrdom and Religion.* New York: Oxford University Press.

Cornford, Francis Macdonald. 1912. *From Religion to Philosophy: A Study in the Origins of Western Speculation.* London: E. Arnold.

Cragg, Kenneth. 2005. *Faith at Suicide, Lives Forfeit: Violent Religion—Human Despair.* Brighton: Sussex Academic Press.

Cunliffe, Richard. 1963. *A Lexicon of the Homeric Dialect.* Norman: University of Oklahoma Press.

Dakake, Maria Massi. 2007. *The Charismatic Community: Shi'ite Identity in Early Islam.* Albany: State University of New York Press.

Darmesteter, James. 1892–93. *Le Zend Avesta.* 3 vols. Paris: Annales du Musée Guimet.

Davidson, Hilda Ellis, ed. 1998. *Saxo Grammaticus, The History of the Danes, Books I–IX.* Suffolk: D. S. Brewer.

Davidson, William. 1948. "A Method for Studying Religious Cult and Healing Ceremonies and Its Application to a Guatemalan Indian Curing Ceremony." M.A. thesis, Duke University Graduate School of Arts and Sciences.

Davis, Natalie Zemon. 1975. "The Rites of Violence." In *Society and Culture in Early Modern France,* pp. 152–87. Stanford, CA: Stanford University Press.

De Luca, Tom, and John Buell. 2005. *Liars! Cheaters! Evildoers! Demonization and the End of Civil Debate in American Politics.* New York: New York University Press.

Detienne, Marcel. 1996 (French original 1967). *The Masters of Truth in Archaic Greece.* New York: Zone Books.

Detienne, Marcel, and Jean-Pierre Vernant. 1989 (French original 1979). *The Cuisine of Sacrifice among the Greeks.* Chicago: University of Chicago Press.

Diamond, Eliezer. 2004. *Holy Men and Hunger Artists: Fasting and Asceticism in Rabbinic Culture.* Oxford: Oxford University Press.

Dodds, E. R. 1951. *The Greeks and the Irrational.* Berkeley: University of California Press.

———. 1965. *Pagan and Christian in an Age of Anxiety: Some Aspects of Religious Experience from Marcus Aurelius to Constantine.* Cambridge: Cambridge University Press.

Donner, Fred. 1981. *The Early Islamic Conquests.* Princeton, NJ: Princeton University Press.

Drake, H. A. 2000. *Constantine and the Bishops: The Politics of Intolerance.* Baltimore: Johns Hopkins University Press.

Dresden, M. J. 1966. *Dēnkart: A Pahlavi Text; Facsimile Edition of the Manuscript B of the K. R. Cama Oriental Institute, Bombay.* Wiesbaden: Otto Harrassowitz.

Driscoll, M. J., ed. 1995. *Ágrip af Nóregskonunga sǫgum.* London: Viking Society for Northern Research.

Droge, Arthur, and James Tabor. 1992. *A Noble Death: Suicide and Martyrdom among Christians and Jews in Antiquity.* San Francisco: Harper.

Dronke, Ursula. 1969–. *The Poetic Edda.* Oxford: Clarendon Press.

Dronke, Ursula, and Peter Dronke. 1977. "The Prologue of the *Prose Edda*: Explorations of a Latin Background." In *Sjötiu ritgerðir helgaðar Jakobi Benediktssyni,* edited by Einar Petursson and Jonas Kristjansson, pp. 153–76. Reykjavik: Stofnun Arna Magnussonar.

Duban, Jeffrey M. 1980. "Poets and Kings in the *Theogony* Invocation." *Quaderni Urbinati di Cultura Clasica*, n.s., 4: 7–21.

Duchesne-Guillemin, Jacques. 1962. *La religion de l'Iran ancien*. Paris: Presses Universitaires de France.

———. 1979. "La Royauté iranienne et le *x*ᵛ*arᵊnah*." In *Iranica*, edited by Gherardo Gnoli and Adriano V. Rossi, pp. 375–86. Naples: Istituto Universitario Orientale.

Eddy, Samuel K. 1961. *The King Is Dead: Studies in the Near Eastern Resistance to Hellenism, 334–31 B.C.* Lincoln: University of Nebraska Press.

Edwards, H. J. ed. 1919. *Caesar, The Gallic War*. London: William Heinemann.

Egilsson, Sveinbjörn. 1931. *Lexicon Poeticum Septentrionalis: Ordbog over det Norsk-Islandske Skjaldesprog*. 2nd ed. Revised by Finnur Jónsson. Copenhagen: S. L. Møller.

Eilers, Wilhelm. 1967. "Stern—Planet—Regenbogen." In *Der Orient in der Forschung: Festschrift für Otto Spies*, edited by Wilhelm Hoenerbach, pp. 112–16. Wiesbaden: Otto Harrassowitz.

Einarsson, Bjarni, ed. 1984. *Ágrip af Nóregskonunga Sögum [ok] Fagrskinna—Nóregs Konunga Tal*. Rejkhavík: Íslenzka Fornritafélag.

Ekrem, Inger, and Lars Boje Mortensen, eds. 2003. *Historia Norwegie*. Translated by Peter Fisher. Copenhagen: Museum Tusculanum Press.

Eliade, Mircea. 1949 (Paris: Gallimard). *Le mythe de l'éternel retour*. Translated by Willard Trask under the title *The Myth of the Eternal Return*. Princeton, NJ: Princeton University Press, 1954.

———. 1963. *Myth and Reality*. New York: Harper Torchbooks.

———. 1990. *Journal*. Translated by Mac Linscott Ricketts. 4 vols. Chicago: University of Chicago Press.

Emerson, Oliver Farrar. 1921. "Grendel's Motive in Attacking Heorot." *Modern Language Review* 16: 113–19.

Falk, Henry. 1986. "Vedisch *upaniṣad*." *Zeitschrift der deutschen morgenlandischen Gesellschaft* 136: 80–97.

Farriss, Nancy. 1984. *Maya Society under Colonial Rule: The Collective Enterprise of Survival*. Princeton, NJ: Princeton University Press.

Faulkes, Anthony, ed. 1982–89. *Snorri Sturluson: Edda; Prologue and Gylfaginning*. 4 vols. Oxford: Clarendon Press.

———. 1983. "Pagan Sympathy: Attitudes to Heathendom in the Prologue to Snorra Edda." In *Edda: A Collection of Essays*, edited by R. J. Glendinning and H. Bessason, pp. 282–314. Winnipeg: University of Manitoba Press.

———. 1993. "The Sources of Skáldskaparmál: Snorri's Intellectual Background." In *Snorri Sturluson*, edited by Alois Wolf, pp. 59–76. Tübingen: Gunter Narr.

Feist, Sigmund. 1939. *Vergleichendes Wörterbuch der Gotischen Sprache*. Leiden: E. J. Brill.

Ferguson, Kitty. 2002. *The Nobleman and His Housedog: Tycho Brahe and Johannes Kepler; The Strange Partnership That Revolutionized Science*. London: Review.

Février, Paul-Albert. 1990. "Les chrétiens dans l'arène." In *Spectacula I: Gladiateurs et amphitheatres*, edited by Claude Domerge et al., pp. 265–73. Lattes, France: Éditions Imago.

Finkler, Kaja. 1994. *Women in Pain: Gender and Morbidity in Mexico*. Philadelphia: University of Pennsylvania Press.

Finlay, Alison, trans. 2004. *Fagrskinna: A Catalogue of the Kings of Norway.* Leiden: E. J. Brill.

Fitzgerald, Tim. 2006. "Bruce Lincoln's 'Theses on Method': Antitheses." *Method and Theory in the Study of Religion* 18: 392–423.

Fix, Hans, ed. 1998. *Snorri Sturluson: Beiträge zu Werk und Rezeption.* Berlin: De Gruyter.

Flach, Hans. 1876. *Glossen und Scholien zur hesiodischen Theogonie.* Leipzig: B. G. Teubner (reprint ed. Osnabrück, 1970).

Forbes, Christopher. 1995. *Prophecy and Inspired Speech in Early Christianity and Its Hellenistic Environment.* Tübingen: J. C. B. Mohr.

Fränkel, Hermann. 1955. "Drei Interpretationen aus Hesiod." In *Wegen und Formen frühgriechischen Denkens,* pp. 316–34. Munich: Beck.

Frankfort, Henri. 1948. *Kingship and the Gods: A Study of Ancient Near Eastern Religion as the Integration of Society and Nature.* Chicago: University of Chicago Press.

Frankfurter, David. 2006. *Evil Incarnate: Rumors of Demonic Conspiracy and Ritual Abuse in History.* Princeton, NJ: Princeton University Press.

Frend, W. H. C. 1965. *Martyrdom and Persecution in the Early Church: A Study of a Conflict from the Maccabees to Donatus.* Oxford: Blackwell.

Friedlander, Judith. 1975. *Being Indian in Hueyapan.* New York: St. Martin's.

Friesen, Steven J. 2001. *Imperial Cults and the Apocalypse of John.* Oxford: Oxford University Press.

Frisk, Hjalmar. 1973. *Griechisches etymologisches Wörterbuch.* 2 vols. Heidelberg: Carl Winter.

Fustel de Coulanges, Numa Denis. 1980 (French original 1864). *The Ancient City: A Study on the Religion, Laws, and Institutions of Greece and Rome.* Baltimore: Johns Hopkins University Press.

Futrell, Alison. 1997. *Blood in the Arena: The Spectacle of Roman Power.* Austin: University of Texas Press.

Gaddis, Michael. 2005. *There Is No Crime for Those Who Have Christ: Religious Violence in the Christian Roman Empire.* Berkeley: University of California Press.

Gager, John. 1982. "Body-Symbols and Social Reality: Resurrection, Incarnation, and Asceticism in Early Christianity." *Religion* 12: 345–64.

Gaukroger, Stephen. 2006. *The Emergence of a Scientific Culture: Science and the Shaping of Modernity, 1210–1685.* Oxford: Oxford University Press.

Geary, Patrick. 2003. *The Myth of Nations: The Medieval Origins of Europe.* Oxford: Oxford University Press.

Geib, R. 1976. "Food and Eater in Natural Philosophy of Early India." *Journal of the Oriental Institute, Baroda* 25: 223–35.

Geldner, Karl F., ed. 1886–96. *Avesta: The Sacred Books of the Parsis.* 3 vols. Stuttgart: W. Kohlhammer.

Gignoux, Ph., and A. Tafazzoli, eds. 1993. *Anthologie de Zādspram.* Paris: Association pour l'avancement des études iraniennes.

Gilder, Joshua, and Anne-Lee Gilder. 2004. *Heavenly Intrigue: Johannes Kepler, Tycho Brahe, and the Murder behind One of History's Greatest Scientific Discoveries.* New York: Doubleday.

Gillin, John. 1948. "Magical Fright." *Psychiatry* 11: 387–400.

———. 1951. *The Culture of Security in San Carlos: A Study of a Guatemalan Community of Indians and Ladinos*. New Orleans: Middle American Research Institute, Tulane University.

———. 1957. "San Luis Jilotepeque: 1942–55." In *Political Changes in Guatemalan Indian Communities*, edited by Richard Adams, pp. 23–27. New Orleans: Middle American Research Institute, Tulane University.

———. 1969. *Human Ways*. Pittsburgh: University of Pittsburgh Press.

Gingrich, Owen. 1993. *The Eye of Heaven: Ptolemy, Copernicus, Kepler*. New York: American Institute of Physics.

Girard, Réné. 1977 (French original 1972). *Violence and the Sacred*. Baltimore: Johns Hopkins University Press.

Girardet, Klaus Martin. 2006. *Die konstantinische Wende: Voraussetzungen und geistige Grundlägen der Religionspolitik Konstantins des Grossen*. Darmstadt: Wissenschaftliche Buchgesellschaft.

Girardot, N. J. 1987. "Chaos." In *The Encyclopedia of Religion*, edited by Mircea Eliade, 3:213–18. New York: Macmillan.

Gleijesis, Piero. 1991. *Shattered Hope: The Guatemalan Revolution and the United States, 1944–1954*. Princeton, NJ: Princeton University Press.

Gnoli, Gherardo. 1996. "Über das iranische *huarnah*-: Lautliche, morphologische und etymologische Probleme; Zum Stand der Forschung." *Altorientalische Forschungen* 23: 151–80.

Goody, Jack. 1987. *The Interface between the Written and the Oral*. Cambridge: Cambridge University Press.

Goudineau, Christian. 2001. *Le dossier Vercingétorix*. Paris: Errance.

Gradel, Ittai. 2002. *Emperor Worship and Roman Religion*. Oxford: Clarendon Press.

Grieb, Kenneth. 1979. *Guatemalan Caudillo: The Regime of Jorge Ubico, Guatemala, 1931–1944*. Athens: Ohio University Press.

Grottanelli, Cristiano. 1982. "Healers and Saviors of the Eastern Mediterranean." In Bianchi and Vermaseren, *La soteriologia dei culti orientali nell' Impero Romano*, pp. 649–70.

———. 1985. "Archaic Forms of Rebellion and Their Religious Background." In *Religion, Rebellion, Revolution*, edited by Bruce Lincoln, pp. 15–45. New York: St. Martin's Press.

———. 1999. *Il Sacrificio*. Rome: Laterza.

Grottanelli, Cristiano, and Nicola Parise. 1988. *Sacrificio e società nel mondo antico*. Rome: Laterza.

Grübel, Isabel. 1991. *Die Hierarchie der Teufel: Studien zum christlichen Teufelsbild und zur Allegorisierung des Bösen in Theologie, Literatur und Kunst zwischen Frühmittelalter und Gegenreformation*. Munich: Tuduv.

Guatemala. London: Catholic Institute for International Relations, 1988.

Guatemala: A Government Program of Political Murder. London: Amnesty International, 1981.

Guatemala: A Nation of Prisoners. New York: Americas Watch, 1984.

Guatemala: Getting away with Murder. New York: Americas Watch; Somerville, MA: Physicians for Human Rights, 1991.

Guatemala: Human Rights Violations under the Civilian Government. New York: Amnesty International, 1989.

Guatemala: Seminario sobre la Realidad Etnica ([Mexico City]: Centro de Estudios Integrados de Desarrollo Communal, 1990).

Guatemala—Tyranny on Trial: Testimony of the Permanent People's Tribunal. San Francisco: Synthesis Publications, 1984.

Gundarson, Mark. 1996. "The Ideology of the Arena." *Classical Antiquity* 15: 113–51.

Hafez, Mohammed M. 2007. *Suicide Bombers in Iraq: The Strategy and Ideology of Martyrdom.* Washington, DC: United States Institute of Peace Press.

Hale, Edward Everett et al., eds. 1909. *The Young Folks Treasury.* Vol. 2, *Myths and Legendary Heroes.* New York: University Society.

Handy, Jim. 1984. *Gift of the Devil: A History of Guatemala.* Boston: South End Press.

———. 1989. "Insurgency and Counter-Insurgency in Guatemala." In *Sociology of "Developing Societies": Central America,* edited by Jan Flora and Edelberto Torres Rivas, pp. 112–39. New York: Monthly Review Press.

———. 1994. *Revolution in the Countryside: Rural Conflict and Agrarian Reform in Guatemala, 1944–1954.* Chapel Hill: University of North Carolina Press.

Havelock, Eric Alfred. 1963. *Preface to Plato.* Cambridge, MA: Harvard University Press.

Hawkins, John. 1984. *Inverse Images: The Meaning of Culture, Ethnicity and Family in Postcolonial Guatemala.* Albuquerque: University of New Mexico Press.

Heim, François. 1987. "Les panegyriques des martyrs ou l'impossible conversion d'un genre littéraire." *Revue des Sciences des Religion* 61: 105–28.

Helder, Willem. 1987. "The Song of Creation in *Beowulf* and the Interpretation of Heorot." *English Studies in Canada* 13: 243–55.

Helm, Karl. 1946. *Wodan: Ausbreitung und Wanderung seines Kultes.* Giesen, Germany: W. Schmitz.

Henten, J. W. van, ed. 1989. *Die Entstehung der jüdischen Martyrologie.* Leiden: E. J. Brill.

———. 2002. *Martyrdom and Noble Death: Selected Texts from Graeco-Roman, Jewish, and Christian Antiquity.* New York: Routledge.

Hinnells, John. 1973. "The Zoroastrian Doctrine of Salvation in the Roman World: A Study of the Oracles of Hystaspes." In *Man and His Salvation: Studies in Honor of S. G. F. Brandon,* edited by E. J. Sharpe and J. R. Hinnells, pp. 125–48. Manchester: Manchester University Press.

Hintze, Almut, ed. and trans. 1994. *Der Zamyād-Yašt: Edition, Übersetzung, Kommentar.* Wiesbaden: Ludwig Reichert.

Hofinger, M. 1975. *Lexicon Hesiodeum.* Leiden: E. J. Brill.

Höfler, Otto. 1934. *Kultische Geheimbünde der Germanen.* Frankfurt: Moritz Diesterweg.

Holder, Alfred. 1961–62. *Altceltischer Sprachschatz.* Graz: Akademische Druck.

Holoka, James P., ed. 2003. *Simone Weil's The Iliad; or, The Poem of Force: A Critical Edition.* New York: Peter Lang.

Horsley, Richard A. 1988. *Bandits, Prophets, and Messiahs: Popular Movements in the Time of Jesus.* San Francisco: Harper & Row.

Hosking, Geoffrey, and George Schöpflin, eds. 1997. *Myths and Nationhood.* New York: Routledge.

Houdard, Sophie. 1992. *Les sciences du diable: Quatre discours sur la sorcellerie, XVe-VIIe siècle.* Paris: Éditions du Cerf.

Hourcade, Juan Luis Garcia. 2000. *La rebellion de los astónomos: Copérnico y Kepler.* Madrid: Nivola Libros Ediciones.

Hubert, Henri, and Marcel Mauss. 1964 (French original 1899). *Sacrifice: Its Nature and Function.* Chicago: University of Chicago Press.

Hultgård, Anders. 1998. "Persian Apocalypticism." In Collins, ed., *Encyclopedia of Apocalypticism,* 1:39–83.

Humbach, Helmut, and Pallan R. Ichaporia, trans. 1998. *Zamyād Yasht: Yasht 19 of the Younger Avesta; Text, Translation, Commentary.* Wiesbaden: Harrassowitz Verlag.

Immerman, Richard. 1982. *The CIA in Guatemala: The Foreign Policy of Intervention.* Austin: University of Texas Press.

Jaafari-Dehaghi, Mahmoud, ed. 1998. *Dādestān ī Dēnīg. Part I: Transcription, Translation, and Commentary.* Paris: Association pour l'avancement des études iraniennes.

Jackson, A. V. Williams. 1928. *Zoroastrian Studies.* New York: Columbia University Press.

Jacobs, Bruno. 1987. "Das *Chvarnah*—Zum Stand der Forschung." *Mitteilungen der Deutschen Orient Gesellschaft* 119: 215–48.

Jal, Paul. 1962a. "Les dieux et les guerres civiles dans la Rome de la fin de la république." *Revue des etudes latines* 40: 170–200.

———. 1962b. "La propagande réligieuse à Rome au cours des guerres civiles de la fin de la république." *L'antiquité classique* 30: 395–414.

———. 1963. *La guerre civile à Rome: Étude littéraire et morale.* Paris: Presses Universitaires de France.

Jandora, John Walter. 1990. *The March from Medina: A Revisionist Study of the Arab Conquests.* Clifton, NJ: Kingston Press.

Jay, Alice et al. 1993. *Persecution by Proxy: The Civil Patrols in Guatemala.* New York: Robert F. Kennedy Memorial Center for Human Rights.

Johnson, David M. 1999. "Hesiod's descriptions of Tartarus (*Theogony* 721–819)." *Phoenix* 53: 8–28.

Johnstone, Nathan. 2006. *The Devil and Demonism in Early Modern England.* Cambridge: Cambridge University Press.

Jonas, Susanne. 1991. *The Battle for Guatemala: Rebels, Death Squads, and U.S. Power.* Boulder, CO: Westview Press.

Jones, Grant. 1989. *Maya Resistance to Spanish Rule: Time and History on a Colonial Frontier.* Albuquerque: University of New Mexico Press.

Judet de la Combe, Pierre. 1996. "La dernière ruse: 'Pandora' dans la *Théogonie.*" In Blaise et al., *Le métier du mythe,* pp. 263–99.

Judet de la Combe, Pierre, and Alain Lernould. 1996. "Sur la Pandore des *Travaux*: Esquisses." In Blaise et al., *Le métier du mythe,* pp. 303–13.

Jullian, Camille. 1903. *Vercingétorix.* Paris: Hachette.

Kafka, Franz. 1937. *The Great Wall of China: Stories and Reflections.* Translated by Willa Muir and Edwin Muir. New York: Schocken Books.

Kambylis, Athanassios. 1965. *Die Dichterweihe und ihre Symbolik.* Heidelberg: Carl Winter.

Kaske, R. E. 1971. "Beowulf and the Book of Enoch." *Speculum* 46: 421–31.

Katz, Joshua, and Katharina Volk. 2000. "'Mere Bellies'?: A New Look at *Theogony* 26–8." *Journal of Hellenic Studies* 120: 122–31.

Keith, A. B. 1925. *The Religion and Philosophy of the Veda and Upanishads*. Cambridge, MA: Harvard University Press.

Kershaw, Priscilla. 2000. *The One-Eyed God: Odin and the (Indo-)Germanic Männerbünde*. Washington, DC: Journal of Indo-European Studies.

Kiefer, Jom. 2005. *Exil und Diaspora: Begrifflichkeit und Deutungen im antiken Judentum und in der Hebräischen Bibel*. Leipzig: Evangelische Verlagsanstalt.

Kierkegaard, Søren. 1983 (Danish original 1843). *Fear and Trembling*. Edited and translated by Howard V. Hong and Edna H. Hong. Princeton, NJ: Princeton University Press.

Kippenberg, Hans, ed. 1991. *Die Vorderasiatischen Erlösungsreligionen in ihrem Zusammenhang mit der antiken Stadtherrschaft*. Frankfurt am Main: Suhrkamp.

Klaeber, Fr., ed. 1950. *Beowulf and the Fight at Finnsburg*. 3rd ed. Lexington, MA: D. C. Heath.

Klingenberg, Heinz. 1999. *Heidnisches Altertum und nordisches Mittelalter: Strukturbildende Perspektiven des Snorri Sturluson*. Freiberg: Hochschul Verlag.

Kojève, Alexandre. 1969 (French original 1947). *Introduction to the Reading of Hegel: Lectures on the Phenomenology of Spirit*. Translated by James H. Nichols. New York: Basic Books.

Koller, Hermann. 1965. "ΘΕΣΠΙΣ ΑΟΙΔΟΣ." *Glotta* 43: 277–85.

Koskikallio, Petteri. 1995. "Baka Dalbhya: A Complex Character in Vedic Ritual Texts, Epics and Puranas." *Electronic Journal of Vedic Studies* 1, no. 3; online at http://www1 .shore.net/~india/ejvs0103/index.html#art1 (accessed June 6, 2011).

Kozhamthadam, Job. 1994. *The Discovery of Kepler's Laws: The Interaction of Science, Philosophy, and Religion*. Notre Dame, IN: University of Notre Dame Press.

Kreutzer, Gert. 1994. "Das Bild Harald Schönhaars in der altisländischen Literatur." In *Studien zum Altgermanischen: Festschrift für Heinrich Beck*, edited by Heiko Uecker, pp. 443–61. Berlin: Walter de Gruyter.

Kugel, James, ed. 1990. *Poetry and Prophecy: The Beginnings of a Literary Tradition*. Ithaca, NY: Cornell University Press.

Kuhn, Thomas S. 1962 (2nd ed. 1970; 3rd ed. 1996). *The Structure of Scientific Revolutions*. Chicago: University of Chicago Press.

Kuhrt, Amélie. 1990. "Nabonidus and the Babylonian Priesthood." In *Pagan Priests: Religion and Power in the Ancient World*, edited by Mary Beard and John North, pp. 119–55. Ithaca, NY: Cornell University Press.

Laks, André. 1996. "Le double du roi: Remarques sur les antecedents Hésiodiques du philosophe-roi." In Blaise et al., *Le métier du mythe*, pp. 83–91.

Lancellotti, Maria Grazia. 2000. *The Naassenes: A Gnostic Identity among Judaism, Christianity, Classical and Ancient Near Eastern Traditions*. Münster: Ugarit Verlag.

Latte, Kurt. 1946. "Hesiods Dichterweihe." *Antike und Abendland* 2: 152–63.

Leclerc, Marie-Christine. 1993. *La parole chez Hésiode: À la recherché de l'harmonie perdue*. Paris: Les Belles Lettres.

Lee, Alvin A. 1998. *Gold-Hall and Earth-Dragon: Beowulf as Metaphor*. Toronto: University of Toronto Press.

Lévèque, Pierre. 1988. "Pandora ou la terrifiante féminité." *Kernos* 1: 49–62.

Lincoln, Bruce. 1986. *Myth, Cosmos, and Society: Indo-European Themes of Creation and Destruction*. Cambridge, MA: Harvard University Press.

———. 1989. *Discourse and the Construction of Society*. New York: Oxford University Press.

———. 1991. *Death, War, and Sacrifice: Studies in Ideology and Practice*. Chicago: University of Chicago Press.

———. 1997. "Pahlavi *Kirrēnīdan* and Traces of Iranian Creation Mythology." *Journal of the American Oriental Society* 117: 681–85.

———. 1999. *Theorizing Myth: Narrative, Ideology, and Scholarship*. Chicago: University of Chicago Press.

———. 2001a. "Revisiting 'Magical Fright.'" *American Ethnologist* 28: 778–802.

———. 2001b. "The Center of the World and the Origins of Life." *History of Religions* 40: 311–26.

———. 2003a (2nd ed. 2005). *Holy Terrors: Thinking about Religion after September 11*. Chicago: University of Chicago Press.

———. 2003b. "Hegelian Meditations on 'Indo-European' Myths." *Papers from the Mediterranean Ethnographic Summer Seminar* 5: 59–76.

———. 2007a. "Concessions, Confessions, Clarifications, Ripostes: By Way of Response to Tim Fitzgerald." *Method and Theory in the Study of Religion* 19: 163–68.

———. 2007b. *Religion, Empire, and Torture: The Case of Achaemenian Persia; With an Appendix on Abu Ghraib*. Chicago: University of Chicago Press.

———. 2009. "Cēšmag, the Lie, and the Logic of Zoroastrian Demonology." *Journal of the American Oriental Society* 129: 45–55.

———. 2010. "Cristiano Grottanelli, in Memoriam et Gratitudinem." *Asdiwal* 5: 7–16.

———. Forthcoming a. *"Happiness for Mankind": Achaemenian Religion and the Imperial Project*. Leuven: Peeters, Acta Iranica vol. 53.

———. Forthcoming b. *Between History and Myth: Stories of Harald "Fairhair" and the Founding of the State*.

Lindow, John. 1994. "Bloodfeud and Scandinavian Mythology." *Alvíssmál* 4: 51–68.

Lindqvist, S. "Ynglingättens gravskick." *Fornvännen* (1921), pp. 83–194.

Lipschitz, Oded. 2005. *The Fall and Rise of Jerusalem: Judah under Babylonian Rule*. Winona Lake, IN: Eisenbrauns.

Loew, Cornelius. 1967. *Myth, Sacred History, and Philosophy: The Pre-Christian Religious Heritage of the West*. New York: Harcourt, Brace and World.

Lommel, Herman. 1927. *Die Yäšt's des Awesta*. Göttingen: Vandenhoeck & Ruprecht.

———. 1930. *Die Religion Zarathustras nach dem Awesta dargestellt*. Tübingen: J. C. B. Mohr.

Lopez, Carlos. 1997. "Food and Immortality in the Veda: A Gastronomic Theology?" *Electronic Journal of Vedic Studies* 3; online at http://www1.shore.net/~india/ejvs0303/ejvs0303.txt (accessed June 6, 2011).

Lucrezi, Francesco. 1996. *Messianismo, Regalità, Impero: Idee religiose e idea imperiale nel mondo romano*. Florence: Editoriale La Giuntina.

MacKenzie, D. N. 1964. "Zoroastrian Astrology in the *Bundahišn*." *Bulletin of the School of Oriental and African Studies* 27: 511–29.

———. 1971. *A Concise Pahlavi Dictionary*. London: Oxford University Press.

MacMullen, Ramsay. 1966 (reprint ed. 1992). *Enemies of the Roman Order: Treason, Unrest, and Alienation in the Empire*. New York: Routledge.

———. 1986. "Judicial Savagery in the Roman Empire." *Chiron* 16: 81–96.

Madan, Dhanjishah Meherjibhai, ed. 1911. *The Complete Text of the Pahlavi Dinkard*. Bombay: Society for the Promotion of Researches into the Zoroastrian Religion.

Madelung, Wilferd. 1997. *The Succession to Muhammad: A Study of the Early Caliphate*. Cambridge: Cambridge University Press.

Magennis, Hugh. 1996. *Images of Community in Old English Poetry*. Cambridge: Cambridge University Press.

Maggi, Armando. 2006. *In the Company of Demons: Unnatural Beings, Love, and Identity in the Italian Renaissance*. Chicago: University of Chicago Press.

Malamoud, Charles. 1972. "Observations sur la notion de 'reste' dans le brâhmanisme." *Wiener Zeitschrift für die Kunde Südasiens*: 5–26.

Markale, Jean. 1995. *Vercingétorix*. Monaco: Éditions du Rocher.

Marquardt, Patricia A. 1982. "Hesiod's Ambiguous View of Woman." *Classical Philology* 77: 283–91.

Martin, Paul M. 2000. *Vercingétorix: Le politique, le stratège*. Paris: Perrin.

Marx, Karl. *A Contribution to the Critique of Hegel's Philosophy of Right: Introduction*. In *Marx, Early Political Writings*, edited and translated by Joseph O'Malley. Cambridge: Cambridge University Press, 1994.

Marzal, Manuel. 1985. *El sincretismo iberoamericano: Un estudio comparativo sobre los quechuas (Cusco), los mayas (Chiapas), y los africanos (Bahia)*. Lima: Pontificia Universidad Catolica del Peru.

Mattox, John Mark. 2006. *Saint Augustine and the Theory of Just War*. London: Continuum.

Maurizio, Lisa. 1995. "Anthropology and Spirit Possession: A Reconsideration of the Pythia's Role at Delphi." *Journal of Hellenic Studies* 115: 69–86.

McClintock, Michael. 1985. *The American Connection: State Terror and Popular Resistance in El Salvador and Guatemala*. 2 vols. London: Zed Books.

McDougall, David, and Ian McDougall, trans. 1998. *Theodoricus Monachus: Historia de Antiquitate Regum Norwagiensium; An Account of the Ancient History of the Norwegian Kings*. London: Viking Society for Northern Research.

Mellinkoff, Ruth. 1979. "Cain's Monstrous Progeny in *Beowulf*: Part I, Noachic Tradition." *Anglo-Saxon England* 8: 143–97.

———. 1981. "Cain's Monstrous Progeny in *Beowulf*: Part II, Post-Diluvian Survival." *Anglo-Saxon England* 9: 183–97.

Merkelbach, R., and M. L. West, eds. 1990. *Hesiodi: Theogonia, Opera et Dies, Scutum*. Oxford: Oxford University Press.

Micillo, Valeria. 2000. "The Latin Tradition and Icelandic." In *History of the Language Sciences*, pp. 617–25. Berlin: De Gruyter.

Middleton, Paul. 2006. *Radical Martyrdom and Cosmic Conflict in Early Christianity*. London: T. & T. Clark.

Molé, Marijan. 1963. *Culte, mythe et cosmologie dans l'Iran ancien*. Paris: Presses Universitaires de France.

Momigliano, Arnaldo. 1975. *Alien Wisdom: The Limits of Hellenization*. Cambridge: Cambridge University Press.

———. 1987. *On Pagans, Jews, and Christians*. Middletown, CT: Wesleyan University Press.

Mondi, Robert. 1989. "Chaos and the Hesiodic Cosmogony." *Harvard Studies in Classical Philology* 92: 1–41.

Monier-Williams, Sir Monier. 1899. *Sanskrit-English Dictionary*. Oxford: Clarendon Press.

Mosiq-Walburg, Karin. 1982. *Die frühen sasanidischen Könige als Vertreter und Förderer der zarathustrischen Religion: Eine Untersuchuing der zeitgenössischen Quellen*. Frankfurt am Main: Peter Lang.

Much, Rudolf, ed. 1967. *Die Germania des Tacitus*. 3rd ed. Revised by Herbert Jankuhn. Heidelberg: Carl Winter Universitätsverlag.

Mühlenberg, Ekkehard. 1997. "The Martyr's Death and Its Literary Presentation." *Studia Patristica* 29: 85–93.

Munch, Peter Andreas, and Carl Rikard Unger, eds. 1847. *Fagrskinna: Kortfattet Norsk Konge-Saga*. Christiana [Oslo]: P. T. Malling.

Murray, A. T., ed. 1971. *Homer: The Iliad*. London: William Heinemann.

Nagy, Gregory. 1989. "Early Greek Views of Poets and Poetry." In *The Cambridge History of Literary Criticism*, vol. 1, *Classical Criticism*, edited by George A. Kennedy, pp. 1–77. Cambridge: Cambridge University Press.

———. 1992. "Authorisation and Authorship in the Hesiodic *Theogony*." *Ramus* 21: 119–30.

Nasr, Seyyed Hossein et al., eds. 1989. *Expectation of the Millennium: Shi'ism in History*. Albany: State University of New York Press.

Näsström, Britt-Mari. 1989. *The Abhorrence of Love: Studies in Rituals and Mystic Aspects in Catullus' Poem of Attis*. Stockholm: Almqvist & Wiksell.

Neckel, Gustav, ed. 1962. *Edda: Die Lieder des Codex Regius*. Heidelberg: Carl Winter.

Neitzel, Heinz. 1980. "Hesiod und die Lügenden Musen." *Hermes* 108: 387–401.

Nestle, Wilhelm. 1940. *Vom Mythos zum Logos: Die Selbstentfaltung des griechischen Denkens von Homer bis auf die Sophistik und Sokrates*. Stuttgart: A. Kröner.

Neugebauer, Otto. 1956. "The Transmission of Planetary Theories in Ancient and Medieval Astronomy." *Scripta Mathematica* 22: 165–92.

Ninck, Martin. 1935. *Wodan und germanischer Schicksalsglaube*. Jena, Germany: Eugen Diederich.

Nutini, Hugo. 1988. *Todos Santos in Rural Tlaxcala: A Syncretic, Expressive, and Symbolic Analysis of the Cult of the Dead*. Princeton, NJ: Princeton University Press.

Nutini, Hugo, and Betty Bell. 1980. *Ritual Kinship: The Structure and Historical Development of the Compadrazgo System in Rural Tlaxcala*. Princeton, NJ: Princeton University Press.

Nyberg, H. S. 1974. *A Manual of Pahlavi*. Wiesbaden: Otto Harrassowitz.

Odahl, Charles Matson. 2004. *Constantine and the Christian Empire*. New York: Routledge.

Öhlig, Karl-Heinz, and Gerd-Rainer Puin, eds. 2006. *Die dunklen Anfänge: Neue Forschungen zur Entstehung und frühen Geschichte des Islam*. Berlin: Hans Schiller.

Olivelle, Patrick, ed. and trans. 1998. *The Early Upaniṣads*. New York: Oxford University Press.

Ong, Walter. 1982. *Orality and Literacy: The Technologizing of the Word*. London: Methuen.

Onians, Richard Broxton. 1951. *The Origins of Greek Thought*. Cambridge: Cambridge University Press.

Oosten, Jarich. 1985. *The War of the Gods: The Social Code in Indo-European Mythology*. London: Routledge & Kegan Paul.

Oppenheim, A. Leo. 1964. *Ancient Mesopotamia: Portrait of a Dead Civilization*. Chicago: University of Chicago Press.

Pakzad, Fazlollah, ed. 2005. *Bundahišn: Zoroastrische Kosmogonie und Kosmologie; Band I: Kritische Edition*. Tehran: Centre for the Great Islamic Encyclopaedia.

Panaino, Antonio. 1990–95. *Tištrya*. Rome: Istituto Italiano per il Medio ed Estremo Oriente.

———. 1995. "Uranographia Iranica I: The Three Heavens in the Zoroastrian Tradition and the Mesopotamian Background." In *Au Carrefour des religions: Mélanges offerts à Philippe Gignoux*, edited by Rike Gyselen, pp. 205–25. Paris: Groupe pour l'Étude de la Civilisation du Moyen-Orient.

———. 1998. *Tessere il Cielo: Considerazioni sulle Tavole astronomiche, gli Oroscopi, e la Dottrina dei Legamenti tra Induismo, Zoroastrismo, Manicheismo e Mandeismo*. Rome: Istituto Italiano per l'Africa e l'Oriente.

———. 2001. "A Few Remarks on the Zoroastrian Conception of the Status of Angra Mainyu and of the Daēvas." *Res Orientales* 13: 99–107.

Patterson, Orlando. 1982. *Slavery and Social Death: A Comparative Study*. Cambridge, MA: Harvard University Press.

Pedahzur, Ami. 2005. *Suicide Terrorism*. Cambridge, MA: Polity.

Petersen-Szemeredy, Griet. 1993. *Zwischen Wentstadt und Wüste: Römische Asketinnen in der Spätantike*. Göttingen: Vandenhoeck & Ruprecht.

Pettazzoni, Raffaele. 1947–48. "Verità del Mito." *Studi e Materiali di Storia delle Religioni* 21: 104–16. Translated by H. J. Roses under the title "The Truth of Myth," in Pettazzoni, *Essays on the History of Religions*, pp. 11–23. Leiden: E. J. Brill, 1967.

Pingree, David. 1963. "Astronomy and Astrology in India and Iran." *Isis* 54: 229–46.

———. 1987. "History of Astronomy in Iran." *Encyclopaedia Iranica*, 2:858–62. London: Routledge & Kegan Paul.

———. 1997. *From Astral Omens to Astrology, from Babylon to Bīkāner*. Rome: Istituto Italiano per l'Africa e l'Oriente.

Pirart, Éric. 2007. *Georges Dumézil face aux démons iraniens*. Paris: Éditions L'Harmattan.

Podbielski, H. 1986. "Le Chaos et les confins de l'univers dans la Théogonie d'Hésiode." *Les Études Classiques* 54: 253–63.

Potter, David S. 1993. "Martyrdom as Spectacle." In *Theater and Society in the Classical World*, edited by Ruth Scodel, pp. 53–88. Ann Arbor: University of Michigan Press.

Pritchard, James, ed. 1969. *Ancient Near Eastern Texts relating to the Old Testament*. 3rd ed. Princeton, NJ: Princeton University Press.

Pucci, Pietro. 1977. *Hesiod and the Language of Poetry*. Baltimore: Johns Hopkins University Press.

Radhakrishnan, S., ed. 1953. *The Principal Upaniṣads*. London: George Allen & Unwin.

Ramnoux, Clémence. 1986. *La nuit et les enfants de la nuit dans la tradition grecque*. Paris: Flammarion.

Renou, Louis. 1955. "Remarques sur la *Chāndogya-Upaniṣad*." In *Études védiques et pāṇinéennes* 1:91–102. Paris: E. de Boccard.

Report on the Situation of Human Rights in the Republic of Guatemala. Washington, DC: General Secretariat of the Organization of American States, 1983.

Reydams-Schils, Gretchen. 2005. *The Roman Stoics: Self, Responsibility, and Affection.* Chicago: University of Chicago Press.

Riesebrodt, Martin. 2010. *The Promise of Salvation: A Theory of Religion.* Chicago: University of Chicago Press, 2010.

Rives, J. B. 1999. *Tacitus, Germania.* Oxford: Clarendon Press.

Rosada Granados, Hector Roberto. 1987. *Indios y Ladinos (Un estudio Antropológico-Sociológico).* San Carlos, Guatemala: Editorial Universitaria.

Rosen, Edward. 1986. *Three Imperial Mathematicians: Kepler Trapped between Tycho Brahe and Ursus.* New York: Abaris Books.

Ross, Margaret Clunies. 1994. *Prolonged Echoes: Old Norse Myths in Medieval Icelandic Society.* 2 vols. Odense, Denmark: Odense University Press.

Roth, Catharine P. 1976. "The Kings and the Muses in Hesiod's *Theogony.*" *Transactions of the American Philological Association* 106: 331–38.

Rubel, Arthur, Carl O'Nell, and Rolando Collado-Ardón. 1984. *Susto: A Folk Illness.* Berkeley: University of California Press.

Rudhardt, Jean. 1986. "Pandora: Hésiode et les femmes." *Museum Helveticum* 43: 231–46.

———. 1996. "Le préambule de la *Théogonie:* La vocation du poète; Le langage des Muses." In Blaise et al., *Le métier du mythe*, pp. 25–40.

Sachs, A., trans. 1969. "Temple Program for the New Year's Festival at Babylon," lines 396–400. In Pritchard, *Ancient Near Eastern Texts*, p. 334.

Ste. Croix, G. E. M. de. 2006. *Christian Persecution, Martyrdom, and Orthodoxy.* New York: Oxford University Press.

Saintillan, Daniel. 1996. "Du festin à l'échange: Les graces de Pandore." In Blaise et al., *Le métier du mythe*, pp. 315–48.

Saliba, George. 2007. *Islamic Science and the Making of the European Renaissance.* Cambridge, MA: MIT Press.

Salis, Sabrina. 2002. "Le due facce del βασιλεύς in Esiodo: Alcune Osservazioni." *Annali della Facoltà di Lettere e Filosofia dell' Università di Cagliari* 20: 97–107.

Samandú, Luis. 1990. *Guatemala: Retos de la iglesia católica en una sociedad en crisis.* San José, Costa Rica: DEI/CSUCA.

———, ed. 1991. *Protestantismos y procesos sociales en Centroamérica*, pp. 67–114. San José, Costa Rica: EDUCA.

Sander, Fredrik, trans. 1893. *Edda, Sämund den Vises: Skaldeverk av Fornnordiska mYt-och Hjältesånger om de Götiska eller Germanska Folkens Gamla Gudatro, Sagominnen och Vandringar.* Stockholm: P. A. Norstedt & Söner.

Scalera McClintock, Giuliana. 1989. *Il Pensiero dell' invisibile nella Grecia arcaica.* Naples: Tempi Moderni Edizioni.

Schäfer, Peter. 1981. *Der Bar Kokhba-Aufstand: Studien zum zweiten jüdischen Krieg gegen Rom.* Tübingen: J. C. B. Mohr.

Schlesinger, Stephen, and Stephen Kinzer. 1982. *Bitter Fruit: The Untold Story of the American Coup in Guatemala.* Garden City, NY: Doubleday.

Schmeidler, Bernhard, ed. 1917. *Adam von Bremen, Hamburgische Kirchengeschichte.* 3rd ed. Hannover: Hahn, 1917.

Schmidt, Hanns-Peter. 1996. "The Non-Existence of Ahreman and the Mixture (*Gumēzišn*) of Good and Evil." In K. R. *Cama Oriental Institute: Second International Congress Proceedings*, pp. 79–95. Bombay: K. R. Cama Oriental Institute.

Schmidt, K. H. 1957. *Die Komposition in gallischen Personennamen.* Tübingen: Max Niemeyer.

Schmitt, Rüdiger. 2009. *Die altpersischen Inschriften der Achaimeniden.* Wiesbaden: Reichert.

Scholten, Clemens. 1987. *Martyrium und Sophiamythos im Gnostizismus nach den Texten von Nag Hammadi.* Münster: Aschendorff.

See, Klaus von. 1988. *Mythos und Theologie im skandinavischen Hochmittelalter.* Heidelberg: Carl Winter.

Seitz, Christopher. 1989. *Theology in Conflict: Reactions to the Exile in the Book of Jeremiah.* Berlin: De Gruyter.

Sellars, John. 2006. *Stoicism.* Berkeley: University of California Press.

Sexton, James. 1978. "Protestantism and Modernization in Two Guatemalan Towns." *American Ethnologist* 5: 280–302.

Shaked, Shaul. 1967. "Some Notes on Ahreman, the Evil Spirit, and His Creation." In *Studies in Mysticism and Religion Presented to Gershom G. Scholem,* edited by E. E. Urbach et al., pp. 227–34. Jerusalem: Magnes Press.

———. 1971. "The Notions Mēnōg and Gētīg in the Pahlavi Texts and Their Relation to Eschatology." *Acta Orientalia* 33: 59–107.

———. 1994. *Dualism in Transformation: Varieties of Religion in Sasanian Iran.* London: School of Oriental and African Studies: University of London.

Shaw, Brent. 1996. "Body/Power/Identity: Passions of the Martyrs." *Journal of Early Christian Studies* 4: 269–312.

Sherman, Nancy. 2005. *Stoic Warriors: The Ancient Philosophy behind the Military Mind.* New York: Oxford University Press.

Signorini, Italo. 1989. *Los tres ejes de la vida: Almas, corpo, enfermedad entre los Nahuas de la Sierra de Puebla.* Xalapa, Mexico: Editorial UV.

Simon, Jean-Marie. 1987. *Guatemala: Eternal Spring—Eternal Tyranny.* New York: W. W. Norton.

Siverts, Henning. 1969. "Ethnic Stability and Boundary Dynamics in Southern Mexico." In *Ethnic Groups and Boundaries: The Social Organization of Cultural Difference,* edited by Fredrik Barth, pp. 101–16. Boston: Little, Brown.

Skjærvø, P. Oktor. 1983. "*Farnah*: Mot mède en vieux-perse." *Bulletin de la Société Linguistique* 78: 241–59.

Slade, Doren. 1992. *Making the World Safe for Existence: Celebration of the Saints among the Sierra Nahuatl.* Ann Arbor: University of Michigan Press.

Smith, Anthony D. 2003. *Chosen Peoples: Sacred Sources of National Identity.* Oxford: Oxford University Press.

———. 1999. *Myths and Memories of the Nation.* Oxford: Oxford University Press.

Smith, Brian K. 1990. "Eaters, Food, and Social Hierarchy in Ancient India: A Dietary Guide to a Revolution in Values." *Journal of the American Academy of Religion* 58: 177–205.

———. 1994. *Classifying the Universe: The Ancient Indian Varn a System and the Origins of Caste.* New York: Oxford University Press.

Smith, Carol, ed. 1990. *Guatemalan Indians and the State, 1540–1988.* Austin: University of Texas Press.

———. 1995. "Race-Class-Gender Ideology in Guatemala: Modern and Anti-Modern Forms." *Comparative Studies in Society and History* 37: 723–49.

Smith, Daniel. 1989. *The Religion of the Landless: The Social Context of the Babylonian Exile.* Bloomington, IN: Meyer-Stone Books.

Smith, Jonathan Z. 1978. *Map Is Not Territory: Studies in the History of Religions.* Leiden: E. J. Brill.

————. 1990. *Drudgery Divine: On the Comparison of Early Christianities and the Religions of Late Antiquity.* Chicago: University of Chicago Press.

————. 2004. *Relating Religion: Essays in the Study of Religion.* Chicago: University of Chicago Press.

Smith, W. Robertson. 1889. *Lectures on the Religion of the Semites: First Series; The Fundamental Institutions.* New York: Appleton.

Smith, Wilfred Cantwell. 1963. *The Meaning and End of Religion: A New Approach to the Religious Traditions of Mankind.* New York: Macmillan.

Snell, Bruno. 1977. "φρένες—φρόνησις." *Glotta* 55: 34–64.

Soden, Wolfram von. 1983. "Kyros und Nabonid: Propaganda und Gegenpropaganda." In *Kunst, Kultur und Geschichte der Achamenidenzeit und ihr Fortleben*, edited by Heidemarie Koch and D. N. MacKenzie, pp. 61–68. Berlin: Dietrich Reimer.

Södergård, J. Peter. 1993. "The Ritualized Bodies of Cybele's Galli and the Methodological Problem of the Plurality of Explanations." In Ahlbäck, *The Problem of Ritual*, pp. 169–98.

Songe-Møller, Vigdis. 2002. *Philosophy without Women: The Birth of Sexism in Western Thought.* London: Continuum.

Sordi, Marta, ed., 1990. *Dulce et decorum est pro patria mori: La morte in combattimento nell' antichità.* Milan: Vita e pensiero.

Speiser, E. A. trans. 1969. "A Cosmological Incantation: The Worm and the Toothache." In Pritchard, *Ancient Near Eastern Texts relating to the Old Testament*, pp. 100–101.

Spiller, Elizabeth. 2004. *Science, Reading, and Renaissance Literature: The Art of Making Knowledge, 1580–1670.* Cambridge: Cambridge University Press,

Spineto, Natale. 1994. *L'histoire des religions a-t-elle un sens? Correspondance, Mircea Eliade et Raffaele Pettazzoni 1926–1959.* Paris: Éditions du Cerf.

Stausberg, Michael. 2002–4. *Die Religion Zarathushtras: Geschichte—Gegenwart—Rituale.* 3 vols. Stuttgart: W. Kohlhammer.

Stavenhagen, Rudolfo. 1969. "Classes, Colonialism, and Acculturation." In *Comparative Perspectives on Stratification: Mexico, Great Britain, Japan*, edited by Joseph Kahl, pp. 31–63. Boston: Little, Brown.

Stein, Philipp vom. 2006. *"Entsagst du, glaubst du?" Die Religion der Sachsen vor der Christianisierung: Das altsächsische Taufgelöbnis.* Wuppertal, Germany: Bergische Universität.

Stewart, Charles, and Rosalind Shaw, eds. 1994. *Syncretism/Anti-Syncretism: The Politics of Religious Synthesis.* New York: Routledge.

Stoddard, Kathryn. 2003. "The Programmatic Message of the 'Kings and Singers' Passage: Hesiod, *Theogony*, 80–103." *Transactions of the American Philological Association* 133: 1–16.

Stoll, David. 1990. *Is Latin America Turning Protestant? The Politics of Evangelical Growth.* Berkeley: University of California Press.

Storm, Gustav, ed. 1880. *Monumenta Historica Norvegæ: Latinske Kildeskrifter til Norges Historie in Middelalderen.* Christiana [Oslo]: A. W. Brøgger.

Strauss, Otto. 1931. "Udgīthavidyā." *Sitzungsberichte der preussischen Akademie der Wissenschaften* 13: 243–310.

Stroumsa, Guy. 2009. *The End of Sacrifice: Social Transformations in Late Antiquity*. Translated by Susan Emanuel. Chicago: University of Chicago Press.

Sullivan, Shirley Darcus. 1989. "Phrenes in Hesiod." *Revue Belge de Philologie et d'Histoire / Belgisch Tijdschrift voor Filologie en Geschiedenis* 67: 5–17.

Sundqvist, Olof. 2002. *Freyr's Offspring: Rulers and Religion in Ancient Svea Society*. Uppsala: Acta Universitatis Uppsaliensis. Historia Religionum.

Sussman, Linda. 1978. "Workers and Drones: Labor, Idleness and Gender Definition in Hesiod's Beehive." *Arethusa* 11: 27–37.

Svenbro, Jesper. 1976. *La parole et le marbre: Aux origins de la poétique grecque*. Lund, Sweden: Studentlitteratur.

Tafazzoli, A. 2000. *Sassanian Society*. New York: Bibliotheca Persica.

Taylor, Paul Beekman. 1966. "Heorot, Earth, and Asgard: Christian Poetry and Pagan Myth." *Tennessee Studies in Literature* 11: 119–30.

Thieme, Paul. 1957. "Vorzarathustrisches bei den Zarathustriern und bei Zarathustra." *Zeitschrift der deutschen morgenlandischen Gesellschaft* 107: 67–104.

Thomassen, Einar. 2006. *The Spiritual Seed: The Church of the Valentinians*. Leiden: E. J. Brill.

Tilley, Maureen. 1996. *Donatist Martyr Stories: The Church in Conflict in Roman North Africa*. Liverpool: Liverpool University Press.

———. 1997. *The Bible in Christian North Africa: The Donatist World*. Minneapolis: Fortress Press.

Timuš, Mihaela. 2003–4. "The 'Eschatological Body' (*tan ī pasēn*) according to the Zoroastrian Theology." *Studia Asiatica* 4–5: 779–808.

Tumin, Melvin. 1952. *Caste in a Peasant Society*. Princeton, NJ: Princeton University Press.

Turner, John Douglas. 2001. *Sethian Gnosticism and the Platonic Tradition*. Louvain: Éditions Peeters.

Vaziri, Mostafa. 1992. *The Emergence of Islam: Prophecy, Imamate, and Messianism in Perspective*. New York: Paragon House.

Vermaseren, M. J. 1977. *Cybele and Attis: The Myth and the Cult*. London: Thames & Hudson.

Vernant, Jean-Pierre. 1982 (French original 1962). *The Origins of Greek Thought*. Ithaca, NY: Cornell University Press.

———. 1989 (French original 1979). "At Man's Table: Hesiod's Foundation Myth of Sacrifice." In *The Cuisine of Sacrifice among the Greeks*, edited by Marcel Detienne and Jean-Pierre Vernant, pp. 21–86. Chicago: University of Chicago Press.

———. 1996. "Les semblances de Pandora." In Blaise et al., *Le métier du mythe*, pp. 381–92.

Villamar, Marco Antonio. 1993. *Significado de la decada 1944–1954 conocido como la revolucion guatamalteca de octubre*. Guatemala City: n.p.

Visnara, Cinzia. 1990. *Il supplizio come spettacolo*. Rome: Quasar.

Vogt, Evon Z. 1993. *Tortillas for the Gods: A Symbolic Analysis of Zinacanteco Rituals*. Norman: University of Oklahoma Press.

Vries, Jan de. 1930. "Ginnungagap." *Acta Philologica Scandinavica* 5: 41–66.

———. 1942. "Harald Schönhaar in Sage und Geschichte." *Beiträge zur Geschichte der deutschen Sprache* 66: 55–116.

———. 1970. *Altgermanische Religionsgeschichte*. 3rd ed. 2 vols. Berlin: Walter de Gruyter.

———. 1977. *Altnordisches etymologisches Wörterbuch*. Leiden: E. J. Brill, 1977.

Wagley, Charles. 1941. *Economics of a Guatemalan Village*. Menasha, WI: American Anthropological Association.

———. 1949. *The Social and Religious Life of a Guatemalan Village*. New York: American Anthropological Association.

Wägner, Wilhelm, and Jakob Rover. 1908. *Nordisch-germanische Götter und Heldensagen für Schule und Volk*. Leipzig: Otto Spamer.

Wald, Priscilla. 2008. *Contagious: Cultures, Carriers, and the Outbreak Narrative*. Durham, NC: Duke University Press.

Waller, James. 2002. *Becoming Evil: How Ordinary People Commit Genocide and Mass Killing*. Oxford: Oxford University Press.

Wanner, Kevin. 2008. *Snorri Sturluson and the Edda: The Conversion of Cultural Capital in Medieval Scandinavia*. Toronto: University of Toronto Press.

Warmind, Morten Lund. 1993. "The Cult of the Roman Emperor before and after Christianity." In Ahlbäck, *The Problem of Ritual*, pp. 211–20.

Warren, Kay. 1978. *The Symbolism of Subordination: Indian Identity in a Guatemalan Town*. Austin: University of Texas Press.

Wasserstrom, Robert. 1975. "Revolution in Guatemala: Peasants and Politics under the Arbenz Government." *Comparative Studies in Society and History* 17: 443–78.

Watanabe, John. 1990. "From Saints to Shibboleths: Image, Structure, and Identity in Maya Religious Syncretism." *American Ethnologist* 17: 131–50.

———. 1992. *Maya Saints and Souls in a Changing World*. Austin: University of Texas Press.

Weber-Brosamer, Bernhard. 1988. *Annam: Untersuchungen zur Bedeutung des Essens und der Speise im vedischen Ritual*. Rheinfelden: Schauble.

Weil, Simone. 1988–. *Oeuvres complètes*. Edited by André A. Devaux and Florence de Lussy. Paris: Gallimard.

West, Jessamyn. *The Friendly Persuasion*. New York: Harcourt, Brace, 1945.

West, M. L., ed. 1966. *Hesiod, Theogony*. Oxford: Clarendon Press.

———. 1978. *Hesiod, Works and Days*. Oxford: Clarendon Press.

Whaley, Diana. 1991. *Heimskringla: An Introduction*. London: Viking Society for Northern Research.

Widengren, Geo. 1965. *Die Religionen Irans*. Stuttgart: W. Kohlhammer.

Williams, David. 1982. *Cain and Beowulf: A Study in Secular Allegory*. Toronto: University of Toronto Press.

Wilson, Richard. 1995. *Maya Resurgence in Guatemala: Q'eqchi' Experiences*. Norman: University of Oklahoma Press.

Wistrich, Robert, ed. 1999. *Demonizing the Other: Antisemitism, Racism and Xenophobia*. Amsterdam: Harwood Academic Publishers.

Zaehner, R. C. 1955. *Zurvān: A Zoroastrian Dilemma*. Oxford: Oxford University Press.

Zanker, Paul. 1988. *The Power of Images in the Age of Augustus*. Ann Arbor: University of Michigan Press.

Zeitlin, Froma. 1996. "L'origine de la femme et la femme origine: La Pandore d'Hésiode." In Blaise et al., *Le métier du mythe*, pp. 349–80.

INDEX

Note: Italicized page numbers indicate illustrations; numerals in boldface denote chapter numbers of texts.